DATE DUE

12/19/12		
01/03/13		

Demco

American Dream Visions

Studies on Themes and Motifs in Literature

Horst Daemmrich
General Editor
Vol. 5

PETER LANG
New York • Washington, DC/Baltimore • San Francisco
Bern • Frankfurt am Main • Berlin • Vienna • Paris

Deborah Davis Schlacks

American Dream Visions

Chaucer's Surprising Influence on F. Scott Fitzgerald

PETER LANG
New York • Washington, DC/Baltimore • San Francisco
Bern • Frankfurt am Main • Berlin • Vienna • Paris

Library of Congress Cataloging-in-Publication Data

Schlacks, Deborah Davis.
  American dream visions: Chaucer's surprising influence on F. Scott
Fitzgerald / Deborah Davis Schlacks.
     p.   cm. — (Studies on themes and motifs in literature; vol. 5)
  Includes bibliographical references (p.) and index.
  1. Fitzgerald, F. Scott (Francis Scott), 1896–1940—Knowledge—
Literature. 2. Medievalism—United States—History—20th century.
3. American literature—English influences. 4. Chaucer, Geoffrey,
d. 1400—Influence. 5. Visions in literature. 6. Dreams in literature.
I. Title. II. Series. III. Series: Studies on themes and motifs in literature;
v. 5.
PS3511.I9Z842   1994   813'.52—dc20   93-14219
  ISBN 0-8204-2246-0   CIP
  ISSN 1056-3970

Die Deutsche Bibliothek - CIP-Einheitsaufnahme

Schlacks, Deborah Davis:
American dream visions: Chaucer's surprising influence on F. Scott Fitzgerald
/ Deborah Davis Schlacks. - New York; San Francisco; Bern; Baltimore;
Frankfurt am Main; Berlin; Wien: Paris: Lang, 1994.
  (Studies on themes and motifs in literature; Vol. 5)
  ISBN 0-8204-2246-0
NE: GT

The paper in this book meets the guidelines for permanence and durability of
the Committee on Production Guidelines for Book Longevity of the
Council on Library Resources.

For Eric and Elizabeth

ACKNOWLEDGMENTS

I owe many debts of gratitude to the people who have provided support as I have worked on this book. To my husband, Eric Schlacks; to my daughter, Elizabeth Lois Schlacks; to my parents, Bettye and Ralph Davis; to the chairperson of my dissertation committee, the late Joyce Thompson; to committee members J. Dean Bishop, Charles Bruce, Lavon B. Fulwiler, and Florence Winston; to Robert B. Beck; and to Beth McLaren, I offer heartfelt thanks.

. . .

Excerpts from the poems of Geoffrey Chaucer are from Robinson, F. N. (Editor), *The Works of Geoffrey Chaucer*, Second Edition. Copyright © 1957 by Houghton Mifflin Company. Used with permission.

Excerpts from F. Scott Fitzgerald's *The Great Gatsby* are reprinted with permission of Charles Scribner's Sons, an imprint of Macmillan Publishing Company, from THE GREAT GATSBY (Authorized Text) by F. Scott Fitzgerald. Copyright 1925 Charles Scribner's Sons; renewal copyright 1953 by Frances Scott Fitzgerald Lanahan. Copyright © 1991, 1992 by Eleanor Lanahan, Matthew J. Bruccoli and Samuel J. Lanahan as Trustees u/a dated 7/3/75 created by Frances Scott Fitzgerald Smith.

Excerpts from Fitzgerald's "The Diamond as Big as the Ritz" are reprinted with permission of Charles Scribner's Sons, an imprint of Macmillan Publishing Company, from TALES OF THE JAZZ AGE by F. Scott Fitzgerald. Copyright 1922 Charles Scribner's Sons; renewal copyright 1950 by Frances Scott Fitzgerald Lanahan.

Excerpts from Fitzgerald's "The Ice Palace" and "The Offshore Pirate" are reprinted with permission of Charles Scribner's Sons, an imprint of Macmillan Publishing Company, from

CONTENTS

INTRODUCTION

Francis Scott Key Fitzgerald has generally been considered a master of the tale of the modern world, an author in touch primarily with his own glittering yet sad Jazz Age. When critics have looked beyond Fitzgerald's contemporaries for evidence of influence, they have most often turned to figures of the romantic era such as John Keats. Seldom has Fitzgerald's possible indebtedness to the literature of the medieval era—in particular, to the works of Geoffrey Chaucer—been recognized or examined. Perhaps the medieval era seems simply too far removed from early twentieth-century America—and far removed it is in many ways. Or perhaps Fitzgerald simply seems an unlikely candidate to have been influenced by an author so distant in time and culture from his own. Nevertheless, something about the era and about Chaucer resonated for F. Scott Fitzgerald; for, in exploring Fitzgerald's works, one does encounter the presence of Chaucer. Certain of Fitzgerald's early works—namely, "The Offshore Pirate" (1920); "The Ice Palace" (1920); "The Diamond as Big as the Ritz" (1922); *The Vegetable or From President to Postman* (1923); and, most of all, *The Great Gatsby* (1925)—distinctly echo Chaucer's four dream visions: *The Book of the Duchess*, *The House of Fame*, *The Parliament of Fowls*, and the Prologue to *The Legend of Good Women*. They echo in particular Chaucer's theme of the artist seeking renewal of creativity, making an interior journey toward increased self-knowledge. Each author reinforces—indeed communicates—this theme through the structure of a dream and through similar characters and settings.

Chapter one of this study details the external evidence of a Chaucer-Fitzgerald connection and suggests specific aspects of medieval culture and medieval (primarily Chaucerian) literature that apparently attracted Fitzgerald. Then, chapters two through five examine the features shared by these works of Fitzgerald and of Chaucer.

This investigation is valuable for several reasons. First, this study makes a startling and illuminating discovery: that, almost certainly, Chaucer's dream visions significantly influenced F. Scott Fitzgerald. Determining influence is surely of intrinsic interest to the literary critic. But, in discovering signs of influence, this study does more: it demonstrates that, to a degree sometimes underestimated, Fitzgerald is a decidedly conscious and subtle artist. He is an artist more attracted to and better educated in things medieval—and things Chaucerian—than has generally been supposed, and one fully able to identify ideas and techniques found in Chaucer's works and to translate them into "Jazz-Age terms" for use in his own works. Also, apart from the matter of influence, the comparison of the works of these two authors sheds new light on important issues—some rather new, and others, perenniel—in Fitzgerald studies: his portrayal of female artist figures as compared to his portrayal of male artist figures; his complex reactions to such conflicting literary movements as the medieval revival of the early twentieth century, romanticism, and modernism; and the conflict he so often experienced between commercial and artistic success.

CHAPTER ONE

A CHAUCER-FITZGERALD CONNECTION

"Each night he added to the pattern of his fancies...."
—F. Scott Fitzgerald, The Great Gatsby

In 1921, Edna St. Vincent Millay compared F. Scott Fitzgerald to a "stupid old woman with whom someone has left a diamond," about which the woman can make only the most "inept" of remarks (cited in Wilson, "F. Scott Fitzgerald" 27). Edmund Wilson added that although Fitzgerald was not stupid, he

> has been left with a jewel he doesn't know quite what to do with. For he has been given imagination without intellectual control of it; he has been given the desire for beauty without an aesthetic ideal; and he has been given a gift for expression without many ideas to express. (Wilson, "F. Scott Fitzgerald" 27)

Even one of Fitzgerald's professors at Princeton, Gordon Hall Gerould, in subsequent years downgraded Fitzgerald's intellectual attainments. Gerould said that anyone with English grades as bad as Fitzgerald's could not have written *The Great Gatsby* (cited in Donaldson, "F. Scott Fitzgerald" 151). Such comments might seem to preclude the possibility that such a supposedly ill-educated man would even have been acquainted with the works of an author such as Geoffrey Chaucer, no less that he would have been influenced by him.

Adding to the apparent unlikelihood of such an influence is the gulf between the late fourteenth-century English world of Chaucer and the early twentieth-century American world of Fitzgerald, as well as that between Chaucer's Middle-English poetry and Fitzgerald's modern prose. Chaucer's England was, after all, a largely rural country dependent upon agriculture, with only five percent of the population dwelling in cities and with a capital city, London, boasting a population of only about 35,000. (Chaucer himself lived in London much of his life.) His was a world in which the horse was the prime means of transportation and communication was exceedingly slow. His was also a pre-scientific and pre-psychoanalytical world in which, for example, a phenomenon such as a dream was deemed meaningful only if prophetic, and dreams caused by the dreamer's own internal concerns were generally considered insignificant (Shelton 21–22). And Chaucer's world was a monarchy in which social class—particularly whether one was or was not of the gentry—was of much importance. Chaucer himself was a courtier who throughout his adulthood held a series of offices in the court of Edward III and Richard II; for instance, he was a customs officer and a clerk of the King's Works. His was an era, too, of strong religious faith: as Derek Brewer puts it, even in the face of such crises as the Hundred Years War, plagues, the Peasants' Revolt, and much political turmoil (including the deposition of Richard II), the age was "committed to belief in a fundamentally good and morally just governance of the universe which extended beyond mortal existence. Life could, therefore, never become meaningless" (37). In contrast, early twentieth-century America was a time and place of rapid urbanization, much industrialization, the automobile, the telephone, science, democracy, the *nouveaux riches*, and the post-World-War-I disillusionment that found expression in such phenomena as jazz, flappers, and bathtub gin.

The gulf between literatures can seem just as wide as the gap between eras. Chaucer wrote poetry (and a little prose) in Middle English, and it is literature written in a pre-romantic era that had precious little interest in either originality or individuality. His poetry was so well-received that during his own lifetime he was recognized as England's greatest poet. Yet Chaucer made a living by holding a series of court-appointed offices, not from writing poetry; and his primary audience for his poetry was the court, where he would often deliver orally his creations and distribute copies upon request. In contrast,

Fitzgerald wrote prose (and a little unsuccessful poetry) in a very modern English, and his is literature that is part of a post-romantic era that values originality and individuality. Also in contrast to Chaucer's reception as an author, after Fitzgerald's first early success, his work was sometimes not well received at all, to the extent that during the 1930s, Fitzgerald was widely considered "washed up." And Fitzgerald made—often barely—a living from his writing, whose audiences (such folk as the readers of the *Saturday Evening Post)* seem quite different from the courtly audience of Chaucer.

Nonetheless, much external evidence suggests that despite such differences, and perhaps in some instances because of them, a Chaucer-Fitzgerald connection is highly likely. This chapter will examine that evidence—showing in the process that Fitzgerald had a much more beautiful "diamond" than some have supposed, a "diamond" he was capable of using most adeptly, one "facet" of which was a knowledge of and interest in the medieval era and Chaucer. Fitzgerald also had the ability to find in the era and in Chaucer ideas and techniques that resonated for him, that he could transform and use in his own way in his own works. Along the way, the chapter will also explore the relationship between the medieval and the modern eras, as well as the sometimes atypical nature of Chaucer within his own era. The gulf between the modern era and the late medieval era may not be as unbridgeable as first might appear.

Evidence reveals, first of all, that Fitzgerald's education was precisely of the sort that would have made him sufficiently knowledgeable about the medieval era and Chaucer to have been influenced significantly by Chaucer. To be sure, the comments about his lack of intellectual prowess, particularly coming from those who knew Fitzgerald, might seem at first to belie any such notion. But as damning as these remarks seem, their context must be recognized; for all concern impressions Fitzgerald made during his college days or during the early part of his career and therefore may well distort the truth about his intellectual accomplishments. The distortion occurs not just because these comments do not account for his later, more mature period; they may even distort the truth about his early accomplishments. After all, Fitzgerald's relatively weak showing in his Princeton English classes may reflect only that Fitzgerald was intrigued more with the social than with the academic side of college life. Fitzgerald also disliked how some professors in the Princeton English Department taught their classes—as if they "really hated it [poetry] and didn't know what it was about," as he told his daughter, Frances Scott Fitzgerald (Scottie), in a letter of August 3, 1940 (*Letters* 88). Additionally, shortly after his Princeton days, as a young, suddenly successful author, Fitzgerald and his wife, Zelda Sayre Fitzgerald, were concerned more with presenting devil-may-care, brash personae to the world than with flaunting Fitzgerald's scholarly side, what with such exhibitions as their jumping into fountains fully clothed, adventures that undoubtedly had something of the aura of the publicity stunt about them.   Fitzgerald may well have created an anti-intellectual persona in much the way that Samuel Clemens created Mark Twain.[1]

More recently, some critics have considered the circumstances just mentioned, delved more deeply into the available evidence, and reached conclusions quite different from those of Millay, Wilson, and Gerould.   After having examined Fitzgerald's school records, Bruce Michelson concludes that Fitzgerald "had a classic imagination, classically trained.... The Newman School [in New Jersey] dedicated itself to preparing its Roman Catholic boys to succeed at the Protestant Yales and Princetons.   Princeton required three years of Latin simply for admission...."   Michelson adds that late in Fitzgerald's life, "when he prided himself on little else, Fitzgerald was still vain about his knowledge of literature, and all through his career he could use that background gracefully when it pleased him to do so" (564–65).   John Kuehl, in "Scott Fitzgerald's Reading," provides an extensive list of authors and works Fitzgerald knew—an inventory so sizable that it strongly suggests that Fitzgerald's education was thorough.   Finally, Sheilah Graham's account of Fitzgerald's efforts to educate her during his final days in Hollywood, *A College of One*, contains facsimiles of the voluminous reading lists with which he provided her; these catalogues include authors ranging from Spengler to Keats to Rimbaud. Fitzgerald, in short, was better read and better educated than some people have realized.

Various critics have agreed, however, that Fitzgerald's reading did find its way into his works.   But they have not agreed about whether Fitzgerald was aware of the influences. After commending the form of *The Great Gatsby*, Arthur Mizener comments on the difficulty of determining where Fitzgerald "learned how to make that pattern" since Fitzgerald "was never very conscious of his literary debts" (*Far Side* 184). Yet in a famed study of Fitzgerald's indebtedness to Joseph Conrad (and to other authors), James E. Miller says that "Fitzgerald was far more conscious of what he was doing in his work than is commonly supposed" (1). This controversy regarding the degree of consciousness of literary influences is perhaps unresolvable; the essential point is that both Mizener and Miller (and others, too) realize that Fitzgerald did have "literary debts" to other authors, whether he explicitly or extensively mentioned those authors or not.

Fitzgerald's special love for history in general and medieval history in particular also points to the plausibility of a Chaucer-Fitzgerald connection and suggests that Fitzgerald's attraction to the era may have stemmed in part from a perception of its dissimilarities to the modern era rather than a perception of its similarities. In a September 14, 1940, letter to Zelda Fitzgerald, F. Scott Fitzgerald assessed the value of his Princeton years in a way that shows his interest in history: "I got nothing out of my first two years—in the last I got my passionate love for poetry and historical perspective and ideas in general (however superficially); it carried me full swing into my career" (*Letters* 124). And, in his biography of Fitzgerald, Matthew Bruccoli reports that Fitzgerald took pride in his history library and kept a "histomap" on his study wall. Fitzgerald and his daughter liked to play a card game of Fitzgerald's invention involving the portraits and biographies of French historical figures (*Price* 512).

Furthermore, Fitzgerald came to be interested in a particular theory of history, that of Oswald Spengler, author of *The Decline of the West*. Spengler contends that history is cyclical, that there is no one linear history but instead there have been a number of Cultures, such as those of India; Babylonia; China; Greece; and, most recently, the West. "Each Culture," says Spengler, "has its own possibilities of self-expression which arise, ripen, decay, and never return" (*Today and Destiny* 117). Following every Culture is a Civilization, which Spengler calls the "inevitable *destiny* of the Culture" (120; Spengler's emphasis). Kermit W. Moyer, who has studied Spenglerian themes in Fitzgerald's works, sums up Spengler's distinction between Culture and Civilization as follows: "As a Culture is destiny-driven, vibrant, religious, intuitive, and aristocratic, a Culture which has become a Civilization is rigid, irreligious, money-controlled, soulless, moribund ... " (242n). As Spengler saw it, the birth of Western Culture had occurred at approximately 900 A.D., while the nineteenth century had marked the transition point from Western Culture to Western Civilization. This particular facet of Spengler's theory is prominent in *Tender Is the Night* (1933), in which Dick Diver and, even more, his father represent waning Western Culture whereas Nicole Warren Diver represents ascendant Western Civilization. Spenglerian themes are equally significant in Fitzgerald's unfinished *The Last Tycoon* (1941), in which Monroe Stahr, the titular character, is one of the last remnants of a dying Culture. (See Moyer.) And Spengler's ideas affected Fitzgerald so much that he also used them in composing a work entitled "Philippe, Count of Darkness," set during the Middle Ages, the era Spengler called the time of the birth of Western Culture. Fitzgerald, then, was equipped through his knowledge of this theory to conceptualize the contrast between the Middle Ages as part of the transition from pre-Culture to Western Culture, and his own era as the transition from Western Culture to Western Civilization.

Indeed, the history of the medieval era particularly fascinated Fitzgerald. In an early interview, Fitzgerald numbered among his enthusiasms "'all books about that period which lies between the V and XV centuries'" (qtd. in Baldwin 172). Other strong indications of this interest appear in Fitzgerald's first two novels. In *This Side of Paradise* (1920), the protagonist, Amory Blaine, meets Thornton Hancock when both Blaine and Hancock visit Amory's mentor, Monsignor Darcy. The member of an old, distinguished family, Hancock has authored a history of the Middle Ages. Then, in *The Beautiful and Damned* (1922), protagonist Anthony Patch tours Rome, where he dallies with art, architecture, and the writing of "ghastly Italian sonnets, supposedly the ruminations of a thirteenth-century monk on the joys of the contemplative life" (8). Later, when Anthony tells his grandfather, Adam Patch, that he plans to write a history of the Middle Ages, Adam shows contempt for the project, commenting, "'Dark Ages, we used to call 'em. Nobody knows what happened, and nobody cares, except that they're over now'" (15). Anthony subsequently makes lists of authorities and toys with possible chapter titles and organizational schemes but writes only part of a "Chestertonian essay on the twelfth century by way of introduction to his proposed book" (189).

These artist figures' reactions to the medieval indicate how admirable they are to be considered: the more they can successfully write about the era, the better. Honorable, distinguished Thomas Hancock seems to deserve those appellations all the more because he has written about the medieval era. Fitzgerald based this character on Henry Adams, whom Fitzgerald met through Monsignor Cyril Sigourney Webster Fay, Fitzgerald's mentor and the model for the Monsignor Darcy character in *This Side of Paradise* (Fitzgerald, qtd. in Wasserstrom 295). Fay and Adams' circle regarded the medieval era as one of relative stability and of ordered faith and beauty (Moreland 310–18)—much in contrast to their view of their own chaotic era. Through his largely autobiographical protagonist Amory Blaine and Amory's encounter with Adams' and Fay's fictional counterparts, Fitzgerald indicates the strong impression his own acquaintance with the medieval era and its contemporary advocates had upon him. Indeed, Fitzgerald's knowledge of Adams and of his ideas possibly did more than provide the young author with a model for a minor character in his first novel; according to William Wasserstrom, Adams' *The Education of Henry Adams* was a model for the entire work. In addition, Ruth Christy Funk holds that Adams' ideas about order and chaos, as presented in the autobiography (and elsewhere in Adams' writings), find their way into *The Great Gatsby* as well. It seems that the difference between the perceived faith and order of the medieval era and the disorder of the modern era was part of what attracted Fitzgerald to the former.

Fitzgerald's other character with medieval interests, Anthony Patch, differs ultimately from Henry Adams/Thomas Hancock in that Anthony can never come close to finishing *his* history of the age, a factor that shows his decline. Notably, Anthony at least likes the era and wishes to write about it whereas his non-artistic but wealthy grandfather, who, in his love of money and in his rigidity, would make a perfect example of Spenglerian Civilization, hates the whole idea of the Middle Ages. Interestingly, as Fitzgerald deals with the issue of these artists' success or failure, he judges the matter by whether or not they can complete works about the medieval era.

Additionally, various comments in *This Side of Paradise* point to Fitzgerald's awareness of medieval religion and to his acquaintance with yet another figure involved in the medieval revival of the early twentieth century. In *This Side of Paradise*, about to have a sexual liaison, Amory Blaine hallucinates that he sees a man with a face like yellow wax and feet that are

> all wrong...[Fitzgerald's ellipses] with a sort of wrongness that he felt rather than knew...[Fitzgerald's ellipses] It was like...blood on satin.... He wore no shoes, but, instead, a sort of half moccasin, pointed, though, like the shoes they wore in the fourteenth century, and with the little ends curling up. (108)

Amory believes he has seen the Devil, and he cannot sleep or pray because of the incident. In being "all wrong," like "blood on satin," Amory's Devil is pictured as a figure of incongruity and chaos. Amory, it is said, is not a Catholic, but in the face of such an experience, he desires to turn toward Catholicism, the "only ghost of a code that he had," a religion he associates with Ralph Adams Cram, who was known for "his adulation of thirteenth-century cathedrals" (118). Cram was a Catholic architect active in the early twentieth-century Gothic Revival. Supervising architect at Princeton University while Fitzgerald was a student there, he designed various Princeton buildings in what was often termed "Collegiate Gothic" style (Stillwell 5). In *This Side of Paradise*, Fitzgerald, through Amory, comments poetically and admiringly about the Gothic Princeton architecture. Seventy-Nine Hall, Amory believes, is "brick-red and arrogant," but "topping all, climbing with clear blue aspiration, [are] the great dreaming spires of Holder and Cleveland towers" (46). Amory attains "a deep, reverent devotion to the gray walls and *Gothic* peaks and all they symbolized as warehouses of dead ages"; he likes "knowing that *Gothic* architecture, with its upward trend, was peculiarly appropriate to universities, and the idea became personal to him" (56; emphasis added). Using the term "Oxonion medievalism" for the same style, John Peale Bishop, Fitzgerald's Princeton classmate and friend, describes Cram's Princeton buildings in a way that echoes Fitzgerald's own admiring sentiments. Bishop speaks of "the grave beauty of these towers and spires trembling upward, intricately labored and grey," of "Seventy-Nine stately, in redbrick, and Holder, enclosing with cloisters and arches a square of sunlight and sod" (392). Cram, in short, made a significant impression on Princeton students such as Fitzgerald and Bishop through their seeing his buildings on campus.

For Fitzgerald, however, the impression was also more direct. Cram was a part of the Adams-Fay circle. He helped arrange for the publication of Henry Adams' medieval history, *Mont-Saint-Michel and Chartres*, which Cram hoped would help America adopt some of the values of the medieval era (Moreland 13–14; 24–26). Cram, like Adams, looked upon the Middle Ages as a golden age that the modern world would do well to emulate, as an age of order, reflected in the world of architecture in the Gothic style. Since Cram was a part of this circle, his influence on Fitzgerald was indeed more direct than it would have been if Fitzgerald had known of him simply as supervising architect for Princeton.

Two of Fitzgerald's short stories echo some of the medieval preoccupations of *This Side of Paradise*. In Fitzgerald's "The Camel's Back" (1931), before a costume party, protagonist Perry Parkhurst tries on a camel costume and, upon looking at himself in a mirror, concludes that he looks like "one of those mediaeval pictures of a monk changed into a beast by the ministrations of Satan" (41). Wearing this costume, Perry proceeds to attend a typically wild, chaotic Jazz Age party. Symbolically, in taking part in the wild goings-on, the young man has indeed become "Satanic." Notably, Perry's experience parallels somewhat Amory's vision of Satan. Amory looks upon medieval Catholicism as orderly and the Devil as chaotic and incongruous; Perry similarly contrasts a monk with a beast.

In "A Penny Spent" (1925), Hallie Bushmill mentions the eerie quality of the grey mountains and decaying Italian castles surrounding her and imagines that the latter contain medieval princes ready to poison people (134). Here, the decay of the medieval era results in evil and chaos. Interestingly, in his dream visions, Fitzgerald's dreamers work toward restoration of creativity, a state marked for Fitzgerald by a kind of order that involves the blending of perspective and detachment on the one hand and imagination and even chaos on the other. Thus, Fitzgerald's concept of the conflict between order and chaos echoes medieval—or at least twentieth-century medievalist—dichotomies.

Fitzgerald was also intrigued by the medieval romance concepts of the Grail quest, the knightly hero, and courtly love. In one of his notebook entries, Fitzgerald proclaims that "as a novelist I reach out to the end of all man's variance, all man's villainy—as a man I do not go that far. I cannot claim honor—but even the knights of the Holy Grail were only striving for it, as I remember" (*Notebooks* 324). This statement suggests that Fitzgerald viewed both the artist's struggle to create and the human being's struggle for an honorable, satisfactory life as a Grail quest, that despite differences in the medieval world and the modern, he felt that such concepts remained valid ways to think of such efforts.

A suggestion of Fitzgerald's interest in knights appears in *The Beautiful and Damned.* Anthony Patch may not be able to write *his* history of the Middle Ages, but he does at least create a medieval character, a knight he calls Chevalier O'Keefe, whose one weakness, his desire for women, makes him miserable for years. As Anthony puts it, Chevalier becomes involved with "'a series of women who hated him, used him, bored him, aggravated him, sickened him, spent his money, made a fool of him—in brief, as the world has it, loved him'" (90). To escape all this, Chevalier enters a monastery, where he is to live in contemplation in the Tower of Chastity. But once there, he looks out the window and sees a pretty peasant girl walk by and lift her skirt to adjust her garter. Chevalier leans out, farther and farther, "'as though pulled forward by a gigantic and irresistible hand'" (91), until he falls and is killed. Suspected of suicide, he does not receive a Christian burial.

Chevalier's subservience to his lady-loves, along with their haughty and superior attitude toward him, strongly suggests the medieval concept of courtly love, though it is courtly love with a definite "Jazz-Age slant." Andreas Capellanus' *De Arte Honest Amandi* enumerates the "laws" of this medieval system: (1) Courtly love is sensuous. Such love is a passion stemming from thoughts about the beauty of the opposite sex and culminating in the gratification of physical desires. (2) The love is illicit. (3) The love must be kept secret, or else it will not last. Thus the lovers must carefully guard against spies. (4) Such love cannot be too easily obtained—hence the lady's "coldness and capriciousness" (Dodd 5–8). Because of the lady's coldness, the courtly lover will suffer severe sickness, sleeplessness, loss of speech upon seeing the lady, trembling and paleness when near her, and a dread of being found out by other persons (Dodd 13). Further, according to William Dodd, "as a perfect being, the lady occupies a position of exalted superiority in respect to the lover. He becomes her vassal and protests absolute submission and devotion to her" (10–11). More recently than Dodd, commentators have agreed that Andreas' work was actually a *satire* on courtly love but that, nevertheless, the system was important.

Medieval literature concerning courtly love (of which the medieval dream vision is a prominent part) results, according to Saul N. Brody, "from the perception of man's dual nature, of his conflicting impulses toward transcendent love and carnal love" (221). The best medieval poets were aware of this conflict and therefore dealt with it in their poetry, which is the "record of their struggle to preserve the ideal from destruction" (221). However, other, lesser poets did not recognize this tension; their poetry is "derivative and naive," merely imitative of the "codified and ritualized behavior" of the courtly-love system rather than expressive of the ideas underlying the code.

Understanding yet another strand of courtly-love literature, the satire, requires a look at social and economic conditions in Chaucer's own time, the late fourteenth century, when such satire thrived. (For example, Andreas' work was of this era.) The age was one of more social mobility and social upheaval of a certain sort than there had been even earlier in that same century. Men of the merchant class (Chaucer's father was a merchant—a vintner) could now be knighted, and noblemen married daughters of merchants. Increasingly, merchants were becoming part of the landed gentry (Brewer 19). Despite the continued dominance of agriculture, the city was becoming more and more an important force; and the merchant class an important force within the city. As Brewer states, "the town represented the new spirit of enterprise, endeavour, utility. In it there were no serfs and an escaped serf who could live a year in a town had cast off his bondage" (18–19). These changes were disturbing to the old courtly class. Hence, the courtly-love system increasingly became, according to Joan M. Ferrante and George D. Economou, an "artificial means of preserving differences" between the aristocratic (courtly) class and the wealthy bourgeois, who, when they tried to imitate courtly ways, did so without an understanding of the serious side of the game. "Literature," say Ferrante and Economou, "reflects this stage by satirizing and ridiculing the emptiness of the forms and the lack of nobility of those who adhered to them, or by denouncing the forms as hypocritical and immoral" (Introduction 4–5).

Chaucer's stance on courtly love and the courtly life is a curious mix of admiration for ideal courtly values—loyalty,

service, love, beauty, and valor—and a recognition of their ultimate insufficiency, their temporal nature (Brewer 62). How
much of this stance stems from the social upheavals of his
time, how much from his so-called "conventional Christian pi-
ety," and how much from his attention to the new intellectual
currents of his time is open to question. Whatever its causes,
this "doubleness" about a matter so connected to issues of social standing and of temporal versus eternal values could have
been deeply attractive to Fitzgerald.

In her dissertation "The Medieval Impulse in America:
Evocations of Courtly Love and Chivalry in Twain, Adams,
Fitzgerald, and Hemingway," Kim Ileen Moreland speaks of
the early twentieth-century medieval revival in America, con-
cluding that within the movement, the Middle Ages was often
regarded as possessing ideals (such as courtly love and chivalry) whose "worth was regarded as self-evident." In the revivalists' view, she states, the only trouble was that contemporary society did not seem able to live up to the ideals (57). She
further contends that Fitzgerald was particularly disposed to
such an attitude toward medieval traditions. And he does seem
to have especially linked order and goodness to the era (and in
particular to its Catholicism), and chaos and evil to its decline.
However, Fitzgerald's reaction to the era—particularly, to
medieval courtly love and chivalry—may have been more
complex than Moreland would suggest, just as the medieval
era—and particularly the late fourteenth century—was more
complex than the revivalists seem to have suggested.[2] Just as
Chaucer exhibits a mixed reaction to issues, Fitzgerald had a
"double vision": he could be both attracted to and repelled by
various forces and ideas. Perhaps he had just such a par-
adoxical attitude toward the medieval period. For example, in
Gatsby, although Jay Gatsby is very much a modern man—a
nouveau riche who would like to find entrance into the world of
the socially established old-money class—he is also much like
the "courtly lover" of medieval times, lovesick about his lady-
love. But the medievalist ideal of the beauty of such an ideal
love and the medievalist sorrow that the modern era simply
could not live up to that ideal are not all there is to Fitzgerald's
thinking on Gatsby as courtly lover. Fitzgerald's novel not
only praises but also indicts Gatsby for his courtly-love behavior. Clearly Fitzgerald is aware of Gatsby's desire for Daisy
as an issue of socio-economic mobility—and aware of how disturbing this mobility is for the old-moneyed Buchanans. One

can well imagine Fitzgerald's having noticed a parallel between the increased social mobility of the late fourteenth century and that of his own era. Interestingly, too, Anthony Patch's tale of Chevalier O'Keefe is quite an indictment of "courtly love," although on another basis. Chevalier is torn between the orderly world of transcendent, spiritual love available in the monastery and the chaotic world of carnal desire in which he is subservient not to God but to his lady-loves. This conflict between the temporal and the eternal is, again, quite Chaucerian.

Another medieval tendency of Fitzgerald's, his listmaking, is both a stylistic feature of some of his fiction and a habit of his daily life. The guest list in *Gatsby* and the list of flowers and trees that populate Nicole's garden in *Tender Is the Night* are two examples from his fiction. Also, Sheilah Graham reports that "plans and lists were the spine of his life," that he was "the most orderly man in a state of disorder I ever knew" (59). Fitzgerald made lists of girls, of battles from the beginning of recorded time to his own time, of his meetings with Ernest Hemingway, of painters and their works, of books he had read by the time he had reached certain benchmark ages, of the plots of *Saturday Evening Post* stories, of prices paid to various authors for their works, of football plays, of plans for the next day, of his sleeping pills (Graham 59–64). In *This Side of Paradise*, Monsignor Darcy—and, by implication, Fitzgerald himself—explicitly associates this habit with medievalism in explaining why Amory Blaine likes to make lists of all sorts of things: It is, Darcy says, "'because you're a mediaevalist.... We both are. It's the passion for classifying and finding a type,'" and it is "'the nucleus of scholastic philosophy'" (100). (Notably, since Darcy here classifies himself and Amory, his statement is in itself an example of the passion for classifying of which he speaks.) Chaucer is, of course, also a great list-maker.

Ultimately, however, the clearest indication of Fitzgerald's interest in the Middle Ages comes from two sources: a statement he made about the era, and, perhaps most importantly, his having planned a novel set in that era, a novel he wished to call "Philippe, Count of Darkness." The statement comes from 1924, when, while working on *The Great Gatsby*, Fitzgerald told an interviewer that he was "'going to read nothing but Homer & Homeric literature—and history 540–1200 A.D. until I finish my novel...'" (qtd. in Bruccoli, *Epic Grandeur* 197). Since *Gatsby* bears extensive evidence of medieval influence, it is especially significant that Fitzgerald should have mentioned reading medieval history during the writing of this particular work.

As for Fitzgerald's proposed medieval novel, "Philippe, Count of Darkness," Fitzgerald completed four episodes of the work; they were published as short stories in *Redbook*. The record of Fitzgerald's struggle to continue writing this doomed novel shows how strongly he was drawn to the medieval era, so much so that the record is worth detailed scrutiny. Letters to Fitzgerald's publisher, Maxwell Perkins of Scribner's, in October and November 1934, contain the earliest extant mentions of this work. On October 30, Fitzgerald simply reports that he has completed the first "Red Book [sic] story, which I think is good (& is accepted)" (*Dear Scott* 208). Then on November 1, Fitzgerald says that he has decided "to do a string of these, at least two more after this one [the third]...." The first indication of Fitzgerald's deep interest in the stories appears when Fitzgerald says in this letter that they "bring me approximately half as much money [as a *Saturday Evening Post* story] but I can do them faster because of the feeling of enthusiasm, probably the feeling of escape from the modern world" (*Dear Scott* 209). Then, on November 10, he writes Perkins that he has 30,000 words of "Philippe" finished. And he gives the first extant indication that the work is to be a novel:

> Remember it is a novel and not merely a string of episodes about a single character as in the case of the Basil stories. It just divides itself into fairly complete units and that [Edwin] Balmer [of *Redbook*], thank God, is sold on it. (*Dear Scott* 211)

These comments appear to chart the course of a growing enthusiasm for a plan dear to Fitzgerald's heart. Janet Lewis' examination of papers concerning this series that are housed in the Fitzgerald collection at the Princeton Library confirms this impression. Lewis states that Fitzgerald

> consulted books on French and European history, the fifth volume of Gibbon, Belloc's *Europe and the Faith*, and Jessie Weston's *From Ritual to Romance*. In the eleventh edition of the *Encyclopaedia Britannica*, he checked articles on armour, castles and Charlemagne, on feudalism, fortification and Viking ships. He made

lists of possible names for men and women and copied down terminology and phrases from the witch rituals described in Margaret Murray's *The Witch Cult in Western Europe*. He made notes about the dates of treaties and compiled a long list of outstanding people of the Middle Ages from Odoacer in 476 to Henry the Navigator in 1446. He prepared a historical table of events and rulers in France, Germany, Italy, and the Saracen kingdoms during the ninth century. (9)

Unfortunately, for various reasons, the novel appears to have been doomed from the start. This fact becomes clear as early as December 5, 1934, when a letter to Fitzgerald from his agent, Harold Ober, reveals that Ober had trouble initially in getting a magazine to accept the series (the first three of the stories had already appeared in *Redbook* by this time) and that the fourth story will not appear in print any time soon. Ober states that nearly every editor he contacted felt that because Fitzgerald was known as an author of "very modern" stories, readers seeing a medieval story by him would be shocked. The editor at *Redbook*, Edwin Balmer, was the only publisher willing to take a chance on the stories, a stance that has made the owners of the magazine wonder if Balmer might be "partially crazy." The stories are certainly good, Ober adds, but it would be best not to push *Redbook* about publishing the fourth one (*As Ever* 205–06).

Despite this impasse—*Redbook* was not to publish the fourth story until after Fitzgerald's death—Fitzgerald's interest remained strong. On March 26, 1935, Fitzgerald lists in a letter the works he would want included in a collection if he should suddenly die. He also lists the works to be scrapped. As a handwritten addendum to the typed list of works to be collected, he writes, "And to date four mediaval [sic] stories." In the instructions at the head of the list, he writes, "If the Mediaeval stories are six or more they should be in a small book of their own. If less [sic] than six they should be in one section in this book. Note date above—there may be other good ones after this date" (*Correspondence* 407). Thus, far from having given up on "Philippe," Fitzgerald was sure of its worth and was anticipating moving forward with it. In fact, in a letter of April 17, 1935, he tells Perkins of the overall plan he had by this time formulated for the novel. "It will," he says, "run to about 90,000 words and will be a novel in every sense..."

(*Dear Scott* 221). In a much later letter to Perkins, dated January 4, 1939, Fitzgerald tells in more detail what his plan had been:

> You will remember that the plan in the beginning was tremendously ambitious—there was to have been Philippe as a young man founding his fortunes—Philippe as a middle-aged man participating in the Captian founding of France as a nation—Philippe as an old man and the consolidation of the feudal system. It was to have covered a span of about sixty [sic] years from 880 A.D. to 950. The research required for the second two parts would be quite tremendous and the book would have been (or would be) a piece of great self-indulgence, though I admit self-indulgence often pays unexpected dividends. (*Dear Scott* 253–54)

Fitzgerald, then, obviously kept trying to bring this project to fruition; and even in 1939, he was not ready to give up fully on the possibility of doing so, as his parenthetical shift to the present tense indicates.

Between the occasion of Fitzgerald's disappointment in late 1934 at *Redbook*'s decision not to publish the fourth story and this show of interest in 1939 appear various instances of attempted compromises with Perkins and Ober, all efforts to see more of this work in print. In a series of letters to Ober from July through September 1935, Fitzgerald speaks of having revised the fourth medieval story for *Redbook* and of Balmer's having apparently stalled about even reading the revised version.[3] Sometime later that September, Fitzgerald began to make his plan less ambitious, primarily, it seems, for financial reasons. In a letter to Ober of about September 5, Fitzgerald reveals that the fourth story had made the series 30,000 words long, "almost half enough for a book. The next step I dont [sic] know in that line. Certainly I've got to shoot at the bigger money till Im [sic] out of debt" (*As Ever* 225). The next month found Fitzgerald (in a letter of October 24) trying to get Perkins to see if *Scribner's Magazine* would buy the rest of the series. He obviously wanted the monetary support of serialization to fall back on while he worked on the novel. Fitzgerald also tells Perkins of a plan to publish two Philippe books of 60,000 words each—in this way, he says, one of the books would already be half done (*Dear Scott* 225). In an October 26, letter, Perkins says no to Fitzgerald's plan (*Dear Scott* 226). The following year, 1936, found Fitzgerald still concerned about that fourth story: "Please find out something more definite about the Medieval story," he writes Ober on January 29. "Can't you see how terribly important it is to me?" (*As Ever* 245).

Little more is said about "Philippe" until April 23, 1938, when Fitzgerald writes Perkins from California that "I have again gone back to the idea of expanding the stories about Philippe, the Dark Ages knight, but when I will find time for that, I don't know..." (*Dear Scott* 245). Indeed, 1938 became a year of more and more futile attempts on Fitzgerald's part to have more of "Philippe" in print—somehow. In an August 29 letter to Ober, he requests that Ober ask *Redbook* for a copy of their copy of the fourth story. This request seems to be an excuse that would have allowed Ober to ask Balmer whether or not *Redbook* ever planned to use the story—"or would they use it if they had a couple of others at hand," Fitzgerald adds (*As Ever* 367). Obviously he still was much concerned about the series, much determined to see more of it completed. Then, in a December 24, 1938, letter, he tells Perkins about an idea for a

> Big collection of stories leading off with *Philippe* entirely rewritten and pulled together into a 30,000-word novelette.... The reason for using *Philippe* is this: he is to some extent complete in the fourth story (which you have never read) and, in spite of some muddled writing, he is one of the best characters I've ever "drawn." He should be a long book—but whether or not my M-G-M contract is renewed I'm going to free-lance out here another year to lay by some money, and then do my modern novel [*The Last Tycoon*]. So it would be literally *years* before I got to *Philippe* again—if ever. In my work here I can find time for such a rewrite of *Philippe* as I contemplate—I could finish it by the first of February. (*Letters* 281)

Financial necessity, not flagging interest, clearly caused a shift to a more limited "Philippe." What happened to this plan for a collection that would include "Philippe" is not known, beyond the fact that it did not come to be. Perkins merely replies a few days later that he wished to publish Philippe as a unit

the following summer, but beyond this, nothing more is said of
the series until a March 26, 1940, letter from Fitzgerald to Neal
Begley, in which Fitzgerald says,

> It was a great disappointment for me not being able to
> go on with that series.... I have often considered writ-
> ing a few more and launching them as a book. That,
> however, would be only half my intention as I in-
> tended to carry Philippe through a long life covering
> the latter part of the ninth century, a time that must
> simply be vibrant with change and would be intensely
> interesting in view of new discoveries...and the new
> Marxian interpretation. But if I did publish a shorter
> book to begin with do you think it would have any
> buyers? There are waves of interest in historic fiction
> and I wonder if this is one of those times. (*Cor-
> respondence* 590–91)

Thus, clearly, Fitzgerald's interest stayed alive at least until
March 1940—only about nine months before his death. His
own reputation as a writer of modern stories, lack of financial
backing, lack of time, and perhaps even the quality of the stories doomed the project. Nevertheless, Fitzgerald's determination to go on with it strongly indicates his interest in the medieval era.

Though only four "Philippe" stories were completed and
published, Fitzgerald wrote basic plotlines for four others.
These stories and plotlines are best interpreted in terms of
Spengler's theory of historical cycles, as Moyer has done. The
first story, "In the Darkest Hour" (October 1934), presents
Philippe, Count of Villefranche, a young man who has just arrived in his homeland to claim his birthright—the land his father at one time owned. The countryside is a wasteland:
"During three days Philippe had not seen a human being—only half-burned farmhouses, inhabited here and there by
ghostly ill-nourished pigs and poultry prowling among the ruins..." (513). The peasants are subject to beatings by maraud-
ers. As Moyer explains, "Roman Civilization has long since
fallen and Western Culture has not yet begun: it is an era of
dark and barbaric prehistory, the ahistorical night between
Roman sunset and Faustian dawn" (242–43). Philippe proceeds
to organize the peasants into a makeshift cavalry that defeats a
band of plunderers. Having thus won a measure of loyalty

from the people, Philippe has established the beginnings of a feudal society. Moyer calls Philippe "a figure of destiny, an authentic embodiment of the creative, demiurgic *Geist* which is awakening throughout Europe..." (244). As Philippe puts it, "'Now, somebody's got to make you people stand up on your hind legs so all these heathen won't ride over you. And Providence in its wisdom has chosen me'" (518).

In the second story, "The Count of Darkness" (June 1935), Philippe builds a fort and continues to establish his fiefdom. He decisively orders his subjects around, telling them, for example, that "there would be no marriage permitted in the country save with his permission. He would expect them to choose their mates among his own men" (68). Yet, despite his forceful, hard nature, he is tempted by a beautiful young girl, Letgarde. But Philippe finds his desire for power more potent than his desire for love and beauty. When he treats Letgarde roughly, she leaves and later is found drowned. He, says Moyer, sacrifices love and beauty for power (245). The time is that of the birth of Western Culture; devotion to love, beauty, and art will have to wait until men such as Philippe have established the Culture and thus smoothed the way for these matters.

The third story, "The Kingdom in the Dark" (August 1935), concerns the conflict between the clergy and Philippe as nobleman and between the king and Philippe. Philippe thus continues to strengthen his position yet runs into conflicts with other powerful entities. And the fourth story, "Gods of the Darkness," which was finally published in November 1941, after Fitzgerald's death, concerns the witch cults of the time and the compromise Philippe must make with them to ensure his continued dominance. For Moyer, this turning to the powers of the underworld makes Fitzgerald's thematic point that "at the very foundation of Western Civilization, like a flawed keystone upon which the whole edifice of our history nevertheless rests, lies the Faustian pact and the obsessive will-to-power" (246) exemplified in the figure of Philippe.

A manuscript stored in the Fitzgerald collection of the Princeton University Library gives the plans for four other stories in the series. In the fifth story, the "decision to build castle leads to raid to kidnap artisan + fight to death." In the sixth story, Philippe would be "called to serve King. His Castle Stormed (Ursurper [sic] has made surfs [sic] mutiny) The Fief absolute." In the seventh story, "hard boiled Counts with

Ecclesiastics [would be] inventing Bogus rights to give chivalry a sacrosanct aspect." Finally, the eighth story was to be a "Love Story" (qtd. in Bruccoli, *Epic Grandeur* 388). Notably, the basic plotline for the seventh story appears to indicate something of Fitzgerald's position on courtly love and chivalry—an awareness of the "game-like" nature of the system, its roots in the attempts of the aristocracy to maintain its exclusivity. Perhaps the eighth story would have illustrated this idea.

Aside from Moyer, most critics have been either silent or largely derogatory about the Philippe stories. For instance, in a book-length study of Fitzgerald's short stories, John A. Higgins dismisses the Philippe stories in a footnote that reads, "This work has received strong negative criticism from all studies mentioning it. Its plot is confused and implausible, and its dialog the most banal Fitzgerald ever wrote" (193n). Both Janet Lewis and Bruccoli analyze the series in a bit more detail than does Higgins. For Lewis the stories are "intriguing skeletons in Fitzgerald's literary closet" (29) whose main flaw is Fitzgerald's attempt to have his characters "talk *almost* like contemporary speakers.... Fitzgerald's problems occur when he tries to reinforce the medieval setting by coupling contemporary and 'ninth-century' speech" (27). And Bruccoli lists the following problems Fitzgerald faced: (1) He could not work well with researched materials. (2) The stories lack the "personal quality" that distinguish his best work. (3) They present a linguistic problem—the same one mentioned by Lewis. Bruccoli rather imaginatively compares Philippe's speech to that of a "hard-boiled detective" and the peasants' to that of "southern sharecroppers" (*Price* 512–13).

Unfortunately, most of these negative comments are all too true. The stories are simply not as good as Fitzgerald's modern stories, largely because of the problem with dialogue. For instance, Philippe calls Griselda "baby" and "kid" and tells her to "pipe down." Yet the stories are not as confusing as Higgins maintains. Moyer has provided an important key to an understanding of them in relating them to Spengler's ideas. However, other critics, aside from complaining about the stories, have had little to say about their meaning. Moyer terms the few attempts at analyses that do exist "baffled assessments." Richard Lehan and Robert Sklar, for example, call the series an allegory of modern times (cited in Moyer 241n); more recently, H. R. Stoneback has said that the character Philippe is modeled on Ernest Hemingway and that, consequently, the series is intended as the "real story of modern man." In fact, according to Spengler, "modern times" and "modern man" are part of Civilization, not of the pre-Culture which is the setting of "Philippe." And Fitzgerald said that working on the stories provided him with a sense of escape from the modern world.

The Philippe series, then, serves as a prime piece of evidence of Fitzgerald's great interest in the medieval era. It also shows that, in his adoption of Spengler's theory and his conversion of that theory into dramatic terms, Fitzgerald achieved rather sophisticated ideas about history. Interestingly, the series also exhibits that other side of the usual Fitzgerald hero, that dreamer encountered in Fitzgerald's dream visions. For Philippe is not a sensitive dreamer; he is a man of action never seen dreaming. Again, in terms of Spengler's theory, as a part of pre-Culture, he is that necessary force that will help forge a Culture in which the dreamers—the artists—can thrive, and then, later, as part of Civilization, can still exist, but with ever-decreasing potency. Philippe does, nonetheless, have something in common with these dreamers: like them, he emerges very much as the individual: in his case, as the one, strong, dominant leader who must exist in order for the Culture to come into being.

Fitzgerald's inability to write these stories effectively may well have had to do with his depression during the period of their composition, which coincides with the period of his "crack-up," that dark night of the soul during which his creativity was at a low ebb (Janet Lewis 29). In a May 24, 1938, letter to Fitzgerald, Perkins suggests as much:

> You know I wish you would get back to the Phillippe [sic].—When you were working on that you were worn out and I thought could not do it justice.—But if you could get at it now it would be different, and you could make a fine historical novel of that time, and the basic idea was excellent and would be appreciated and understood now better than when you were writing it. (*Dear Scott* 246)

The plan and the desire were there; but the execution was weak. It is indeed unfortunate that Fitzgerald did not have the second chance that Perkins wished for him.

The saga of Fitzgerald's attempts to write "Philippe, Count of Darkness" is significant, too, in showing the tension Fitzgerald felt throughout his career between his personal inclinations as an artist and his financial needs. Fitzgerald was compelled throughout much of his career to write magazine stories to earn a living, to "lay by some money," as he put it, so that he could work on what he considered his more serious, more artistic works: his novels. That some of these magazine stories are of very high quality and rank among his best works does not diminish this sense Fitzgerald had of not being able to concentrate on what he deemed his most important work. This sort of tension, notably, is one that Chaucer seems never to have personally felt. To be sure, in Chaucer's last poem, "The Complaint of Chaucer to his Purse," the persona does cry out for his purse to be heavy again, and the poem does parody the courtly-love system by characterizing the purse as a lady whose yellowness (according to courtly-love conventions, the lady's hair, but really, gold coins) Chaucer wishes to see once again. But it is well agreed, it seems, that Chaucer's financial distress was only momentary, stemming from the recent ascension of Henry IV to the throne and the resulting delay in Chaucer's receipt of his pay. Otherwise, Chaucer seems to have been financially comfortable—but, again, because he made his living not as a writer but as a government official. If Fitzgerald were familiar with this poem, it could be, however, that he was not familiar with the biographical circumstances of it and thus did see a commonalty between Chaucer's seeming poverty and his own. Whether this poem had any effect upon Fitzgerald or not, and in spite of Chaucer's apparent lack of personal experience with the conflict between material and non-material values, that conflict was nonetheless an important one in Chaucer's day. Chaucer picks up on it in his works, though in the dream visions, he seems to speak more of the folly and temporality of fame than of wealth. In any case, the medieval version of this conflict stemmed in part from the stance of the medieval Church toward the courtly world. As Brewer explains, "the Church, in the name of otherworldliness, constantly attacked courtly values as worldly" and as causing injustice to the poor (62–63). Perhaps because it somewhat echoed his own dilemma, Fitzgerald was attracted to this idea as expressed in Chaucer's works.

Thus, Fitzgerald was attracted to the medieval era; and it makes sense to speak of Fitzgerald's attraction to Chaucer and to his particular part of the medieval era. Yet only a few Fitzgerald critics have previously noted a connection between the two authors—some fleetingly, and others, at length. Tom Burnam speaks of Fitzgerald's desire for order—as reflected in the "Schedule" that Gatsby has written in a copy of *Hopalong Cassidy*—as an "effort to reduce the world to terms in the Chaucerian sense of 'boundaries'" (109). William A. Fahey calls the episode in *This Side of Paradise* in which Amory and friends frolic in Asbury Park a "modern-day spring pilgrimage not unlike Chaucer's" (34). Higgins calls Fitzgerald's short story "One of My Oldest Friends" (1925) a "moral tale in the Chaucerian sense, complete with the climatic miracle" (73). And K. G. Probert has spoken briefly of a link between Chaucer's daisy/Alceste, a major figure in his dream vision the Prologue to *The Legend of Good Women*, and Daisy Fay Buchanan of *The Great Gatsby*. Seeming to assume the parallel is indirect, Probert merely notes that Daisy's name "has a rich history in medieval history"—namely, in the French marguerite poems—and that the name was "brought into English literature by Chaucer in *The Legend of Good Women*" (194). In short, these particular critics have sensed a Chaucerian presence in various works of Fitzgerald but have not pursued the matter further.

However, two other critics, Nancy Y. Hoffman and F. T. Flahiff, *have* pursued the matter further; they are more than slightly aware of a Chaucerian presence in Fitzgerald. Each has published a study concerning the influence of Chaucer's *Troilus and Criseyde* upon Fitzgerald's *The Great Gatsby*. Hoffman notes that in both works the protagonists search for desecrated Grails and are thereby destroyed—that is, Troilus desires the (in Hoffman's view) corrupt Criseyde, and Gatsby, the corrupt Daisy (156). Likewise, Flahiff finds various situations in Fitzgerald's novel reminiscent of Chaucer's poem—for instance, Nick's acting as something of a pander in arranging Gatsby's meeting with Daisy (as compared to Pandarus' role in *Troilus*) Flahiff regards as "pure Chaucer" (91).

Hoffman, Flahiff, and a few other critics present other important evidence linking Fitzgerald to Chaucer. John Kuehl, in his article "Scott Fitzgerald's Reading," not only shows how widely Fitzgerald read but also states that Fitzgerald did read Chaucer (59). More importantly, Hoffman (echoed by Flahiff and Bruccoli) states that, according to records at Princeton University, Fitzgerald took English 303, Chaucer and His Contemporaries, in the fall term of 1916.[4] The course was taught by

Gordon Hall Gerould.[5]   Bruccoli adds that Fitzgerald, in that term, was repeating the course, along with three other courses (*Epic Grandeur* 70); he had taken it before, in that fateful semester in which he left school in November, suffering from tuberculosis and on the verge of failing. The Princeton catalogue in effect in 1916 describes the course as follows: "'Reading will include the greater part of Chaucer's poetry, with selections from Langland, Gower, Wyclif and the author of Sir Gawain and the Green Knight.'"[6] The course required composition of "'a thesis of considerable length, embodying the result of independent investigation'" (Janet Miller, qtd. in Hoffman 157n). Unfortunately, Fitzgerald's thesis has not been found (Miller, cited in Hoffman 157n). However, he must have completed the project; for he finished the course, receiving the grade of 3, the equivalent of a C (Bruccoli, *Epic Grandeur* 70).

Although it can never be known for certain how much time and energy Fitzgerald devoted to this course, the grade of 3, though not high, was surely respectable in the days before grade inflation. Also, Hoffman contends that Fitzgerald, distressed by his previous failure, returned to Princeton that term "apparently determined to really study" (149). Indeed, his willingness in that semester to fall behind his class and to repeat so many classes while also taking two others (Bruccoli, *Epic Grandeur* 68) bespeaks great determination to pay attention to his studies, including the Chaucer course.

In fact, Fitzgerald made an indirect comment about his favorable impression of this class—or at least of its teacher, Gerould; and his friend John Peale Bishop spoke admiringly of the class, too. Years after he took the course, in a 1934 letter to Christian Gauss, Fitzgerald says, "I have a hunch Gerould rather likes me and I like Root whether he likes me or not..." (*Letters* 386). Robert K. Root was editor of the 1926 edition of Chaucer's *Troilus and Criseyde*. It would seem from this comment that the Princeton professors who specialized in the medieval era made a more favorable impression upon Fitzgerald than did most of the other English professors. As for Bishop, as Flahiff points out, he spoke of having gained at Princeton "the ability to pronounce Middle English passably well," as though this accomplishment—which was doubtless achieved in the Chaucer course—were one of the most memorable of his college years.[7]

It was a memorable course for Fitzgerald, too. Indeed, it had a larger impact on Fitzgerald than his remark about its teacher or Bishop's comments about the class would suggest. In his unused preface to *This Side of Paradise*, Fitzgerald mentions Chaucer admiringly, seemingly in connection with Fitzgerald's college days, which were then in the recent past. (Fitzgerald wrote the preface in 1919, just three years after he took the Chaucer course.) At the end of this preface, Fitzgerald offers his novel "to all those argumentative and discoursive souls who once frequented a certain inn whose doors are now dark, whose fabled walls ring no more to the melody of *Chaucer's lesser known poems*."[8] What else could Chaucer's "lesser known poems" be but his four dream visions? And what an impact these poems seem to have had on the then-fledgling novelist, that he should wish to refer to them in the preface to his first novel! (The inn of which Fitzgerald speaks, by the way, is probably the Peacock Inn, which was near the Princeton campus. Bishop reports that he and Fitzgerald first met at this inn as freshmen, and that on that occasion they and other students who gathered around the two of them "talked of books" ["Fitzgerald" 46–47]. In parallel fashion, in *This Side of Paradise*, Amory meets Bishop's counterpart, Thomas Parke D'Invilliers, at an inn called Joe's, where they discuss books [52–55].) Though apparently unaware of this reference of Fitzgerald's to Chaucer, Flahiff makes an astute observation about this Chaucer-Fitzgerald connection when he says, "The tradition is transmitted at odd times and in odd ways, by—and to—unaccountable people. Fitzgerald left Princeton—scrappy, full of promise, seemingly ungrateful—and the words were there, in his pocket" (98).

Indeed, Fitzgerald's admiration for Chaucer seems not to have abated even considerably later in his career; for it is from that era that Fitzgerald's one other direct reference to Chaucer comes. Chaucer appears on Fitzgerald's list, "Men of the Dark Thousand," which he compiled in the mid-1930s as part of his research for the Philippe project.[9] Thus, both early and late in his career, Fitzgerald considered Chaucer significant and evidenced a knowledge of his works.

Other evidence of a Chaucer-Fitzgerald connection derives from an examination of their ideas about dreams. Medieval thinking about the subject included Macrobius' influential commentary on Cicero's *Somnium Scipionis*, in which Macrobius divides dreams into five categories, the first three of which contain prophetic dreams: (1) *somnium* (enigmatic dream), in which the truth is under a veil of symbolism or allegory and

which can be of five types: personal, alien, social, public, and
universal; (2) *visio* (prophetic vision), which comes true as
seen; (3) *oraculum*, in which a revered man speaks the future to
the dreamer; (4) *insomnium*, which occurs through mental or
physical disturbances and simply replays one's waking preoccupations; and (5) *visum*, an illusion of shapes moving to and
fro that occurs when a person is not fully asleep.[10] In attend-
ing so carefully to whether a dream has any use for the discovery of truth, Macrobius shows his overriding concern with the
dream's effect (that is, its revelation of future events).   It is
also notable that Macrobius' interest lay mainly in the first
three categories of dreams, all of which involve the notion of
prophecy or direction from an outside authority figure, as opposed to the promptings of the dreamer's own psyche.   The
dreams that fit into categories four and five—including those
which stem from the dreamer's own waking preoccupations—
he deems worthless, though his system obviously accounts for
their existence.

    At first glance, modern dream theory would seem alto-
gether different.   But an area of overlap becomes apparent
when one examines medieval theory against one particular
modern dream theory, that of Carl Jung. What these two theories have most in common is the idea of a revelation of "truth"
to the dreamer, though in Jung's case, a better phrase would
be "solutions to problems." It is just that for Macrobius, the
revelation would come from a prophet, from an outside authority who would supernaturally appear in the dreamer's dream,
while for Jung, the revelation would come from within, as the
dreamer's own working out of the solution to his or her problem. As Raymond de Becker puts it, for Jung, the dream is not
just a "photograph of the unconscious.... It wants something.
It is a 'something' in progress. It is not a question of the
dream being prophetic...but it certainly is a question of a
dream which *makes* the future" (281). In Jung's own terms, the
dream has a "prospective function"—that is, it is "an anticipa-
tion in the unconscious of future conscious achievements,
something like a preliminary exercise or sketch, or a plan
roughed out in advance" ("General Aspects" 411). Obviously,
Jung's and Macrobius' ideas of the functions of dreams do
have a certain similarity, beyond the very real differences.

    But Jung does not concern himself merely with the after-
math of dreaming. He believes that dreams look both forward
and backward: "In almost every dream," he states, "certain

details can be found which have their origin in the impressions, thoughts, and moods of the preceding day or days" ("General Aspects" 24). Likewise, Macrobius' *insomnium* occurs because of mental and physical upsets, and it concerns waking preoccupations; but, again, Macrobius simply recognized the existence of such a dream without finding it significant. Also, Macrobius' scheme does not connect the idea that dreams are caused by the dreamer's waking experiences and feelings with the notion that dreams work on solutions to problems. However, Chaucer's ideas about dreams as revealed in his dream visions are somewhat more similar to modern theories in this regard than is the general medieval theory; for Chaucer clearly assumes the value of the connection between waking preoccupations and dreams as providing help with those problems.

Both medieval and modern dream theories also concern themselves with the way dreams operate. The theories of both eras mention the symbolic nature of dreams. To be sure, Macrobius' *visio* directly shows what is to happen; but most of his other categories contain symbolic dreams. Most significantly, Macrobius' *somnium*, or enigmatic dream, achieves its effect upon the dreamer precisely through symbolic means. In addition, his *oraculum* involves a universal symbol, the wise individual who comes to speak the truth to another. Somewhat similarly, Jung holds that the typical motifs in a dream form a parable that teaches the dreamer something ("General Aspects" 32). The typical motifs to which Jung refers are the manifestations of the archetypes, those universal molds for ideas, those patterns shared by all people and found in the collective unconscious. Archetypes include the wise old man of the sort that appears in Macrobius' *oraculum*; the anima and animus, which are, respectively, the female component within the male and the male component with the female; the persona and the shadow, or the pleasant surface image of oneself versus the darker, unpleasant, often hidden part of oneself; the mother, which can be an image either of protection or of smothering; and so on.

Also, for medieval and modern thinkers, dreams are structured alogically. Macrobius' definition of the *visum* specifically focuses upon its confusing nature. For Jung, "a dream is a strange and disconcerting product distinguished by many 'bad qualities,' such as lack of logic, questionable morality, uncouth form, and apparent absurdity or nonsense" ("On the Nature of Dreams" 68).

Chaucer and Fitzgerald, then, had access to dream theories with some significant points of similarity. Chaucer was familiar with the dream theories of his time; he lists them in *The House of Fame*, *The Parliament of Fowls*, and *The Nun's Priest's Tale*. It is usually held that he did not adhere to any one explanation of dreams, but that he kept an open mind. Indeed, in various works beyond those which merely list dream categories, Chaucer allows characters to present the full gamut of ideas on the subject. Early in *Troilus and Criseyde*, Troilus says that dreams are prophetic; later, he concludes that they are allegorical. Pandarus, however, contends that the true meaning of a dream must remain elusive because the possible explanations are too many. In "The Miller's Tale," Absolon considers dreams symbolic and thinks that the feasting in his dream symbolizes kissing. In his tale, the Parson considers dream interpretation impious. However, despite Chaucer's failure to commit himself to any one explanation of dreams, the evidence from both outside and within his dream visions suggests Chaucer's almost modern awareness of dreams' psychological import and symbolic nature. In other words, Chaucer viewed the dream as potentially a constructive, renewing, problem-solving event. In addition, however, he was aware of a potential danger for the dreamer who never truly awakens.

Chaucer's first dream vision, *The Book of the Duchess*, concerns a poet-persona who has a sorrowful imagination, probably not because of a real-life loss of a lady but rather because he has been too absorbed in the artificial courtly-love "text." He has a dream in which he meets his shadow, a man who also lacks part of what is needed for full creativity. This man tells the dreamer a fragmented, confusing story that the dreamer questions and otherwise attempts to make sense of. Having awakened renewed in his creativity because of his association with his shadow, the poet-persona is able to compose the poem that is *The Book of the Duchess*.

The second of Chaucer's dream visions, *The House of Fame*, also features a currently uncreative artist-figure—Geffrey—in need of a dream because of a lack of imagination caused by too much adherence to the texts of other people. In his dream, Geffrey visits three places, each of which fails to provide him with a worthy goal for his creativity. At the last place, he meets a man of great authority, who perhaps would have provided him with an eternal goal. But the poem ends, incomplete, at this point.

The Parliament of Fowls concerns a similarly unsuccessful artist who in his dream observes the courtly-love-styled mating ceremony of various birds, an experience that presumably should help him restore his creativity by showing him the need to concentrate on Nature instead of the artificial courtly-love system. But upon awakening, this poet-persona seems to have learned nothing from his dream; for he speaks of needing to look elsewhere for a solution to his problem.

All three of these dream visions show that a dream has at least the potential for providing a dreamer with renewal of creativity, but Chaucer's Prologue to *The Legend of Good Women* indicates just the opposite: that a dream can damage creativity. Here, the poet-persona's creative powers work well before the dream; he is able then to compose an artful tribute to the fresh, natural daisy. But during his dream, he mistakes a manipulative, artificial goddess for a natural daisy; allows this figure to manipulate him; and at her request—while still living within the dream—composes the relatively unsuccessful *Legend of Good Women*. Living too long within a dream—especially the wrong dream—short-circuits creativity, Chaucer seems to say; but dreams do have much potential in helping the artist solve the problem of lack of creativity.[11]

There is, of course, a possible distinction between theories about natural dreams and theories about literary genres. Nonetheless, Chaucer's notions about the natural dream and about the literary genre called the dream vision seem to match closely. To be sure, a few critics, such as the venerable C. S. Lewis, view the use of the dream in the dream vision (whether of Chaucer or of any other medieval author) as a mere convention having no connection to the natural dream as a psychological event (*The Allegory of Love* 167–68); but many others see that, at least in Chaucer's case, the dream form is not just convention but a psychological exploration as well. Of course, Chaucer does use the conventional aspects of the genre, inherited from the French: the discussion of dreams and sleeplessness; the springtime setting (though he does not always follow this convention); the poet-persona's recounting of the dream itself, surrounding by a frame occurring in the waking world; a guide; a courtly-love emphasis (Robinson 266). However, Chaucer also makes this genre a reflection of the natural dream and its psychological dynamics. He transforms the usual trappings of the genre into psychologically valid entities and adds new trappings of his own. For instance, he transforms the discussion of sleeplessness and dreams into a reason for the dream—the insomnia signifies the troubled, uncreative state of the dreamer, who therefore needs a dream to find renewal.   Chaucer also adds the mention of books in the frame of the tale (Stearns 31; Julius 21), with the book whose plot the poet-persona recounts always being in some way transformed into the "plot" of the dream, and always in an alogical, dream-like fashion.   Finally, Chaucer increases the complexity of the poet-persona, who often seems naive yet gives some indication of being experienced. This sort of ambiguity reflects that of the actual dream state. And all of these innovations point to a trait in Chaucer's characterizations that was to come to full fruition in his masterpiece, *The Canterbury Tales*: it is the new degree of realism, the attention to each character as a distinct individual, complete with an psyche of interest.

Chaucer's innovations seem, in other words, more modern than medieval—and thus something that might have appealed to Fitzgerald on that basis, for Fitzgerald was undoubtedly familiar with modern dream theory; Jung's (and Freud's) theories were simply "in the air" during his era.   Also, it is possible than Jungian theory was an influence upon Fitzgerald's depiction of the emotional condition of Nicole Warren Diver in *Tender Is the Night*.[12]

Like both Jung and Chaucer, Fitzgerald also appears to have especially recognized the possibility of both positive and negative dreaming: of dreaming of the wrong thing or staying within the dream, never awakening, and of having positive, constructive dreams that help in problem-solving. In "Pasting It Together" (1936), one of *The Crack-Up* articles, Fitzgerald says:

> In a real dark night of the soul it is always three o'clock in the morning, day after day. At that hour the tendency is to refuse to face things as long as possible by retiring into an infantile dream—but one is constantly startled out of this by various contacts with the world. One meets these occasions as quickly and carelessly as possible and retires once more back into the dream, hoping that things will adjust themselves by some great material or spiritual bonanza. But as

the withdrawal persists there is less and less chance of
the bonanza.... (75–76)

Here, dreams seem the very antithesis of constructive, renewing phenomena. Fitzgerald describes them instead as opiates,
mere escapes that do not help the dreamer live or create;
rather, they prevent the dreamer from doing so. But these, it
must be recalled, are what Fitzgerald calls "infantile dreams,"
and elsewhere in *The Crack-Up*, he explains more about them:

> As the twenties passed, with my own twenties march-
> ing a little ahead of them, my two juvenile regrets—at
> not being big enough (or good enough) to play football
> in college, and at not getting overseas during the
> war—resolved themselves into childish waking dreams
> of imaginary heroism that were good enough to go to
> sleep on in restless nights. ("The Crack-Up" 70)

Additionally, in "Sleeping and Waking" (1934), Fitzgerald
states that these dreams have been "worn thin with years of
usage. The character who bears my name has become blurred.
In the dead of the night I am only one of the dark millions rid-
ing forward in black buses toward the unknown" (67). The infantile dreams of Fitzgerald's dark night of the soul seem,
then, symptoms of his sickness—lack of creativity in art and in
life—and not the cure, the key to solving his problems. They
are old, worn-out dreams good only for inducing or preserving
sleep, not for inducing a happier waking state.

However, buried in Fitzgerald's negativity is the suggestion of another sort of dream outcome. The proof of the positive nature of Fitzgerald's own dreams—the very dreams he so
criticizes—lies in his ability to write *The Crack-Up* itself *after*
having gone through this dark night of the soul, *after* having
had the seemingly altogether destructive infantile dreams.
Significantly, it was *during* this period of depression that Fitzgerald produced the Philippe stories, which are poorly exe-
cuted. Having completed his interior journey through his dark
night, Fitzgerald could produce works—namely, the *Crack-Up*
articles—so effective, in fact, that they had an unintended con-
sequence: they evoked so strongly the sense of Fitzgerald's
despair that they made people think he was forever debilitated.
More recently, critics have hailed them as fine representatives

of the confessional genre. (See, for example, Donaldson, "The Crisis"; Box 82.) Consequently, Fitzgerald's interior journey filled with dreaming proved positive after all, even if, in *The Crack-Up*, at least, Fitzgerald does not say so.

In other places, Fitzgerald does see the value of dreams in enhancing creativity. His notebooks record some of his natural dreams and "daydreams"—apparently as grist for the artistic mill. For instance, he tells of "my blue dream of being in a basket like a kite held by a rope against the wind" (*Notebooks* 311), and of "my extraordinary dream about the Crimean war" (*Notebooks* 259). He also relates that "when I was a boy I dreamed that I sat always at the wheel of a magnificent Stutz...as low as a snake and as red as an Indiana barn" (*Notebooks* 244–45). Other entries capture the illogic of dreams and sound as if Fitzgerald recorded them soon after waking. One drifts into incoherence at various points:

> A trip to Florida with Howard Garrish and many bathing beauties. Asleep standing on the prow the beach and girls dancing. The one one [sic] skates like skiis [sic]. Like Switzerland, far castles and palaces. The horseman in the sea, the motor truck on sand, the horsemen coming ashore, the Bishop rears, falls, the horse saves him. My room, suits and ties, the view, the soldiers drilling under arcs in khaki, the wonderful man is now Tom Taylor, I buy and ties wake in strange room. Blunder into Mother who nags me. My mean remarks. (*Notebooks* 64)

This dream account comes complete with characters who appear and disappear suddenly, shifts in setting, a concern about waking preoccupations (beautiful girls, his mother), and, interestingly, some vaguely medieval trappings, such as the castles and the bishop on a horse. Altogether, the dream account is illogical and on one level nonsensical; yet Fitzgerald felt the dream's worth as an aid to composition, so much so that he chose to write an account of it in the notebook.

Another notebook entry shows that Fitzgerald felt a dream—notably, an implicit one—could be used as a literary device. The dream would help a character learn something:

> Plot—if I were rich. He became such Dream (not told)

starts with who he wouldn't help, unsympathetic. Goes through schemes Princeton, etc. People that he wouldn't help become more and more sympathetic in bad place. Other schemes fail. Wakes up disillusioned. Would now help—those people. (*Notebooks* 101)

Dreams, then, could indeed lead to artistic renewal; and they could be structurally significant in a literary work.

The matter of the alogical structure of the dream vision is important in another regard, too. It is frequently said that *The Great Gatsby*, as a first-person novel full of non-chronological fragments, exemplifies the "modern," as opposed to the "traditional" means of narration—with the term "traditional" referring to the use of a chronological structure and an omniscient narrator to produce "organic unity." "Traditional," however, makes sense in reference to this kind of narrative only if one is limiting the history of narratives to the eighteenth century and later, for the omniscient narrator is, after all, essentially a nineteenth-century invention. In fact, a much older tradition is exemplified in such works of the late Middle Ages as the dream visions of Chaucer. In this tradition, as explained by Judith Davidoff, narrative is inorganic, not organic. In such a narrative, the "core structure" contains inconsistencies and illogic but is held together by a unifying "exposed structural technique" such as a dream frame and a first-person narrator. Such a work manifests an "inorganic unity" that the late medieval audience expected (194–95). It seems to be this older tradition that Fitzgerald picks up on, though he does include much more of a plotline—and much more plot development—than is found in Chaucer's dream visions.

A final consideration also involves the dream-vision genre and exposes one of the prime conflicts found in both Chaucer's and Fitzgerald's treatments of the nature of artistic creativity: the conflict between perspective and objectivity on the one hand, and imaginative, emotional involvement on the other. As part of an illustration of the changes that occurred in late fourteenth-century England, Brewer describes King Edward III as the typical *early* fourteenth-century type (even though the king lived during the late part of the century). "One cannot," says Brewer, "imagine Edward questioning himself nor the nature of the universe.... Edward can never have 'put himself into someone else's place' to see how it felt, can hardly have internalized any values. If he had psychological conflicts they were seen as completely external events..." (84).

Brewer's characterization of this king is intriguing for the contrast with the dreamer depicted in Chaucer's dream visions, and for the sense the reader of Chaucer gets of the divided nature of the poet himself. Chaucer, the late fourteenth-century man, is, in a sense, the ultimate insider, with an appreciation for the courtly life and the courtly values around him, who nevertheless remains an outsider, a spectator, in his courtly poems (such as the dream visions), one who also questions the ultimate value of that existence (Brewer 137). In contrast, the king cannot, as it were, split himself in two, into the person who feels (or who sees others as feeling) and the person who recognizes and articulates the feelings. He cannot recognize himself as having emotions, an inner being. But the late fourteenth century marked a departure from earlier parts of the medieval era, with the beginnings of more legitimacy for the individual and thus for the inner, the emotional. In other words, it was a world edging toward a "modern" civilization that would produce, several centuries later, such phenomena as the romantic era and the sentimental novel. However, it was certainly not yet all right, as it would be those several centuries later, simply to blurt out personal feelings in literature, to think that the individual was quite that important.

Hence the flowering in this era of a genre such as the dream vision, which allows for a persona to be the "I," carefully distanced from the poet's own identity, and also largely an observer within his own dream, expressing his feelings—but indirectly through symbolic people and places within the dream. To be sure, some rather direct expression of emotion on the part of the "I" can seem to take place, too, as when the poet-persona of *The Book of the Duchess* tells of his sorrowful imagination and insomnia, but such passages are often conventional and stylized pieces rather than individualized outpourings, though, again, indirectly, they can *signify* something more personal. As J. Stephen Russell explains, "the lyric persona [in, for example, the romantic poem], moved by some emotion to write a poem, goes ahead and writes a poem about that emotion and about the events that engendered it, while the poet-dreamer never sets out consciously to expose his feelings" (*The English Dream Vision* 116).

In Fitzgerald's era, after the relatively direct emotional outpourings of nineteenth-century romantic poetry, and after what
was often seen by modernists as the excessively sentimental
outpourings of nineteenth-century domestic fiction, came modernism, with its emphases upon analysis, disunity of the human consciousness, irony, the scientific—indeed, a whole set
of attitudes in reaction to what had gone before. Modernists
(writers such as T. S. Eliot and Gertrude Stein and critics such
as Edmund Wilson) sought out a type of literature that involved a larger element of perspective and objectivity.[13] Modernists sometimes "genderized" their concerns by speaking
fearfully of needing to resist the "feminization" of literature.
(See Clark and Kerr.) Terry Eagleton characterizes this facet of
the modernist position as follows:

> Poetry had fallen foul of the Romantics, become a
> mawkish, womanly affair full of gush and fine feeling.
> Language had gone soft and lost its virility: it needed
> to be stiffened up again, made hard and stone-like, re-
> connected with the physical world.... Emotions were
> messy and suspect, part of a clapped-out epoch of
> high-flown liberal-individualist sentiment which must
> now yield to the dehumanized mechanical world of
> modern society.[14]

Fitzgerald's career as a writer can be read in part as a struggle
to deal with this dilemma of "inner" and romantic/sentimental
(feminine) versus "outer" and modernist (masculine)—to find,
that is, the means to express deep emotions while also finding
a way to stand aside and comment upon those feelings, the
means, perhaps, to be both romantic/sentimental and modernist.[15] It seems that in certain of his works—those to be dealt
with in subsequent chapters of this study—he is working toward finding a way to combine these two stances, while also
dealing with the Chaucerian idea of the artist's need for a
permanent, non-material goal, one beyond the popular and the
commercial. The way he finds involves using the enticing
models provided by Chaucer's dream visions.

CHAPTER TWO

SILENCED WOMEN: "THE OFFSHORE PIRATE" AND "THE ICE PALACE"

Be good sweet maid, and let who can be clever;
  Do lovely things, not dream them, all day long;
And so make Life, Death, and that For Ever
  One grand sweet song.
  —Charles Kingsley, "A Farewell"

Two of F. Scott Fitzgerald's earliest professional short stories, "The Offshore Pirate" (1920) and "The Ice Palace" (1920), are also Fitzgerald's earliest dream visions. They manifest elements common in the Chaucerian dream vision, including the Chaucerian theme of the interior journey of the artist toward renewal of creativity—although in neither of Fitzgerald's stories does the character succeed in the quest. But these two Fitzgeraldian "dream visions" also are highly unusual in that, unlike Chaucer's dream visions, and unlike Fitzgerald's other dream visions, they feature women dreamers.

"The Offshore Pirate," first published in the *Saturday Evening Post*, was originally an *explicit* dream vision. The story concerns the rebellious, beautiful, wealthy, potentially creative Ardita Farnam, who lies lazily about on her uncle's yacht reading Anatole France's *The Revolt of the Angels*. She refuses her uncle's suggestion that she meet wealthy Toby Moreland; instead, she wants to join her notorious boyfriend at Palm Beach, despite her uncle's objections. The uncle leaves; and soon Curtis Carlyle, accompanied by six black singers, boards the yacht, his group singing. Most of the story details Ardita and Carlyle's conversations about his past as they travel toward a

beautiful island. Carlyle is a musician who has been torn between playing ragtime with his black friends and being accepted by the socially elite. He has recently turned to bank
robbery. Ardita admires his sense of adventure and thinks
how much they are alike. They are both rebels, but Ardita is
rich and Carlyle is poor. Ultimately, on the island, they kiss
just as they hear a bumping, scraping sound.

What happens next in the story depends on whether one is
reading the published story or the version that Fitzgerald
originally sent to his literary agent, Paul Revere Reynolds.
Apparently, up to the ending, the original version is very
much like the published version, though evidently it does contain in the opening passages some references to a maid who is
on the yacht. But this earlier version does have a markedly
different ending from the published story. The earlier version
ends with a scene in which, just after the kiss, Ardita awakens
to encounter her uncle and her maid. In a conversation with
the maid, it comes to light that the maid once told Ardita about
a vaudeville act called Curtis Carlyle and his Six Black Bud-
dies. Ardita now wonders whether this "real" Curtis Carlyle
resembles her dream Curtis Carlyle. The maid denies any resemblance, saying that the real Carlyle is small, ugly, and bow-
legged. The story concludes with Ardita simply proclaiming
that "'it's a darn funny world'" and the maid agreeing with
this sentiment.[1]

When he originally sent the story to Reynolds, Fitzgerald
expressed some dissatisfaction with this ending: "If you think
the ending spoils it," he writes on January 27, 1920, "clip it
off.... Don't look now but when you come to sit [sic] see if you
think it takes the pep out of the story. Personally I like it as it
is" (*As Ever* 11). Apparently, however, someone—Reynolds,
Harold Ober, or even George Horace Lorimer of the *Saturday
Evening Post*—suggested that instead of simply clipping off the
ending, Fitzgerald revise the story and alter the ending (Atkinson 49). Subsequently, on February 21, 1920, in a letter to
Ober, Fitzgerald says of the revised story, "I think you'll see if
you read this from the beginning that I've put the required
Jazz ending on it and I don't doubt they'll [the *Saturday Evening Post*] buy it." The final new line, he continues, "takes Mr.
Lorimer at his word. Its [sic] one of the best *lines* I've ever
written" (*As Ever* 12).

Indeed, the new ending is quite different from the original
one. In the published version, Ardita does not awaken, so the

foregoing action is not explicitly part of a dream. Instead, Ardita's uncle arrives, revealing that Carlyle is really Toby Moreland. Toby has made up the whole thing to meet the reluctant Ardita and to find out if she is the appropriate mate for him. Amazingly, Ardita welcomes the news of his pretense; she admires Toby for his vivid imagination and asks him to lie to her like that for the rest of their lives. The last line that Fitzgerald liked so much states that Ardita reached up and "kissed him [Toby] softly in the illustration" (266).

Fitzgerald's attitude about the story's ending seems ambivalent. In the letter to Reynolds, his use of the word *personally* implies that he simply thinks the first ending will not be commercially successful, that artistically it poses no problems for him, an idea he possibly reinforces in the letter to Ober, in which he speaks of the new ending as the "required Jazz Age ending." Yet he does seem to admire the new last sentence. This state of affairs is an early example of that conflict between commercial success and artistic success that was Fitzgerald's companion throughout his career. Fitzgerald was under pressure to write stories popular with magazine readers, particularly the readers of the high-paying *Saturday Evening Post* (rather like Chaucer and other medieval courtly poets felt more or less constrained to meet the expectations of the court). Matthew Bruccoli maintains that "it would be foolish to claim that his [Fitzgerald's] awareness of the *Post's* expectations did not exert an influence on his material or that he did not to some extent tailor his stories to his best market" (Introduction, *Price* xv). Fitzgerald's use of the word *pep* in his letter to Reynolds indicates something about the expectations of those readers: they wanted adventure—as well as a sophisticated tone and such Jazz-Age trappings as the brash, rich flapper Ardita and the ragtime pianist Carlyle. They also wanted a happy, romantic ending—which the revised version supplies but the first version does not.

However, despite this sort of pressure, Fitzgerald was able to keep his dream vision a dream vision, although an implicit one. Perhaps this early experience with having to "bury"— possibly rather clumsily in this case—his true intent led him, in all his other dream visions except *The Vegetable*, to be more successfully subtle in his use of the genre. This subtle use of the dream in a dream vision is not without precedent in medieval literature, where certain works that otherwise follow the dream-vision pattern do not contain actual dreams. Examples include the anonymous fifteenth-century Chaucer imitation *The Flower and the Leaf* and John Lydgate's *The Complaint of the Black Knight* (an imitation of *The Book of the Duchess*). Davidoff has suggested the terms "dream-vision analogues" or "waking visions" for such works in order to emphasize that they are "structurally identical to conventional dream vision," aside from the lack of break in consciousness on the part of the poets-personae (89). So the implicitness of Fitzgerald's dream visions does not stop them from belonging to this genre; in making the shift, he is simply behaving as certain fourteenth- and fifteenth-century Chaucer imitators do (whether he was aware of their imitations or not). And perhaps Fitzgerald was wise to be implicit: his one published explicit dream vision, *The Vegetable*, proved an abysmal failure with the public. His original audience (whether for a play or for stories and novels) apparently neither expected nor desired out-and-out dream visions—or at least Fitzgerald's publisher did not believe they did. Their expectations were, then, very much in contrast to those of Chaucer's original audience.

The change from explicit to implicit, though it does not affect membership in the genre, is no small matter in another respect, for it makes a significant difference to present a protagonist who merely has dreamlike experience rather than a protagonist who generates a dream. In the published version, Ardita's experience is dreamlike, not a dream, so she can never be as much the artist as a Chaucerian poet-persona is; for a Chaucerian poet-persona is pictured as actually having generated his own dream. The typical Chaucerian poet-persona's identity is permeated with the idea of the artist in another way as well: as first-person narrator, he creates not only the dream but also the dream account. In *The Book of the Duchess*, there is a third way in which the identity as an artist emerges: this poet-persona also edits the tale of a second artist-figure. Since Fitzgerald's "The Offshore Pirate" does not feature the usual dream-vision point of view, the first-person, its protagonist does not even "write" the account of the dreamlike experience. Ardita's identity as an artist has to stem primarily from her attempts to "shape" the story told by the other artist, Carlyle, during the dreamlike experience. It is Carlyle who emerges as the artist who creates the dream—and then only in the revised version, where it turns out that he is really Toby, who has made up the story of Carlyle. Fitzgerald thus uses in this story only one of Chaucer's means for establishing his protagonist's artistic identity. The same is true of the protagonists of Fitzgerald's next two dream visions, "The Ice Palace" and "The Diamond as Big as the Ritz."

Then, something different occurs in *The Vegetable* and *The Great Gatsby*. In *The Vegetable*, protagonist Jerry Frost actually has a dream, but, since the work is a play, the reporting of the dream is not "his," so he cannot emerge as the artist who creates the dream account. Then, in *Gatsby*, Nick Carraway appears as the artist who actually writes the "dream" account and also edits another artist's tale, yet the "dream" is only implicitly a dream. Nick therefore does not generate the dreamlike experience. Within the dream visions of Chaucer, then, the dream is a real event; within the works of Fitzgerald, dream is simile, with dreamlike events, not dreams. Nonetheless, Fitzgerald is able to create the sense that his protagonists are artists, even if not entirely through the same means Chaucer uses to create the same effect.

"The Offshore Pirate" consists of a frame and of a core that may be interpreted as a dream, or in any case a dreamlike experience, even in the revised version with its lack of direct reference to a dream. In the first part of its frame, a Chaucerian dream vision calls attention to itself as a dream vision and thus as art conscious of itself as art. Chaucer achieves this effect in several ways: by the poet-persona's rather directly referring to the fact that he is about to recount a dream; by his discussing sleep and dreams; by his appearing as a person who, because of a current lack of creativity, needs the renewal that sleep and dreams can bring. In *The Book of the Duchess*, the poet-persona makes clear that he is about to tell of a dream by saying,

> Y fil aslepe, and therwith even
> Me mette so ynly swete a sweven,
> So wonderful, that never yit
> Y trowe no man had the wyt
> To koone wel my sweven rede. (275–79)

He also speaks of his insomnia and its adverse effect upon him. It is this lack of sleep that drives him to pick up a book in which he reads a story which itself concerns sleep and dreams—that of Alcione, who dreams she sees her dead husband, Seys. The poet-persona then calls upon the god of sleep, Morpheus, to make him sleep. Thus the poet-persona feels a need to sleep, as if sleep and dreams will hold the key to his nourishment and renewal.

In the published form of "The Offshore Pirate," though Fitzgerald is committed to using the genre subtly and therefore does not mention the tale as the record of a dream, he does take care to call attention to the story as a story; and he frequently uses imagery suggestive of sleep and dreams. "This unlikely story," the opening sentence reads, "begins on a sea that was a blue dream, as colorful as blue-silk stockings, and beneath a sky as blue as the irises of children's eyes" (17). In the first three words, Fitzgerald calls attention to the story as story, and his inclusion of the adjective "unlikely" implies that this will be a story with the implausibility also associated with dreams. Subsequently, in his emphasis upon dream imagery, Fitzgerald does everything but proclaim that this is a dream vision. Fitzgerald juxtaposes several images to fairly saturate the story with the aura of a dream: the sea, that archetypal symbol of the protective mother, associated with the womb, a place of sleep here associated with a "blue dream"; children's eyes and thus the idea of vision and insight; blue, which for Fitzgerald represents dream and vision.

Further into the opening part of the frame, Fitzgerald continues to use sleep and dream imagery. The third-person narrator calls the silence enveloping the boat "drowsy" and says that Ardita "very faintly but quite unmistakably yawned" (17). But perhaps the most striking imagery suggestive of sleep and dreams—moreover of Ardita's need to experience them—occurs in the description of her lemon. The other half of the lemon Ardita is sucking "lay on the deck at her feet and rocked very gently to and fro at the almost imperceptible motion of the tide" (17). Here, two images form a picture of a mother suckling and rocking her child. The lemon surely serves as a metonymy of the tangy, zestful, even "sour" Ardita. She, like the lemon, is sucked dry, unproductive, just lying there on a yacht doing nothing—though she is capable of much creativity. Notably, if the lemon represents Ardita, it follows that Ardita is sucking herself dry; and, indeed, she is centered fully on herself, wasting her energy in a generalized rebellion against her uncle which seems passive aggressive. She uses her imagination only to create clever taunts with which to mock him. The lemon rocks gently as a result of the motion of the sea, the archetypal mother. Like the Chaucerian poet-persona, Ardita Farnam needs such lulling to sleep so that a dream can renew her.

Chaucer's typical poets-persona and Fitzgerald's Ardita are frustrated artist-figures. The poet-persona of *The Book of the Duchess* feels numb, confused, and unproductive. He is troubled by his "sorwful ymagynacioun," which he finds "alway hooly in my mynde" (14–15) as if no room for a more productive kind of imagination is left. Two other Chaucerian poets-personae feel similarly bereft of artistic imagination. Geffrey, in *The House of Fame*, wants Apollo to make his poem "sumwhat agreable," for he feels that "the rym ys lyght and lewed" and that "som vers fayle in a sillable; / And that I do no diligence / To shewe craft, but o sentence" (1096–1100). The poet-persona of *The Parliament of Fowls*, though professing to be speaking about love, appears to be talking about his difficulties as an artist when he proclaims, "the lyf so short, the craft so long to lerne" (1). Of Chaucer's poets-personae, only the poet-persona of the Prologue to *The Legend of Good Women* is not a frustrated artist at the beginning of his poem; he is instead the inverse: a productive artist whose creativity is stymied *within* his dream. But otherwise, the typical Chaucerian poet-persona begins as a frustrated artist.

Likewise, the opening frame in "The Offshore Pirate" establishes Ardita as an artist. Perhaps the name *Ardita* refers to art. (*Art* becomes *Ard?*) And Ardita reveals how much she values the imagination when she says she wants to marry her boyfriend because "'...he's the only man I know, good or bad, who has an imagination and the courage of his convictions'"(20). Also, when her uncle tries to tell her of this man's affair with a nefarious woman named Mimi, Ardita says,

> "Thrilling scandals by an anxious uncle.... Have it filmed. Wicked clubman making eyes at virtuous flapper. Virtuous flapper conclusively vamped by his lurid past. Plans to meet him at Palm Beach. Foiled by anxious uncle." (20)

Here, Ardita turns a presumably real-life event into a movie scenario. She thus shows her propensity to be a director, to seek artistic control, to take raw experience and make it into art. (See Arnold 44.)

Yet Ardita is currently an unproductive artist with no proper outlet for her ability. Throughout the opening section, she does little except taunt her uncle and suck on her lemon. She also comments that her family has made her the way she is and that she never changes her mind—statements of rigidity and stasis. Ardita's imagination, like that of Chaucer's poets-personae, is askew. Even the reasons for the problem are similar. The poet-persona of *The Book of the Duchess*, for instance, dwells upon the loss of a loved one and therefore is confused and dull; Ardita dwells upon her separation from her beloved and is thus languid, rigid, and irresponsible.

Both Chaucer and Fitzgerald reinforce the idea of artistic frustration by reference to books, a dream-vision attribute seemingly original with Chaucer (Stearns 31; Julius 21). The content of the books mirrors what will occur in the dreams. For instance, in *The Book of the Duchess*, the poet-persona says that he read the tale of Alcyone, who dies after a dream in which her dead husband, Seys, has appeared to reveal to her his death. This tale of a woman who mourns excessively will be reflected in the poet-persona's dream, in which the Man in Black mourns excessively (Hieatt 68–69). The poet-persona's turning to a book stresses his essential problem: he has not turned inward for a renewal of creativity but instead has sought only the external aid of a book. Even his talk of sorrowful imagination is bookish talk, for it makes use of bookish courtly-love conventions.

Similarly, in "The Offshore Pirate," Ardita reads a book, Anatole France's *The Revolt of the Angels*, a work that concerns just what the title suggests. It therefore serves as an appropriate mirror of the dream she is about to have, in which she will meet the rebel Curtis Carlyle and discuss her own desire to rebel. Yet the book also serves to emphasize Ardita's true lack of active imagination. She sleepily reads of risk-taking, talks about loving to live imaginatively, even shows a tendency for creativity in formulating a movie scenario—but one that serves merely to taunt her uncle. Until near the end of the opening frame, she takes no action to direct her own life, to be the artist in control of her own "scenarios."

In the typical Chaucerian dream vision, the poet-persona turns away from his book by beginning to dream. In "The Offshore Pirate," Ardita (rather like one of the angels in *The Revolt of the Angels*) literally throws away her book. Angry at her uncle's threat to disown her, Ardita says, "'Will you stop

boring me!... Do you want me to throw this book at you!'"
(19). And then she does just that. (Later, she throws the
lemon at him, too.) Finally, after lolling about, yawning, and
reading, Ardita takes action, albeit destructive action, but at
least direct. And her action has a definite effect: soon thereafter, her uncle leaves the boat, which leaves her alone and
ready for self-exploration in her "dream."

As with Chaucer's dream visions, Ardita's dream will
combine "real-life" experience and reading material. The poet-
persona in *The Book of the Duchess* has more than books on his
mind; he also is concerned about his past experience of loss—
probably the loss of a lady (Lumiansky). He thus dreams a
dream combining bookish knowledge and "real-life" experience. Likewise, Ardita reads about rebellion; and she dreams
about rebellion. She also is told several things that will show
up in her dream: her uncle says that Toby has come from New
York to meet and go to dinner ashore with her, her maid tells
(in the original opening) of the musical group featuring Curtis
Carlyle, and her uncle informs her of her boyfriend's gift to
Mimi of a diamond bracelet. All of these elements combine in
the dream to form the dream-figure Curtis Carlyle.

In Chaucer's dream visions and in "The Offshore Pirate,"
it is not that books or real life has nothing to offer the artist. It
is instead that the artist has overemphasized these aspects to
the exclusion of another—inner exploration. The overemphasized aspects are the more passive and outward ones. Yet the
artist must take what they have to offer, internalize it, and
reform it through the activity of his or her imagination—that
is, through dreaming. Chaucer and Fitzgerald therefore give a
picture of the necessary materials with which the artist needs
to work: the reading of other authors' works, direct experience
of the world, and the inner exploration of self and imagination
that a dream affords. Again, Chaucer's attention to inner
exploration constitutes a relatively new emphasis for his time:
a newfound, fledgling emphasis upon the significance of the
individual and his psyche. That Fitzgerald picked up on this
emphasis in Chaucer's works should not be surprising: as part
of a post-romantic age, he was well disposed to consider the
psyche of the individual important. As a modernist, however,
Fitzgerald may have worried about the "feminization" of literature, about too much emotional content—hence a reason
(not unlike the reasoning of the a medieval author) to choose
the dream vision as an indirect way to express the inner and

emotional, one that not only allowed for such expression but also disguised it. In light of such considerations, it becomes all the more intriguing that he should have made a woman the artist-figure in this work (and in "The Ice Palace").

The core or dream account of "The Offshore Pirate" is especially similar to that of *The Book of the Duchess*. For one thing, the first parts of the core are much alike. As the dream in Chaucer's poem begins, the dreamer is awakened by "smale foules a gret hep / That had affrayed me out of my slep, / Thorgh noyse and swetnesse of her song" (295–97). Similarly, in "The Offshore Pirate," Ardita's dream (and Part II of the story) begins with her hearing a "chorus of men in close *harmony* and in perfect rhythm to an accompanying sound of oars cleaving the blue waters" (21; emphasis added). Their song includes the words, "Blow us a breeze" (21), and "Who could make clocks / Out of cellos?" (22). Thus, like the poet-persona of *The Book of the Duchess*, Ardita wakes up in her dream to confront a situation far different from her own lazy, unproductive condition. She meets figures using their creative powers full force. Their harmony suggests creativity working well, and their words—with their emphasis upon inspiration ("breezes") and upon imaginative transformations (turning clocks into cellos)—further stress this point.

The rest of each dream account reflects the haziness and illogic of dreams, and each is structured around a journey deep into a dreamlike region where each dreamer meets himself or herself in the person of his or her shadow. Each dreamer serves as "editor" or "director" of the shadow's story and thereby exercises some artistic control over it.

The dream account in *The Book of the Duchess* is filled with suggestions of the haze and illogic of dreams.[2] The dreamer, for instance, suddenly mentions a horse being in his chamber and never wonders how it got there, and just as suddenly he finds himself under a tree and never thinks to explain how he has come to be there. The similarly haziness and illogic of the core of "The Offshore Pirate" becomes evident in several instances. The moon smiles "misty-eyed upon the sea...as the shore faded dimly out"; and the yacht is "quiet as a dream boat star-bound through the heavens" (26). Then when Carlyle and Ardita are on the island, "the dew rose and turned to golden mist, thin as a dream, enveloping them until they seemed gossamer relics of the late night..." (44). Most strikingly, though astonished initially at their presence, Ardita does not question the plausibility of a man and a group of singers in blue uniforms happening to board her boat to elude the law. Indeed, Ardita initially takes their presence seriously enough to demand that they get off the yacht; and although she doubts details of Carlyle's story and dislikes his storytelling method, she never seems to question the basic highly illogical situation.

Journeys into dream world occur in both accounts. In *The Book of the Duchess*, the dreamer travels twice into various parts of the dream world, each time led by a guide or guides. Near the beginning of the dream, he follows by horse the hunters whose horn he has heard. They are hunting a hart—obviously a pun on the word *heart*—so his following them on their quest signifies that his journey is an interior one: a journey to find his heart. Later, on foot now, he follows a dog through a green wood "thikke of trees, so ful of leves" (418) and full of flowers and many animals, including harts, bucks, does, squirrels. The dreamer, in short, has entered a place of abundant natural creativity—symbolizing his own imagination, with its potential for creativity.

In "The Offshore Pirate," a journey deep into a dream world also occurs, with Carlyle serving as guide. As the trip gets under way, Carlyle has Trombone Mose paint over the name of the boat, "Narcissus," and substitute the name "Hula Hula" (25). The name substitution suggests the nature of this journey: it will be an exploration of Ardita's self. The name *Narcissus* indicates the root of her problem: a self-centeredness resulting in a myopic, distorted view of the self. She is, in other words, so intent upon herself that she has no perspective. She will need to explore her self in a different way (hence the change in name)—by playing it off against that of Carlyle. Later, the yacht travels to an island reminiscent of the green wood in *The Book of the Duchess*. It is a "miniature world of green and gold" featuring tropical vegetation and a "golden lake" (32). Like the wood in Chaucer's work, it suggests natural creativity.

In *The Book of the Duchess*, the dreamer meets the Man in Black only after the dreamer has reached the middle of the green wood; in contrast, in "The Offshore Pirate," since Carlyle functions as both guide and shadow, Ardita and he begin their encounter on the way to the green island. Despite the structural difference, the exchanges between Chaucer's poet-persona and the Man in Black and those between Ardita and Carlyle resemble each other significantly.

   The dreamer in *The Book of the Duchess* sees a highborn
man dressed in black sitting under an oak tree. This Man in
Black, unaware of the dreamer's presence, sings a lay concerning the loss of his lady. Eventually, the man notices the
dreamer, and there follows an interchange in which the
dreamer's role has been hotly debated. Despite having just
heard the lay about the lady's death, the dreamer seemingly
cannot understand the man's subsequent comments about why
he (the Man in Black) feels so mournful and sorrowful. Critics
have explained the dreamer's obtuseness in all sorts of ways—
chiefly, that the dreamer is truly naive or that he is actually
quite experienced and simply realizes that the man must work
through his grief and hence goes on asking questions to draw
out the whole story and to get the man to come to grips with
the loss by plainly speaking of it. (See Bronson 877.) Yet another explanation concerns the nature of the man's remarks.
He initially speaks of his loss in a lay, a genre that uses
courtly-love language. Therefore, perhaps the dreamer views
the man's remarks in the song as mere convention (Garbaty
99). Subsequently, when the Man In Black tries to explain his
situation to the dreamer, he still does so in the courtly-love
"code" as it were. He speaks, for example, of how False Fortune has taken away his "fers," not plainly of how he has lost
his lady to death. He also often uses ornate courtly-love
terms, which may make the dreamer believe the man is simply
pining—in the best courtly-love tradition—for an unkind
woman. Perhaps the dreamer on some level realizes the nature
of the man's loss and is trying to get him to speak of it in a
real, personal manner worthy of such a monumental event, not
in unworthy, hackneyed terms. Eventually, the attempts of
the dreamer to edit the Man's remarks pay off: the Man in
Black states plainly that Good Fair White is dead.
   Like the dreamer, the Man in Black has been letting something stand in the way of an active life and a productive
imagination. His opening lay is confusing to the dreamer and
insufficient as a fitting tribute to his lost lady. But in the end,
he is able to express his sorrow effectively (that is, plainly and
realistically) and then go on with his life; and, as an artist, he
has created a fitting tribute (Shoaf 164–47). In helping the man
achieve these ends, the dreamer is really helping himself, too.
The Man in Black, in Jungian terms, is the dreamer's shadow,
his alter ego who represents that part of the dreamer that he
has preferred to keep hidden. Encountering this figure in his

dream, the dreamer becomes aware of his own inability to be creative: he, too, has become caught up in unnatural, excessive grief because of his own loss of a lady; and thus he lacks perspective. (See Tisdale 368–69; Julius 11.)

In "The Offshore Pirate," a similar interchange occurs, and one with similar results. Curtis Carlyle appears, not dressed in black or singing a song but instead accompanied by six black musicians who sing a song. At first glance, the differences between the situation in Chaucer's poem and the one in Fitzgerald's story seem many. Carlyle has not lost a loved one, and he is anything but high-born. And Ardita is a "high-born" Jazz-Age flapper, hardly like the quiet and courteous poet-persona. In fact, if anything the social standings of the characters in Fitzgerald's story are the reverse of those in Chaucer's poem, where the Man in Black is probably of higher standing than is the poet-persona. Yet there are curious parallels, and the central situations are the same: Ardita, like Chaucer's dreamer, does meet her shadow and converse with him, all the while "editing" and exploring his remarks.

As various examples indicate, Carlyle and Ardita are much alike. Ardita considers Carlyle a "romantic figure" who gives the impression of possessing a "towering self-confidence." She believes that, like her, he is an egotist (26). Later she tells him, "'I've been thinking all day that you and I are somewhat alike. We're both rebels—only for different reasons.'" At one time, she continues,

> "we both fitted.... But deep in us both was something that made us require more for happiness. I didn't know what I wanted.... I used to sit sometimes chewing at the insides of my mouth and thinking I was going crazy—I had a frightful sense of transciency." (35)

Carlyle, serves, then, as Ardita's double. However, he does more than reflect what Ardita already knows about herself—which seems to be that she desires a sense of permanence. Carlyle also serves as shadow, revealing the part of herself she would prefer to keep hidden, even from herself.

What is this hidden part of Ardita? She reveals that at one time she resented society and began to desire only to shock people. Now, however, she feels she has discovered something else: "'courage as a rule of life,'" which she defines as the capacity "'to live as I liked always and to die in my own way'" (36). What seems to be hidden from Ardita is the idea that this positive, courageous way of life she has supposedly been following seems rather a matter of recklessly taunting and shocking people, a way of life she thinks she has given up. Ardita is indeed shown as simply reckless; she is like someone who splashes paint of a wall in a fit of rebellion for attention's sake and wants then to call it art, as opposed to an artist who, with imagination and discipline, paints something meaningful on that same wall. The artist's work might involve rebellion, but not exclusively. Thus, Ardita, like Chaucer's dreamer, lacks perspective on herself.

It is Carlyle who can reveal to Ardita her true nature. Like her, he is capable of much creativity in that he exhibits "vividness of...imagination" and also a "rather unusual musical gift" (27). Though in the past he has expressed his creativity, now, he is, as Ardita observes,

> somehow completely pregnable and quite defenseless. When Ardita defied convention—and of late it had been her chief amusement—it was from an intense desire to be herself, and she felt that this man, on the contrary, was preoccupied with his own defiance. (26)

Ardita is rationalizing about her own reasons for rebelling rather than recognizing Carlyle's reasons for his behavior. For Carlyle has had a problem as an artist: a conflict between his artistic inclinations and his desire to attain high social standing. At this point, he has already told Ardita about his past, about his being a fine ragtime pianist with the ability to play traditional African rhythms, a type of music portrayed as expressive of strong emotions. But he has also spoken of his conflicting negative feelings about the fact that this particular type of music meant his being associated with blacks and thus shunned by more restrained, conventional aristocratic society. Though Carlyle's attitudes toward racial matters is certainly repugnant to the late twentieth-century reader, Fitzgerald seems to have been attempting through Carlyle to portray a sense of the artist's being torn between artistic and commercial success, along with a sense of the racist assumptions of the elite society of his time. Carlyle is bitter because his artistic inclinations lead him into a part of society scorned by aristocrats. His conflict echoes that faced by Fitzgerald himself, as he confronted his propensity for the romantic as against the tenets of modernism, as well as the conflict between commercial and artistic success.

Carlyle has chosen not to face his problem at all; instead he robs a bank, retreats from society, and relates the story of his past using every hackneyed plot device imaginable. It is in this sense of retreat from life and submersion in a tale about his past that Carlyle most parallels the Man in Black, who would also rather sit about and tell a tale—poorly—rather than face his problems. It is also in this sense that Carlyle and Ardita are most alike: both retreat from facing their creativity. That Carlyle's attitude mirrors Ardita's becomes clear when Carlyle, unwilling to tell Ardita the details of the robbery he has committed, says he does not want to break down her illusion of *herself*. It is as if learning about him will show Ardita something real about herself rather than about him. Carlyle further comments that the only difference between them is that Ardita is rich and Carlyle is poor. He thus implies that were it not for the security provided by wealth, Ardita would find herself retreating in an illegal way, as he has.

As Carlyle tells the story of his past, Ardita edits and directs it. In many ways, she does so much as the Chaucerian dreamer edits the tale told by the Man in Black. Soon after Carlyle and his man board the yacht, Ardita indicates that she likes to look at her own life in movie terms, that, in other words, she has a propensity to direct. Ardita's "own situation," the reader is told, "affected her as the prospect of a matinee might affect a ten-year-old child" (26). She soon starts acting out this tendency when she asks Carlyle to "'lie to me by the moonlight. Do a fabulous story'" (27). So Carlyle tells of his past: his poor background; his achieving fame because of his imagination and musical talent, which led him to work as a ragtime violinist on the Orpheum circuit and on Broadway; his desire to become a "regular pianist" instead of an "eternal monkey, a sort of sublimated chorus man" not good enough to associate with aristocrats (28); his artistic suicide in leaving this group; his loss of his money; his duties as a war-time bandleader; and, finally, his taking desperate measures to keep from returning to being merely a "'bobbing, squawking clown'" (29). It is indeed a tale full of all the usual hackneyed features of popular film (just as the Man in Black's tale uses hackneyed courtly-love features): the rags-to-riches plotline, the tale of the poor fellow who never got to fight in the war, the yarn about

the poor boy who longs to hob-nob with the rich. And, again,
it is full of stereotypical, degrading racial references that also
were the popular attitudes of that time. Ardita reacts to the
hoary devices, and perhaps even the stereotypical responses,
by making her first editorial comment about the story: the tale,
she says, is an "'interminable history of your life'" worthy only
of retelling in "'dime novels'" (30).

Later, Carlyle tells about his current plans to travel south-
ward to Peru, all the while staying away from the usual routes
of travel. Following this adventure tale, Carlyle moves to comedy as he tells how he and Babe used to play the bassoon and
oboe together, blending "'minor keys in African harmonics a
thousand years old until the rats would crawl up the posts and
sit round groaning and squeaking like dogs will in front of a
phonograph'" (33). Ardita comments on this part of the story
by saying, "'How you can tell 'em!'" (33). She finds it amusing
that Carlyle's life story sounds like the script for a low-budget
film, little realizing, it seems, that hers sounds equally so.

Finally, Carlyle makes what sounds like a proposal to
Ardita. Still the editor, Ardita says, "'Extra! Ardita Farnam becomes pirate's bride. Society girl kidnapped by ragtime bank
robber'" (30). Here, Ardita is newspaper editor, creating of
Carlyle's plans a sensational news story that, if it appeared today, would belong in the tabloids.

By dream's end, however, Ardita, like the Chaucerian
dreamer, seems at first to have accepted this other part of her
being. Her love for Carlyle could indicate that she is prepared
to embrace (both literally and symbolically) all he is. Near the
point of her embrace, the dream imagery in the story intensi-
fies, as if to emphasize that a change is about to occur: the
musicians march about, "weaving in concentric circles, now
with their heads thrown back, now bent over their instruments
like piping fauns" (41). Ardita and Carlyle dance, floating

> like drifting moths under the rich hazy light, and as
> the fantastic symphony wept and exulted and wavered
> and despaired, Ardita's last sense of reality dropped
> away, and she abandoned her imagination to the
> dreamy summer scents of tropical flowers and the
> infinite starry spaces overhead, feeling that if she
> opened her eyes it would be to find herself dancing
> with a ghost in a land created by her own fancy. (41)

Interestingly, in what might seem a paradox, it is when the dreamlike nature of her experience reaches its pinnacle, when she is utterly submerged in her dream, that Ardita has the greatest chance to find herself. She must lose herself to find herself. The finding could come through a kiss: Ardita and Carlyle kiss as though they now have blended into one whole person (44). Then the dream ends, and very much as does the dream in *The Book of the Duchess*, in which the sound of bells ringing marks the end of the dream. Here, a sound—of the rowboat bumping and scraping something—also marks dream's end.

The closing part of the frame of *The Book of the Duchess* is brief but meaningful. The poet-persona awakens in bed with the book he has been reading in his hand, and thinks,

> "Thys ys so queynt a sweven
> That I wol, be processe of tyme,
> Fonde to put this sweven in ryme
> As I kan best, and that anoon."
> This was my sweven; now hit ys doon. (1330b–34)

He has overcome his problem; he can now create an effective piece of writing—*The Book of the Duchess* itself—so he is no longer the numb, confused fellow he was before the dream.

The ending of "The Offshore Pirate" proves more slippery in intent and meaning, and not just because there are two endings available. In the original ending, Ardita simply awakens because of the sound of her uncle's and maid's return. She discovers the whole episode has been a dream brought on by the maid's comment about Curtis Carlyle and his musical group. She learns, too, that the dream Carlyle little resembles the real Carlyle. Ardita's only comment about the dream is that this is a funny world, a remark suggesting that she simply does not know what to make of her dream. But perhaps she does not wish to know. Her questioning of the maid indicates that she would prefer for chance remarks about a musical group instead of her own problems to have caused the dream. She seeks to connect the dream to anything but her own rebellion or to the dream Carlyle's parallels to her boyfriend. It is as if, in short, she wishes to reject any possible insight into herself she could have gained. Her view of her dream seems, in fact, a bit like Macrobius' attitude toward those dreams that stem from the dreamer's personal preoccupations: they both discount the significance of such dreams. Notably, however, Ardita at least remains the dreamer-creator of the story in this version—that is, it is her imagination that has been responsible for weaving the tale of Carlyle.

In the revised ending of the story, just as in the original one, Ardita is pulled back into the everyday world by a sound. But in this case, it is then revealed that Toby Moreland and her uncle have been in cahoots all the time, that Toby and Carlyle are the same person. Toby/Carlyle's wild tales that Ardita has made fun of turn out to have been just that—wild tales created not by Ardita the dreamer but by Toby the suitor. Toby, not Ardita, becomes the imaginative creator, but of a fake dilemma between artistic and commercial success rather than a real one. And Ardita can only commend *him* for *his* fine imagination and ask him to "'lie to me just as sweetly as you know how for the rest of my life'" (46). With this ending, their kiss "deconstructs"; it becomes not a symbol for the wedding of parts of personality to achieve a full measure of creative power, not a sign that Ardita now accepts another part of herself as revealed in Carlyle, not a collaboration, but rather a submergence of one personality in another. Ardita is seemingly prepared to allow Toby to be the storyteller while she serves as the henceforth uncritical audience. Significantly, during her dream, Ardita has at least attained the status of editor/director, and in the original version, of creator of dream; but, given her permission to Toby to tell her lies from now on, it seems that she has relinquished any degree of creative activity. Edwin T. Arnold speaks of Fitzgerald's use of the cinema as metaphor using a distinction that has significance here:

> Here he...found two ideal symbols, personifications of two possible attitudes toward life, in the actor, who enters the illusion and is controlled by it, and in the director, who "dominates" the cheap and mundane around him. For Fitzgerald, the director, not the actor, is the artist.... (44)

During her dream, as it reaches its climactic kiss, Ardita has fully entered the illusion, but she comes out again. Ironically, after she awakens (not while she is "asleep"), she enters fully the illusion, but presumably will never emerge. Toby will create a life of illusion—a dream—for her to "act" in. Jay

Gatsby shares in Ardita's affliction, as does the poet-persona of Chaucer's Prologue to *The Legend of Good Women*.

Technically, Fitzgerald deftly handles the revised ending of "The Offshore Pirate" by reminding the reader of the story as a story and thus bringing the frame to an appropriate close (Atkinson 49). But, thematically, the revised ending, like the original, shows an still uncreative dreamer. In this matter, the story differs from *The Book of the Duchess* but resembles another of Chaucer's dream visions, *The Parliament of Fowls*. In this poem, the poet-persona dreams a wonderful dream about Nature's overseeing the mating of birds, a dream that seems likely to provide the poet-persona with much insight about love, the topic he has desired to learn about. Yet afterwards, he says,

> I woke, and othere bokes tok me to,
> To reede upon, and yit I rede alwey.
> I hope, ywis, to rede so som day
> That I shal mete som thyng for to fare
> The bet, and thus to rede I nyl nat spares. (695–99)

This poet-persona, similar to Ardita, gains no insight from his dream. Seemingly dissatisfied with his foray into his own mind, he retreats to his books, to his passivity (Cleary 109). Ardita is not so different from him in her attempt in the original version to reject any association the dream may have with her own life. Her dream meant to renew creativity does not work, but at least in the original version she is still creator of the dream.

Linked to "The Offshore Pirate" is another Fitzgerald story from 1920, "The Ice Palace." These two stories appeared as the first and second stories, respectively, in the first collected volume of Fitzgerald's short stories, *Flappers and Philosophers* (1920). This book appeared later the same year as did Fitzgerald's wildly popular first novel, *This Side of Paradise*, and thus was published in the flush of Fitzgerald's early success. It therefore seems apparent that these two stories were very popular with their original (magazine) readers. But was there more to Fitzgerald's (and his publisher's) placing them in these preeminent positions in this selection? Was Fitzgerald convinced also of their artistry, and if so, to what extent did his reliance on Chaucerian models in writing them affect his perception of their artistic merit? Fitzgerald was later to make

quite disparaging remarks about "The Offshore Pirate," calling
it a cheap story (cited in Mizener, Introduction 15). But why?
Did he find it cheap because he had to change the ending and
otherwise to kowtow to the Jazz-Age audience or a profit-
minded publisher? Or could he have felt the story was misunderstood? For example, Arthur Mizener, in one of the few
critical commentaries on the story (and his is very brief), concentrates on Toby/Carlyle as the main character in the story,
neglecting Ardita's role altogether (Introduction 14–15). These
are all intriguing and perhaps unanswerable questions. What
is clear is that these stories, for whatever reason, were considered of importance early in Fitzgerald's career. It is tempting
to speculate that Fitzgerald originally found these two stories
significant in part because of his use of the Chaucerian models
in writing them.

"The Ice Palace" uses *The House of Fame* as its primary
Chaucerian model. The story concerns Sally Carrol Happer, a
young woman who lies lazily about in the languid South yet
wants to go to the energetic North where she feels she can accomplish something. Like "The Offshore Pirate," this story
shares with Chaucer's dream visions a frame that surrounds a
dream account—though the "dream" is implicit in Fitzgerald's
story.

Fitzgerald takes care, in the opening frame of "The Ice Palace," to include most of the usual emphases found in the
opening frame of Chaucer's dream visions. Although his subtle use of the genre does not allow for a proclamation that a
dream is to be told, Fitzgerald establishes an aura of sleepiness. For instance, "Sally Carrol gazed down sleepily. She
started to yawn, but finding this quite impossible unless she
raised her chin from the window-sill, changed her mind..."
(47). Sally Carrol's surroundings prove equally "sleepy": Sally
Carrol's friend, Clark, spends his time "dozing round the lazy
streets of his home town..." (48); and, downtown, the citizenry
"idled casually across the streets," the street-car seems "plac-
id," and the shops appear to be "yawning their doors and
blinking their windows in the sunshine before retiring into a
state of utter and finite coma" (49). Thus the very buildings
take part in the sleepiness of the citizens, including Sally Carrol. Even here in the waking world, buildings are significant;
they are even more important in the dream account, just as
they are to Chaucer in *The House of Fame*, which J. A. W. Bennett has called a "supremely architectural poem" (x).

The typical Chaucerian poet-persona needs sleep and a dream of a certain sort. In *The Book of the Duchess*, for instance, the poet-persona needs sleep and dreams because he is an artist currently uncreative and dull because of love-sickness. In *The House of Fame*, a more complicated situation exists. In that poem, the artistic poet-persona, Geffrey, fears that his "rym ys lyght and lewed" and that "som vers [may] fayle in a sillable" (1096; 1098). Notably, however, he voices these fears after having the dream, but before the telling of it, so they do not represent his attitude before the dream, or at least not exclusively so. But as reflections of his state during the initial stages of composing the poem, they may suggest that not only having a dream but also creating a meaningful account of it can be essential parts of the interior journey toward renewal of creativity. This complexity is lost in "The Ice Palace," where Sally Carrol is not first-person narrator.

Besides his telling of his fears, Geffrey also shows erudition by listing various possible explanations for dreams. He never says, though, that he himself has dreamed a meaningful dream before. He, like other Chaucerian dreamers, possesses bookish knowledge without personal experience. This notion is later emphasized when, during the dream account, the eagle reveals that Geffrey has "no tydynges / Of Loves folk" (644b–645a) but instead spends his time sitting "at another book / Tyl fully daswed ys thy look" (657b–58). Geffrey, in short, stands in much need of a dream.

Other indications of Geffrey as frustrated artist appear within the dream account, but they describe Geffrey's waking condition. The eagle implies that Geffrey is usually an ineffective artist. And, as his dream starts, Geffrey first visits a place mirroring his own psychic state (Joyner 6): a desert containing the temple of Venus, empty of Venus herself but complete with a picture of the goddess and a table of brass on which is written *The Aeneid*, part of which Geffrey retells. As symbolically revealed here, Geffrey has a barren imagination (the desert); all he has going for him is a knowledge of old stories (the table of brass). Geffrey shows some willingness to leave his barren state behind and make the essential interior journey when he says that he will go out looking for "any stiryng man" (478b) who can tell him where he is. He shows, in other words, a willingness to take action, to explore the "desert."

In "The Ice Palace," Sally Carrol faces a plight much like that of Geffrey and most other Chaucerian dreamers. In the

opening part of the frame, Sally Carrol is indeed passive; she
does little except gaze out her window. But more specifically,
like Geffrey, she is preoccupied with a received "text." Sally
Carrol is comfortable with ideas and ideals from the Old South,
with its notions of courtly love and chivalry. She is described
as one of the "gracious, soft-voiced girls, who were brought up
on memories instead of money" (49). The southern climate is
an important image of the conditions under which this particular ingredient for artistry can be fostered. The opening sentence of the story reads, "The sunlight dripped over the house
like golden paint over an art jar, and the freckling shadows
here and there only intensified the rigor of the bath of light"
(47). Shortly thereafter, Clark's car is described as "hot—being
partly metallic it retained all the heat it absorbed or evolved..."
(47). These two initial images—of light and heat—recur many
times in the opening frame and suggest the limited role of the
South as a fosterer of creativity. The South can provide only a
part of what the artist needs: it provides only light and heat,
symbolizing the knowledge and energy gained from outside
sources—literally the sun, but symbolically the Old South received "text." Both the sun and old texts are givens. For the
farmer growing crops, the sun is a force that simply exists
through no effort of his own; for the artist, texts of other artists—whether actual books or old traditions handed down
orally—just exist, too. Though reading or listening to such
texts is a somewhat active process, neither involves the artist's
active exploration of the contents of his or her own imagination. The artist can remain essentially passive. Like the sun's
role in the growing of crops, old texts are indeed necessary but
not sufficient for full creativity; and they are necessary only
temporarily. Just as the winter should follow the summer, the
dark and cold of the North (which call, symbolically, for the
artist to generate his or her own "light" and "heat" through
exercise of the imagination) should balance the light and heat
of the South.

Later, within the dream, Sally Carrol reveals more about
her waking-world identification with the text of the Old South.
In visiting the graveyard, she encounters some written texts
that are part of the Old South tradition: the inscriptions on the
gravestones, which make her recall the more extensive oral
tales she knows of the Old South. Particularly she is interested in one inscription, that of the ante-bellum Margery Lee.

In addition, she tells Harry of her great love for the entire Old South text:

> "I've tried in a way to live up to those past standards of noblesse oblige—there's just the last remnants of it, you know, like the roses of an old garden dying all round us—streaks of strange courtliness and chivalry in some of these boys an' stories I used to hear from a Confederate soldier who lived next door...." (53)

Sally Carrol's graveyard is as apt a symbol for her passivity as the desert is for Geffrey's similar state. Sally Carrol, like Geffrey, has only one of the three components necessary for creativity: knowledge of texts created by others. She lacks much direct experience of life, a factor revealed when she says how much she wants to "'go places and see people'" and wants "'my mind to grow. I want to live where things happen on a big scale'" (50). She wants what has been lacking in her life thus far. And Sally Carrol also lacks as yet the interior journey of a dream, one which would show her the need for an active, self-begotten creativity.

Like Chaucer's dreamers, Sally Carrol is a frustrated artist. As the story opens, she is stationary at her window, but soon occurs one of the few series of movements that she makes during the opening frame:

> Sally Carrol sighed voluminously and raised herself with profound inertia from the floor, where she had been occupied in alternately destroying parts of a green apple and painting paper dolls for her younger sister. She approached a mirror, regarding her expression with a pleased and pleasant languor, dabbed two spots of rouge on her lips and a grain of powder on her nose, and covered her bobbed corn-colored hair with a rose-littered sunbonnet. Then she kicked over the painting water, said, "Oh, damn!"—but let it lay—and left the room. (48)

Ironically, Sally Carrol destroys the apple, a natural creation, a fresh, newly created object suggestive of current creativity. She instead has been constructing painted dolls and currently is making of herself a kind of painted doll. The doll image strongly recalls the past age of Old Southern chivalry, with its beautiful but cardboard courtly-love ladies, celebrated and worshipped for their outer "paint." However, Sally Carrol's earlier abandonment of even this limited creative activity in favor of lolling about the window and kicking over the painting water indicates her frustration with this particular role as artist. Later, she tells Clark that she has two sides: "'there's the sleepy old side you love, an' there's a sort of energy—the feelin' that makes me do wild things. That's the part of me that may be useful somewhere, that'll last when I'm not beautiful any more'" (50). Sally Carrol, then, senses the opposition between her creation of herself as a beautiful object in the mold of the Old South's courtly ideal and her potential role as a truly active, creative artist, both out in the contemporary world, gathering material from it, and from within (finding "a part of me"). Also, much like Geffrey, she shows a willingness to explore, to kick over the unsatisfactory painting water, to go to new places and find something better to do—in short, to become actively creative.

Sally Carrol makes her remarks about seeing new things and becoming useful as she rides along with friends in Clark's car. Interestingly, it is during this same ride that Sally Carrol falls asleep, an event that marks the start of the story's implicit "dream." As she falls asleep, she increasingly encounters objects suggestive of a gradual entrance into a dream world, such as a "savory breeze" (50), symbolic of inspiration, which blows in her face, "tangled growths of bright-green coppice and grass and tall trees that sent sprays of foliage to hang a cool welcome over the road," and workers in "lazy cotton-fields" who seem like "intangible shadows" (51).

The dream accounts of *The House of Fame* and "The Ice Palace" are quite similar. First, the seasonal settings match, with both dreams occurring in winter. Geffrey proclaims that he had his dream on December 20, the eve of the winter solstice, and therefore, according to David Bevington, "the date of all dates least poetically suggestive of love and springtime" (292). Chaucer thus moves as far away as possible from the traditional spring setting of the typical dream vision. Geffrey no doubt knows already about the French code for such poems—he has much bookish knowledge, after all—and has no further need to think of that side of things. What he does need is to explore the other—the darker, more inward—side.

Likewise, the dream in "The Ice Palace" occurs in the winter. Harry Bellamy, the reader is told, arrives in the South in November; Sally Carrol and Harry travel north in January. Like Geffrey, Sally Carrol will confront another side of herself in her dream; so, appropriately, the time of year of the dream is the opposite of the summer setting of the frame. Notably, this frame also avoids the traditional spring setting. Sally Carrol's South, with its emphasis upon chivalric ideals and courtly love, is *akin* to a traditional dream vision from which Sally Carrol needs to "awaken"—into another sort of dream. Yet it is not just like a traditional dream vision, for the setting would be spring if it were just like it. In picturing the South as summery, not springlike, perhaps Fitzgerald intends the intense heat and light of summer to suggest the extreme, oppressive nature of the south's contribution to creativity: knowledge of the Old South text. In short, the hot, sunny southern summer is a traditional dream vision with a vengeance. The wintry dream, as in *The House of Fame*, will reveal the other side—the inner attributes necessary to creativity—and the other extreme.

Each dream concerns the dreamer's journeys to a series of edifices. In the dream account of *The House of Fame*, in contrast to that same portion of *The Book of the Duchess*, the dreamer does not project a part of himself onto any one other character (i.e., the Man in Black) but instead onto various locales and edifices in the dream world. The same occurs in the dream account of "The Ice Palace." Sally Carrol goes to the southern graveyard, and Geffrey visits the temple of Venus. Then Sally Carrol journeys by Pullman; and Geffrey is carried by a golden eagle. In the North, Sally Carrol first visits Harry's house, which shares features with the other two places she goes: the ice palace, which parallels the House of Fame, Geffrey's next encounter; and the labyrinths beneath the ice palace, where she meets the ghost of Margery Lee as well as Roger Patton. Sally Carrol's visit to the labyrinths parallels Geffrey's entry into the whirling house of twigs, where he meets a man of great authority.

Geffrey first visits Venus' temple, which he describes as

> a temple ymad of glas;
> In which ther were moo ymages
> Of gold, stondynge in sondry stages,
> And moo ryche tabernacles,

And with perre moo pynacles,
And moo curiouse portreytures,
And queynte maner of figures
Of olde werk, then I saugh ever.
For certeynly, I nyste never
Wher that I was, but wel wyste I,
Hyt was of Venus redely,
The temple; for in portreyture,
I sawgh anoon-ryght hir figure
Naked fletynge in a see.
And also on hir hed, pardee,
Hir rose garlond whit and red,
And hir comb ot kembe hyr hed,
Hir dowves, and daun Cupido,
Hir blynde sone, and Vulcano,
That in his face was ful broun.   (120b–39)

Geffrey also sees a table of brass on which are written old tales
of love. Notably, all is stationary here; no living, breathing
figures appear, apart from Geffrey. Nor are there actual
mythological creatures: Venus, symbol of love, exists only as a
portrait, and everything else (including the tales of love) is a
mere artistic replica, too (Sanders 4). The images in the temple
are called "queynte"—that is "elaborate," or "ornamented"
(Robinson 972); the word emphasizes that past artists have created these images. The story set in brass—and thus complete
and unchanging—also stresses past creativity. In short, the
place, along with the surrounding desert, appropriately represents Geffrey's barren imagination, which contains only information culled from old books, parallel to the artistic replicas of
the temple.
    Sally Carrol's first stop, at the southern graveyard, is de-
scribed as follows:

They [Sally Carrol and Harry] passed through the
gateway and followed a path that led through a wavy
valley of graves—dusty-gray and mouldy for the fif-
ties; quaintly carved with flowers and jars for the sev-
enties; ornate and hideous for the nineties, with fat
marble cherubs lying in sodden sleep on stone pil-
lows, and great impossible growths of nameless granite flowers.... Over most of the graves lay silence and
withered leaves with only the fragrance that their own

shadowy memories could waken in living minds.
(51–52)

Sally Carrol sees the grave of Margery Lee, on which is in-
scribed, "'Margery Lee...1844–1873'" (52). Sally Carrol then
tells the story of Margery Lee: "'she was dark, I think; and she
always wore her hair with a ribbon in it, and gorgeous hoop-
skirts of alice blue and old rose'" (52). Further, Margery Lee

"was sweet, Harry! And she was the sort of girl born
to stand on a wide, pillared porch and welcome folks
in. I think perhaps a lot of men went away to war
meanin' to come back to her; but maybe none of 'em
ever did." (52)

Like the depiction of the temple of Venus, the cemetery description emphasizes stillness, sterility, lack of current creativity. While a few people are there to offer flowers to the dead,
otherwise, instead of real flowers and people, the graveyard
primarily contains granite flowers, marble cherubs, and of
course the graves themselves, complete with stones to com-
memorate the once-living. The only real vegetation is withered—all but dead. The fat marble cherubs are reminiscent of
the cherubic Cupid mentioned in Geffrey's description. And,
altogether, these details suggest the same sort of stasis as in
the temple. Particularly striking is the mention of the granite
flowers as "great impossible growths." The word *growth* surely
becomes ironic when used to describe hard, lifeless granite, as
incapable of growth as the marble or the gravestone. Also,
these objects are described as "quaintly carved" (just as the
images in Venus' temple are called "queynte")—that is, as with
the temple images, some unnamed artists at some point created
them—but altogether in the past. In addition, like the story
set in brass in the temple, the inscriptions on the headstones
are set in stone, unchanging, part of the past. The inscription
on Margery Lee's grave is capable only of summoning up in
Sally Carrol a story of the Old South based, as noted earlier, on
old tales of Confederate soldiers. The story itself has courtly-
love trappings—the beautiful girl waiting for a man who is at
war on her behalf—and it is also reminiscent of the stories of
love on the table of brass in Geffrey's dream. Thus both inscriptions and story are "set in stone." In telling the story of
Margery Lee, Sally Carrol might as well be spouting off the

lists of information from old texts or telling stories of love from *The Aeneid* as Geffrey does. The graveyard, in short, becomes as inverse an image of a fertile, productive garden of real flowers, of current creativity, as is the desert surrounding Venus' temple. The graveyard and the locale in Chaucer's poem are instead barren places of artificial past creations.

But neither the graveyard nor the temple is to be considered as wholly negative. Surely it is not bad to know stories of the chivalrous Old South; nor is it harmful in itself to read *The Aeneid*, as Geffrey does in Venus' temple. Sally Carrol herself states of the graveyard (and its association with the Old South text) that she gets "'a sort of strength from it'" (7). The problem is, again, that to stop at this point, to be satisfied with only old stories created by someone else is not to be a true, productive artist. It is intriguing to consider that Fitzgerald may have been dealing in such a passage with his own desire to use models (such as Chaucer's poems)—that is, he was dealing with the conflict between the use of literary models and the need to be original. The romantic era of the century just past had favored originality, but, with the modernists' general questioning of the romantic period, could Fitzgerald have been questioning this particular dictum and finding in his Chaucerian models that very conflict portrayed in a way that resonated for him?

In any case, next, to further bind these two dream visions, the two dreamers journey toward the other edifices of their dreams. Each one is accompanied by a guide: Geffrey's golden eagle and Sally Carrol's Harry. Geffrey and the eagle travel by air; Sally Carrol and Harry go north by train. Geffrey and Sally Carrol then visit buildings that serve as complements to the temple and the graveyard.

Geffrey sees the House of Fame, a place filled with all the activity and liveliness absent from his previous stop. This palace stands upon a rock of ice with the names of many famous people carved into its sides. The north side contains names still easily read because of the shade, but the names on the sunny southern side have melted beyond recognition. The palace itself is of beryl, a transparent, semiprecious stone (Braswell 106); and the dwelling features grotesque figures ("babewynnes"), carved work ("ymageries"), spires ("pynacles"), tents ("tabernacles"), niches ("habitacles"), and many windows. Here, Geffrey sees a vast variety of artists—"many

thousand tymes twelve" (1216)—both musicians and storytellers, all seeking renown. Furthermore, when Geffrey hears a
great sound, the eagle says that it

> "rumbleth up and doun
> In Fames Hous, full of tydynges,
> Bothe of feir speche and chidynges,
> And of fals and soth compouned." (1026b–29)

Finally Geffrey hears the company shouting,

> "'God save the lady of thys pel,
> Our oune gentil lady Fame,
> And hem that wilnen to have name
> Of us!'" (1311–13a)

Then he sees the goddess Fame capriciously dole out renown
to various groups.

This place is not utterly different from Venus' temple; both
are ornate representations of human creativity. The difference
lies in the amount of activity in each place and in the goal for
the activity. Much creative action is occurring in the House of
Fame; work is still in progress. In contrast, no action is currently occurring in the temple. Significantly, however, neither
place is totally positive nor totally negative. The House of
Fame features much activity, but to what end? The artists create only in order to receive fame from the goddess, an undependable and transitory objective, as is clear both from the nature of the melting icy rock on which the names of the famous
are carved, only for some of them to quickly disappear. These
ideas are also clear from the nature of the goddess herself. She
is a "femynyne creature, / That never formed by Nature / Nas
such another thing yseye" (1365–67). Further, she has many
eyes, hair of gold, ears that stand up, tongues, and winged
feet. However, she is not only unnatural but also changeable:
at first she appears tiny; but then, in a while, she has grown
so that "with hir hed she touched hevene" (1375). In addition,
in her behavior toward her minions, she is utterly capricious,
granting without logic fame, infamy, and oblivion to various
supplicants. In short, fame from the goddess of Fame is hardly
a wise or proper goal for one's creative productions. In contrast, the temple of Venus is a shrine to love, which is surely a

worthier object.   Yet the "real" Venus is absent, and there is
no one available to actively create anything.   What is needed is
some combination of the qualities of these places: active creativity and a worthy focus for that creative effort.

In "The Ice Palace," before going to the ice palace itself,
Sally Carrol visits Harry's house.   Then, she goes to the ice
palace, which is indeed similar to the House of Fame.   The ice
palace is described as follows:

> On a tall hill, outlined in vivid glaring green against
> the wintry sky, stood the ice palace.   It was three sto-
> ries in the air, with battlements and embrasures and
> narrow icicled windows, and the innumerable electric
> lights inside made a gorgeous transparency of great
> central hall.   (65)

The ice palace is reminiscent of the rock of ice on which the
House of Fame stands: both structures are of the here-and-
now, nothing permanent.   The parapets complete with flared
opening and windows suggest the House of Fame "ful eke of
wyndowes" (1191) and its "sondry habitacles [niches]" (1194)
in which minstrels and storytellers stand.   Windows suggest
the imagination, busy looking in many directions.   Also both
structures are transparent: the House of Fame is made of the
transparent stone beryl; the ice palace, of ice itself, which features a "gorgeous transparency."   Sitting in it, Sally Carrol
notes that "the blocks...had been selected for their purity and
clearness to obtain this opalescent, translucent effect" (66).
This quality of transparency perhaps indicates, as do the windows, the imaginative faculty of seeing much in many directions.   But it also suggests the ephemeral nature of these
places: from the outside, they seem as if they are barely there;
and because they are built on or of ice, they are apt to disappear any time.   Both ice palace and the House of Fame are,
then, humanly created places—temporary, but at least expressive of active creativity.

The ice palace, like the House of Fame, also features much
sound, especially music: "A band in a far corner struck up
'Hail, Hail, the Gang's All Here' which echoed over to them
[Sally Carrol and Harry] in wild muddled acoustics..." (66).
Then, after the lights have been turned out, the various
"marching clubs" enter, each wearing a different color, chant-
ing loudly, and carrying "a phantasmagoria of torches waving

in great banks of fire, of colors and the rhythm of soft-leather steps...." To Sally Carrol, the reader is told, the entire procession is "the North offering sacrifice on some mighty altar to the gray pagan God of Snow" (67).

This scene is much like that in *The House of Fame* in which the company of people creates music and other art and then comes before Fame group by group to petition her for renown. Importantly, this passage from "The Ice Palace" reveals, just as the parallel passage from *The House of Fame*, the other ingredients needed for creativity. In "The Ice Palace," they are the attributes offered by and developed by life in the North. The description mentions much light and heat—but manufactured light and heat (the torches), products of people and not of the sun. The southern sun, as has been mentioned, is a given, an outside object providing light and heat. In contrast, the North is cold and, of itself, dark in winter; the sun is often hidden. Only through human design—the lighting of torches, the creation of the ice palace itself, with all its electric lights—are light and heat generated. Symbolically, then, in the North, darkness and cold create the need for people to generate their own light and heat—their own inner knowledge and energy. The scene in the ice palace becomes a visual (and auditory) manifestation of this process.

Like the House of Fame, the ice palace is neither altogether positive nor altogether negative. Although much action occurs, so do much distortion and chaos. Sounds echo weirdly through the palace; light "stream[s] in luridly," and the torches constitute a "phantasmagoria" (67). The trouble is that, as with the House of Fame, the creativity lacks a proper focus. To Sally Carrol at least, the action is but a sacrifice to the so-called pagan God of Snow. The North has no fine traditions of courtly love or of anything else that could serve as a focus; instead, there is only snow, a sign of drifting, of the fleeting, of the perishable. Earlier in the story, snow is called "a powdery wraith...that travelled in wavy lines" (64). The snow may also represent darkness in that it *covers* light, making of the sky a "dark, ominous tent" that almost covers the "brown-and-green glow of lighted windows," making the houses seem covered with "tombing heaps of snow" (64–65). But as negative as these characteristics are, they are also necessary. They call for people to produce their own light and heat.

At the House of Fame, Geffrey meets a second guide: a man to whom Geffrey complains about having found in the

structure "'no such tydynges / As I mene of'" (1894b–95a). So
he willingly allows the man to lead him to another place where
he may find that he seeks: tidings of love's folk, or answers to
the riddle of creativity. Similarly, Sally Carrol lets Harry lead
her into another area of the ice palace, the labyrinths below.

In a valley beneath the House of Fame lies the house of
twigs, the final building that Geffrey visits. This place represents the furthest extreme of the sort of creative though ultimately purposeless existence found in the House of Fame. It is
the multi-colored, swiftly whirling house of twigs, also called
"Laboryntus" (1920). The structure has many entries and
features "so gret a noyse" (1926b) that it might be heard all the
way to Rome. Geffrey says that the house is "founded to
endure / While that hit lyst to Aventure" (1981b–82). In the
shack he sees "a congregacioun / Of folk" (2034b–35a), so many
that each has little space to himself. These people begin to
leap up and climb upon each other, at which point Geffrey notices one who "semed for to be / A man of gret auctorite..."
(2157b–58; editor's ellipses). Here the poem ends, incomplete.

According to various critics, the house of twigs serves as a
"suburb" to the House of Fame. (See Bennett 165.) It is, in
other words, like a ramshackle version of that rich castle, a
display of the problems with the House of Fame taken to their
extreme, stripped of their opulent trappings. Here, Geffrey
sees a wandering, confused, labyrinthine scrambling for something. Here, Geffrey finds not even the unsatisfactory goddess
Fame present to offer a modicum of order and purpose. Here,
Geffrey sees the thoroughly dark side of the ingredients for
creativity offered by the House of Fame. Attention to the here-
and-now and to action reach their zenith here, with utter chaos
resulting. Without some tempering, these characteristics lead
to destruction, not creation, as the behavior of the mob shows.
However, at the end, there appears a man of great authority.
Though it is impossible to know with certainty how he was to
have functioned, his being called a person of authority offers
some clue. Perhaps he would have brought the much-needed
element of purpose to the scene. Would he have supplied the
missing Venus as object of the action of these people, or would
he have revealed to Geffrey that this place provides the very
antithesis of an answer to Geffrey's problem, that a blend of
Venus' temple and the House of Fame would allow Geffrey to
renew his creativity? Or perhaps Chaucer himself did not
know what to do with the man of great authority. Brewer has

suggested that the reason Chaucer never completed *The House of Fame* is that he "simply cannot bring himself to be a mouthpiece for authority. In this respect the poem expresses the general social unrest, the seeking of new ways, of that troubled time" (124). After all, previous to the appearance of the man of great authority, the dreamer encounters other guides who eventually disappear, leaving him still seeking. Only one thing is certain: Chaucer's intent will never be known. But apparently, even some good comes out of this fragment of a trip to a seemingly fully negative place. Apparently, only by delving into the very nadir of the mind, the primitive, uninhibited part, can a person hope to reach what he or she is seeking. Geffrey must symbolically reach a state of utterly confused and chaotic action before he can seek the necessary balance.

In "The Ice Palace," Harry leads Sally Carrol into the labyrinths beneath the ice palace, a place that echoes the house of twigs. This lower region consists of many chutes, one of which leads to a "long empty room of ice"; Harry and Sally Carrol find their way into this area. Various "glittering passages" open into this room, and Harry soon disappears into one of them, leaving Sally Carrol behind (67). Frightened, Sally Carrol calls to Harry and then hears

> a faint muffled answer far to the left, and with a touch of panic fled toward it. She passed another turning, two more yawning alleys.... She reached a turn...took the left and came to what should have been the outlet...but it was only another glittering passage with darkness at the end. She called again but the walls gave back a flat, lifeless echo with no reverberations. Retracing her steps she turned another corner, this time following a wide passage. It was like the green lane between the parted waters of the Red Sea, like a damp vault connecting empty tombs. (68)

Like the house of twigs, this is a tangled, confusing labyrinth. It represents the deepest recesses of Sally Carrol's mind, just as the house of twigs represents that same part of Geffrey's mind. In such a region of the psyche, primary process thought, which is not subject to the strictures of logic or propriety, reigns supreme. Unchecked, such thought leads to chaos and confusion. Subjected to strictures, it is useful in providing imaginative material for the creative process. Here, as in the house of twigs, it is unchecked whereas in the upper part of the ice palace, the God of Snow, however ultimately unsuitable, has provided a purpose.

Ultimately the lights go out, and Sally Carrol sinks to the floor and thinks about how she is "alone with this presence that came out of the North.... It was an icy breath of death; it was rolling down low across the land to clutch at her" (68). She imagines that "on both sides of her along the walls she felt things creeping, damp souls that haunted this palace, this town, this North" (69). These creeping souls remind one of the scrambling mob in Chaucer's poem; like the mob, the creeping souls move chaotically, without discernible purpose. Likewise, Sally Carrol is at a loss in this atmosphere where the coldness and darkness of the North become excessive and fail to be balanced by any semblance of heat or light. Ideally, the northerners know how to create their own (the torches). But Sally Carrol, used to the southern sun, has trouble doing so.

Next, Sally Carrol meets someone somewhat parallel to Geffrey's man of great authority: the ghost of Margery Lee. She imagines that someone sits down and "take[s] her face in warm, soft hands" (69). The ghost of Margery Lee looks "just as Sally Carrol had known she would be, with a young, white brow, and wide, welcoming eyes, and a hoop-skirt of some soft material that was quite comforting to rest on" (69). Sinking ever more into her hallucination, Sally Carrol thinks she sees the southern cemetery. Soon after, however, Roger Patton rescues her. Sally Carrol tells him, "'Oh, I want to get out of here! I'm going back home'" (70).

In these passages, having reached the ultimate in darkness and coldness, in the inner and primitive, Sally Carrol, asleep now even within her dream, is able to provide the complementary ingredient for creativity. The ghost of Margery Lee— paradoxically inasmuch as a ghost usually suggests coldness— gives her warmth and light. Margery Lee's ghost, it will be recalled, is parallel to the portrait of Venus. Venus represents love, a worthy object upon which to base one's artistic efforts. Margery Lee, similarly, represents courtly love. But Sally Carrol meets only Margery Lee's ghost, just as she did earlier in the graveyard, just as Geffrey meets only a picture of Venus in her temple. The encounter is a bit more "real" here than in the cemetery: earlier, Sally Carrol could only tell stories of Margery Lee and speak of the ghost; here, she sees and feels the ghost there with her. Still the ghost is ultimately unreal, a remnant of the past, just as the courtly Old South is.

Thus, if the interpretation of Geffrey's man of great authority as one who would bring together the parts is correct, then Margery Lee is not really parallel to this figure after all. Instead, Roger Patton, who arrives torch in hand to pick up Sally Carrol, is. However, even though Roger has perhaps achieved for himself the blend of outer and inner attributes, he cannot do so for Sally Carrol, for she will not let him.

In an earlier scene, Sally Carrol's visit to Harry's house, Roger, a professor of literature, has revealed his capacity to blend qualities necessary for creativity. Sally Carrol encounters at Harry's house both the positive and the negative about the North as milieu for creativity; but it takes Roger to explain the significance of what she senses. Before a party to be held at this house, Sally Carrol spends "a breathless indescribable hour crammed full of half-sentences, hot water, bacon and eggs and confusion..." (56) and visits the family library, which appears not to have been used much. At the party, Sally Carrol admits to her confusion in this atmosphere and to her fear when she sees flurries of snow that look like "'somethin' dead was movin'"" (59). Yet, along with all the activity, the northern girls sit "in a haughty and expensive aloofness" (57). At this point, Roger reveals his theory that northerners are becoming Ibsenesque, that they are freezing up. This propensity to freeze up could mean that they are becoming unable to produce light and heat, and thus are letting cold overcome them. The ice-palace revelry later reveals that this is not entirely the case, but Sally Carrol's misadventure in the labyrinth—particularly when the lights go out—shows that the possibility is real. Without a goal better than worship of the God of Snow, perhaps the freezing up will indeed occur, just as Roger thinks. In any case, Roger does here indicate a knowledge here of the condition of northerners; furthermore, Roger, a professor of literature, is a self-proclaimed devotee of books. However, Roger makes his statements about the North and about books while at a party full of movement and people; and in the labyrinth, he carries a torch, symbol of the imagination. Perhaps he possesses the blend of inner and outer ingredients needed for creativity, and perhaps his ability to find his way through the labyrinth and to rescue Sally Carrol further indicates that he has both qualities. However, Sally Carrol chooses Margery Lee rather than Roger. She retreats to the

South, to bask yet again in outer-created light and heat—that is, in both the sun and the received Old South text that can provide only part of what is needed for active creativity. Like Geffrey's man of great authority, Roger seems to promise answers but does not deliver.

The ending of *The Parliament of Fowls* parallels the ending of "The Ice Palace," just as it does the ending of "The Offshore Pirate." In Chaucer's poem, the poet-persona appears to reject the insight that his dream might have provided; he merely returns to his books (Cleary 109). Likewise, Sally Carrol returns to her received Old South text. She leaves behind Roger, the one person who might have helped her reconcile the forces within and without her. In the closing passage of the story, she is as she was at the start: sitting amid a "wealth of golden sunlight" which

> poured a quite enervating yet oddly comforting heat over the house.... Two birds were making a great to-do...and...a colored woman was announcing herself melodiously as a purveyor of strawberries. It was an April afternoon. Sally Carrol Happer, resting her chin on her arm, and her arm on an old window-seat gazed sleepily down over the spangled dust whence heat waves were rising for the first time this spring. (70)

Significantly, in this passage, the birds and the woman sing; but Sally Carrol just sits at the window, much as before. She is eating fruit—this time, a green peach. Clark comes by, asking her to go swimming; also as before, she reluctantly agrees to go although she "'hate[s] to move'" (71). This time, however, all signs of creativity occur apart from Sally Carrol: she paints no dolls. And even though she agrees to go with Clark, an action that at the first of the story led to her falling asleep in his car and having her dream, now the action means nothing. Even if she does dream again, what good will it do? She has chosen inactive, complacent reliance on the past with its tales of chivalry over a life of creativity and imagination. The green peach she munches on symbolizes vividly her choice of an "unripe" existence—and of a fully southern one, too, in that peaches are decidedly southern (as in a "Georgia peach"). Sally Carrol seems destined to live in a traditional spring-set, courtly-love-filled dream vision full of springtime, birds, and sweet peaches and strawberries, a dream vision not even of her own making, just as Ardita will live in a dream created by Toby Moreland. This last scene of "The Ice Palace" is even set in April to further accentuate Sally Carrol's choice.

Both "The Offshore Pirate" and "The Ice Palace," then, present remarkable resemblances to Chaucer's dream visions. They are particularly intriguing, however, not only for their similarity to Chaucer's works but also for their difference in point of view. In each story, Fitzgerald uses as point of view not only third person instead of first person but also female instead of male. Perhaps Fitzgerald's altering of Chaucer's dream-vision point of view from first person to third person occurs in part because of his relative immaturity as an artist in 1920. As a young artist writing about the artist's struggle to create, could Fitzgerald have unconsciously or consciously transferred onto his protagonists his feelings of lack of full control over and lack of integration of the various components of his own creativity, creating in them a lack of control over their own stories, signaled in part by the avoidance of the first person? Perhaps the alteration was made by a Fitzgerald still striving to find his way as a romantic cum modernist who desired that his characters express both imaginative involvement and perspective but did not yet see the possibilities for this dual expression that are part of the usual dream-vision point of view. Perhaps, also, having had "The Romantic Egotist," the earlier, first-person version of *This Side of Paradise*, rejected by his publisher led to a reluctance to try using that point of view so soon again.

And what of Fitzgerald's use of female protagonists versus Chaucer's use of male poets-personae? Perhaps Fitzgerald's and/or his readership's ideas about women made it easy for him to think of casting them in the role of passive artists who cannot overcome their passivity. Or, in the case of Sally Carrol at least, with her southern connection to a courtly past, having a woman as artist figure might have allowed Fitzgerald a protagonist who, as an artist committed only to the received text of these ideals, could actually make of *herself*—not just of paper dolls or the heroine of a chivalric tale—a piece of art, a courtly-love lady. She could become enmeshed, in the end, in the sentimental southern story, the very sort of "feminized" literature so out of favor with modernists. Similarly, Ardita ultimately lives in the romantic tale produced by Toby/Carlyle.

Fitzgerald was thinking of his southern wife when he created Sally Carrol; perhaps Zelda Fitzgerald was partial model

for Ardita, too. Zelda Fitzgerald's artistic aspirations did not
find public expression until the 1930s, when she wrote,
painted, and took ballet lessons, though these two stories indicate that Fitzgerald knew much earlier of her interests in being
creative. In any case, Fitzgerald's response to his wife's creative endeavors of the 1930s has sometimes been thought negative. Indeed, he did demand changes in her novel, *Save Me the
Waltz* (1932), because it was to cover the same time span and
draw on the same set of experiences as would the novel he was
working on, *Tender Is the Night*. (For instance, she meant to
name the "hero" of the novel Amory Blaine, the name of the
protagonist of *This Side of Paradise*.) Fitzgerald also stipulated,
for the same reason, that her play *Scandalabra* (1933), not use
certain material. Yet, according to the Fitzgeralds' daughter,
Scottie Fitzgerald Smith, Fitzgerald was otherwise supportive
of his wife's creative efforts, arranging for the first showing of
her paintings and paying for her ballet lessons. It was, Smith
concedes, a competitive relationship (v–vi).

Fitzgerald's view in these two stories of women as artist-
figures is interesting to examine in terms of his later responses
to his wife's creative endeavors. Fitzgerald seems clearly able
to regard the two protagonists as creative individuals, yet just
as able to cast them as passive about their creativity, though
willing to change to a more active stance. He also gives each
woman a male "guide" whom she needs to rescue her from her
creative problems. Then, he gives each story a negative ending; neither artist gains from her dream the impetus to become
actively creative. Ardita even turns over, as it were, her creativity to Toby, letting him henceforth be the imaginative one,
with the result that the story has an ostensibly happy ending.
In contrast, Sally Carrol's rejection of Roger's help results in an
avowedly negative ending. Do such dynamics echo the early
relationship between the Fitzgeralds? Or is Fitzgerald simply
recognizing the problems women can face in trying to be creative in a society that would prefer painted dolls who either ac-
quiesce to the men in their lives or else retreat to a childhood
world? In locating herself ultimately within a dream (whether
it be Toby/Carlyle's illusion or Margery Lee's Old South illusion), each woman is thus locating herself within the "feminine" dream-garden forever.

Or, as suggested also by the switch from first- to third-
person, is Fitzgerald identifying with the female artists of these
stories (and with his wife, too), examining through them his

own problems as a young, possibly unsure artist? The idea garners some support from the fact that Fitzgerald's next dream vision, "The Diamond as Big as the Ritz," features a male protagonist (John Unger) often read as partially autobiographical (despite the fantastic plot of the story); this male artist also fails to learn from his dream. Perhaps Ardita and Sally Carrol are in some sense earlier versions of John Unger.

One thing is clear: using women as artist-figures within dream visions is an idea that Fitzgerald did not pick up from Chaucer's dream visions—though one should not quickly dismiss the effect on Fitzgerald that Chaucer's use of women as storytellers in *The Canterbury Tales* may have had. With typical medieval dream visions (including Chaucer's), whether their concern is romance or not, a highly sexual symbolism permeates the overall situation: the male poet-persona penetrates the fertile dream-garden (or dream forest) (McMillan 28–29).

Only two medieval dream visions would necessarily involve a different symbolism, for only two feature female poets-personae: the anonymous fifteenth-century dream visions (and Chaucer imitations) *The Flower and the Leaf* and *The Assembly of Ladies*, which, until the nineteenth century, were considered part of the Chaucer canon.[3] Ann McMillan holds that these dream visions, whether by women poets or not, speak to the medieval woman's concerns. *The Flower and the Leaf* emphasizes that through chastity, women are protected from observation and betrayal and thus gain the ability to lead active, useful lives, to reach their potentials. *The Assembly of Ladies* calls this same notion into question. Both works feature female, not male, guides. And both end negatively: *The Flower and the Leaf* ends with the dreamer understanding that chastity is necessary for her to reach her potential yet closing her poem with a modest plea for her little poem to blush like a maiden about the fact that it must become public. Chastity and the creative life do not seem so readily combined after all. *The Assembly of Ladies*, during which women have complained to Lady Loiaulte (Loyalty) of having been chaste yet having gone unrewarded for it, ends with frustration at the lack of clear-cut response to the complaints. (See McMillan.) How is the medieval woman to live the active, creative life? Each work asks this question yet offers little real answer.

It is indeed a difficult question, and one that Fitzgerald updates to apply in "The Offshore Pirate" and "The Ice Palace" to the problems of the early twentieth-century woman—again,

for whatever reasons, with little in the way of positive or definitive answers. Fitzgerald was to attempt the female point of
view again—in, for instance, *Tender Is the Night*, in which
Rosemary Hoyt is the central consciousness during the first
part of the novel, and in the unfinished *The Last Tycoon*, which
is narrated in first person by Cecelia Brady. But until these
works of the 1930s and 1940s, Fitzgerald, instead of allowing
the promise of his fictional female artists to be fulfilled, shows
their voices being heard, but then silenced.

CHAPTER THREE

AMERICAN NIGHTMARES: "THE DIAMOND AS BIG AS THE RITZ" AND *THE VEGETABLE*

Because a man has shop to mind
In time and place, since flesh must live,
Need spirit lack all life behind,
All stray thoughts, fancies fugitive,
All love except what trade can give?
—Robert Browning, "Shop"

F. Scott Fitzgerald's next forays into the dream-vision genre occur with the 1922 short story "The Diamond as Big as the Ritz" and the 1923 play *The Vegetable or From President to Postman.* Both works are fantasies as illogical and outlandish—and as "architectural"—as Chaucer's fantastic *The House of Fame.* In each of these works, as he considers the plight of a male artist-figure, Fitzgerald widens his concern with the renewal of creativity through dreams from a personal and/or regional focus to a focus upon Americans' collective need for insight into the dangers of the traditional American dream of material wealth and power. Heretofore called upon to use his own creativity only in an ultimately destructive pursuit of this American dream, each of Fitzgerald's protagonists has a vision of the nightmare version of this dream. One of the dreamers gives in to the nightmare (and thus, like the female dreamers before him fails to learn from his dream). The other dreamer learns something from his dream and changes his life, becoming creative in a personally satisfying way.

Like a Chaucerian dream vision, "The Diamond as Big as the Ritz" features an opening waking-world section that establishes the story as self-conscious piece of art and the protagonist as a frustrated artist. This section—also as in Chaucer's dream visions—offers certain pieces of information that recur, transformed and often distorted, in the dream account. The phrase calling attention to the work as self-conscious art occurs in this sentence: "Now in Hades—*as you know if you ever have been there*—the names of the more fashionable preparatory schools and colleges mean very little" (141, emphasis added). This brief, amusing apostrophe to the reader produces keen awareness of the artificiality of the story.

Like most Chaucerian dreamers, John Unger, the protagonist of the story, is an artist figure who currently uses his imagination only in a limited, misdirected way. He needs a dream to show him what missing ingredients he needs to be truly creative. His identity as artist figure is shown in three ways: his attention to texts, his imaginative description of jewels, and one rather explicit narrative remark about John's imagination. John's attention to texts—echoing a similar attention on the part of the Chaucerian poet-persona—is seen in his liking for the "old-fashioned Victorian motto" over the gates to Hades (142). Also, while on the train with Percy Washington, John speaks of having read the *World Almanac*. In it, he has learned about the relative monetary worth of various wealthy Americans. And he describes jewels: "'Vivian Schnlitzer-Murphy,'" he tells Percy Washington, has "'rubies as big as hen's eggs, and sapphires that were like globes with lights inside them'"; and the family has "'diamonds as big as walnuts...'" (144). Here, John uses figurative language quite imaginatively. Finally, the reader learns that John's trip to visit Percy's family "promised rich confectionery for his curiosity" (143)—surely a statement of John's imaginative capacity.

But perhaps the best indication that John is an artist figure occurs not in the frame but rather in the dream account itself (just as in *The House of Fame*, certain indications of Geffrey's artistic identity appear within the dream account). The world of John's dream is overdone—extremely extravagant, outrageous; the Washington chateau is particularly gaudy. Robert Emmet Long says that "the material form this paradise of wealth takes...is like a dream of bad taste" (65). Marius Bewley calls this part of the story a fantasy in a style he terms "Babylonian-Hollywood" (266). Similar to Ardita's, John's imagination is imbued with the imagery of Hollywood; movies are "texts" with which he is undoubtedly familiar. Like a director or screenwriter, in his dream, he creates a "movie" of sorts. Bewley further comments that the story is movie-like: it has "the sense of a colossal Hollywood set, and a 'plot' that unwinds along the lines of an old time movie scenario" (267). Notably, too, Bewley speaks of the ambivalence of an audience's response to a movie—the mixture of disbelief and acceptance (267). This sort of ambivalence could just as readily apply to the dreamer's response to a dream. The movie thus becomes for Fitzgerald a highly charged metaphor suggesting at once both the dream experience and its relationship to the artist's creativity. John's love of imagery reminiscent of movies shows that his creativity has no proper goal, for Fitzgerald apparently intends that Hollywood be seen as a main propagator of a very material American dream.

John is indeed a frustrated artist. His very name, *Unger*, suggests hunger, unfulfilled longings. Additionally, the name and description of his hometown, Hades, mark it as a wasteland where people lack imagination.[1] All the talented young men leave Hades to go to school elsewhere. And the townspeople are isolated and must put up a mere pretense of imaginative involvement with life and art: "The inhabitants have been so long out of the world that, though they make a show of keeping up to date in dress and manners and literature, they depend to a great extent on hearsay..." (141) (rather like the second-hand information from old books that Geffrey depends upon). John's father has tried, to no avail, to have a new motto put up over the city gates, "something with a little more push and verve about it" (142). But most residents are satisfied to leave things as they are, to remain uncreative. John himself appears to be a young man who has been sent away for the first time from an insular atmosphere and thus is, like Chaucer's poets-personae, ignorant about the world.

Religious worship may be viewed as a creative exercise: it involves the creation of ritual, prayer, even story; so it is significant to examine what the residents of Hades select to worship. The opening description of Hades establishes it as a place bereft of traditional Christianity, as might be expected considering its name. But, on an allegorical level, this Hades is not representative of the Hell spoken of in the Bible, a Hell that is the place of punishment for sins, of removal from the presence of God, though in important ways this Hades is

somewhat parallel to that Hell. Instead of being the place of
removal from the presence of the Christian God, Hades is a
place of removal from the presence of the god Wealth. But
even though the residents are removed from wealth itself, they
worship it from afar. The situation is reminiscent of James
2:19: "You [Christians] believe that God is one. You do well;
the demons also believe, and shudder." Outside Hades, in the
"Heaven" of the god Wealth, people believe in this god; inside
Hades, its citizens (demons) also believe in Wealth, though
they are far away from it. This twisted worship of money
shows in the Ungers' desire to send John to St Midas' school.
Midas, changer of objects into gold, is in their eyes a saint, an
object of religious devotion. He is a strange substitute for
actual saints, and even for Christ Himself, known for producing miraculous changes of a much different sort. But this
sort of creativity is not recognized in Hades whereas Midas'
sort is both recognized and worshipped.

Even John's parents fail to use for a worthy end what creativity they possess. Mr. Unger is the one who wants a new
town motto of something like "'Hades—Your Opportunity'" or
the word *welcome* accompanied by a handshake made of electric
lights (142). He is like an advertising executive creating a text
meant only to "sell" the town—and in what sounds like a mis-
leading way. (After all, what irony there is in suggesting a
town called Hades offers wonderful opportunities!) Mrs.
Unger makes political addresses; thus she creates texts only to
seek political influence. And it is Mr. and Mrs. Unger who
have determined that John must have a prestigious New England education at St. Midas' School. In short, then, John's
parents' association with creativity is sullied because the goal
is gold and power. Mr. Unger rather explicitly shows his priorities when, before he gives any advice or shows any affection
to his departing son, he presents him with "an asbestos
pocket-book stuffed with money" (141).

In his choice of reading material (*The World Almanac*'s sta-
tistics about wealthy Americans) and in his descriptions of the
Schnlitzer-Murphy jewels, John reveals that he, too, is ob-
sessed with wealth. In shape, the eggs, walnuts, and globe of
light to which he compares the jewels suggest testicles and
thus reproductive creativity. In addition, the eggs normally
suggest rebirth, particularly since John saw the jewels on Eas-
ter, traditional occasion of rebirth. Eggs and walnuts, though
hard like jewels outside, on the inside are far different: "soft,"

flexible, changing, still capable of producing life. A globe of light, to which he compares sapphires, is also hard outside— perhaps made of glass—but spreads the light and heat that exist inside it. Thus John compares a symbol of creative inspiration, an object with light of its own, to a sapphire capable only of reflecting light from an outside source. In short, seeming not to see the difference, John has compared hard, fixed objects of great material value to relatively inexpensive objects either still capable of natural growth or else symbolically indicative of creative inspiration. John thereby reveals that wealth is the one "subject" he finds appropriate for any creative "text" he might produce.

Also as in Chaucer's dream visions, certain waking-world material will appear, transformed, in the dream account. Not only does John speak of huge jewels, but also his rich friend Percy Washington says that his father has "'a diamond bigger than the Ritz-Carlton Hotel'" (144). Percy's outlandish statement can be reasonably explained: he is bragging. Having heard John talk about the Schnlitzer-Murphy jewels, Percy exaggerates, wanting to "top" John's remarks. But in terms of the dream John will soon have, Percy's statement becomes an example of waking-world material that is magnified and distorted in the dream. In this case, a nonliteral statement is taken literally in the dream, in which a diamond mountain figures prominently.

Before the dream proper begins, a journey into the dream world occurs, one that parallels the journey in *The Book of the Duchess*. Near the beginning of his dream, the dreamer of Chaucer's poem follows hunters after he hears the sound of their horn. Similarly, in "The Diamond as Big as the Ritz," John and Percy travel by train to visit Percy's family in Montana, which in this story is the dream world where he will visit the village of Fish and then the Washington chateau on the diamond mountain. The difference between this journey and that in *The Book of the Duchess* is that John's trip occurs while John is still awake. Perhaps as with Sally Carrol's car trip in "The Ice Palace," John's train ride represents the process of falling asleep, of going deeper and deeper into the dream world. Bewley implies such a situation when he comments that during this train trip, the dream qualities of the story are intensified, and that although the reader does not know for sure when the dream begins, begin it has by the time of John's arrival at Fish (262–63).

The dream account in "The Diamond as Big as the Ritz" parallels the dream account in *The House of Fame*. J. A. W. Bennett's description of *The House of Fame* as "supremely architectural" (x) could well apply to Fitzgerald's story, too; for it, like Chaucer's poem, is built around a series of edifices.

Percy and John first arrive at Fish, a town from which they will take a car to Percy's home on the diamond mountain. Various critics have commented on the dreamlike nature of Fish as described in the first two paragraphs in section two of the story. Bewley has commented on how these paragraphs "create the atmosphere of dream" and present "grotesque and distorted Christian connotations" and "a religion that is sick and expressing itself in disjointed image and associations, as if it were delirious" (263–64). Likewise, Long has said that the passage is "like a dream that has become diseased and incoherent" (62). A look at this description confirms Bewley's and Long's impressions and also reveals great affinities with Chaucer's description of the desert and temple of Venus: Fish, the reader is told, is in an area in which the sun peers from between two mountains "like a gigantic bruise" (144) in a "poisoned sky." The village, "minute, dismal, and forgotten," contains twelve men who suck only "a lean milk from the almost literally bare rock"; it is as if some "mysterious populatory force" has created and then "abandoned them to struggle and extermination." Whenever the Transcontinental Express comes in, the twelve men "gathered like ghosts" (145) to watch its lights, and, on the rare occasion that the train stops, to watch someone disembark. This ritual is described in the story as follows:

> The observation of this pointless and preposterous phenomenon had become sort of a cult among the men of Fish. To observe, that was all; there remained in them none of the vital quality of illusion which would make them wonder or speculate, else a religion might have grown up around these mysterious visitations. But the men of Fish were beyond all religion...so there was no altar, no priest, no sacrifice....
>
> On this June night, the Great Brakeman, whom, had they deified any one, they might well have chosen as their celestial protagonist, had ordained that the seven o'clock train should leave its human (or inhuman) deposit at Fish. (145-46)

Like the desert surrounding the temple of Venus in *The House of Fame*, the village of Fish indicates the barren condition of the dreamer's mind (Joyner 6)—and of his waking environment, too. The desert in *The House of Fame* is

> Withouten toun, or hous, or tree,
> Or bush, or grass, or eryd lond;
> For al the feld nas but of sond
> As smal as man may se yet lye
> In the desert of Lybye;
> Ne no maner creature
> That ys yformed be Nature
> Ne sawgh I.... (484–90a)

Likewise, the most prominent feature of Fish is a bare rock so nearly completely devoid of fertility that the men can suck only "a lean milk" from it. Even the lack of living creatures characteristic of the desert is mirrored in Fish; for there only twelve strange, largely immobile men live. Their lack of humanity is emphasized when they are called "a race apart, these twelve men of Fish, like some species...abandoned..." (145). These barren places echo the lack of creativity within both dreamers, and in the entire town of Hades. It is as if this region is another version of Hades.

Similar buildings appear in the desert and in Fish. The temple of Venus stands in the middle of the desert. It contains only golden figures and only a portrait of the goddess. No living beings and no actual goddess are present. All active worship of Venus has long since ceased. Similarly, the shanty depot in Fish is marked by almost complete lack of activity or imagination. Here, the men of Fish come nightly to watch for the train and its Great Brakeman. Notably, as they wait, these men remain as stationary as the golden figures in Venus' temple; they merely observe the train when it finally does go by—and often, it never appears. And these men do not have sufficient imagination to make an active religion of this event.

In the temple of Venus, a portrait of Venus appears to suggest a proper goal for creative endeavors. At least Venus does symbolize Love, surely a worthy goal. The problem is that the real thing is not there, nor are any worshipers present. In the shanty depot are potential worshipers—the twelve men of Fish—but they do not have sufficient creativity to worship anything; they say only "a prayer of dim, anaemic wonder" (145).

No creative formulation of ritual, no creation of prayers, no creation of a deity to worship exist among the men of Fish. Also, the one thing possibly available for worship is unsatisfactory. All they might find to worship—or, as Fitzgerald puts it, have as their "celestial protagonist"—would be the Great Brakeman who—infrequently—brings them the train and takes it away again. The Great Brakeman thus signifies the impermanent and meaningless. The train he drives only brings people to a barren place. Reminiscent initially of the twelve apostles of Jesus, these men, unlike the apostles, lack a Jesus to worship creatively.

Next, John and Percy travel by car to Percy's home. As they travel, Percy takes on a resemblance to the golden eagle, Geffrey's guide in *The House of Fame*. This eagle appears as Geffrey stands in the desert after having visited the temple of Venus. Grasping Geffrey in his claws, the eagle soars upward, taking the frightened dreamer to the House of Fame. On the way, besides commenting on the poet-persona's supposed obtuseness, the eagle gives Geffrey a lengthy, rather scientific explanation about how all sounds reach Fame's castle:

> Every word, ywys,
> That lowd or pryvee spoken ys,
> Moveth first an ayr aboute,
> And of thys movynge, out of doute,
> Another ayr anoon ys meved,
> As I have of the watir preved,
> That every cercle causeth other.
> Ryght so of ayr, my leve brother;
> Everych ayr another stereth
> More and more, and speche up bereth,
> Or voys, or noyse, or word, or soun.
> Ay through multiplicacioun,
> Til hyt be atte Hous of Fame,—
> Take yt in ernest or in game. (809–22)

Similarly, on their way to the Washingtons' chateau, Percy makes John seem obtuse when he intimates that John does not really know who the wealthiest men in the land are. And Percy provides John with a rather scientific explanation of how his father has avoided letting the government survey their land. Using scientific methods, Braddock Washington

"fixed it so that their compasses were in the strongest
magnetic field ever artificially set up. He had a whole
set of surveying instruments made with a slight defec-
tion that would allow for this territory not to appear,
and he substituted them for the ones that were to be
used. Then he had a river deflected and he had what
looked like a village built up on its banks—so that
they'd see it, and think it was a town ten miles farther
up the valley." (148-49)

The goddess of Fame controls sound, not only luring all
sounds into her house but also transforming them into people.
Conversely, Mr. Washington controls the magnetic field to
keep most people away from his abode. Both, then, have a
measure of control over forces of nature. Notably, by appeal-
ing to a desire to be near wealth, Braddock and his children do
lure some people to their house, but only to get pleasure or
work out of them, and then to discard—kill—them when finished with them. Altogether, the Washingtons' capricious,
controlling actions mirror the goddess Fame's equally capricious, controlling actions.

The car in which Percy and John travel to the chateau is
similar in color, decoration, and movement to the Geffrey's
golden eagle. The eagle is "of gold, and shon so bryghte /
That never sawe men such a syght" (503–04); it speaks ornately, using all the colors of rhetoric; it appears out of nowhere twice during the dream; and it bears Geffrey high up
into the air, to a high place (the House of Fame, which is on
the icy rock). Similarly, the car is made of "gleaming metal"
(146) and has "cloth of gold" (147) upholstery. The upholstery
is also ornate, with "a thousand minute and exquisite tapestries of silk, woven with jewels and embroideries" and the
"ends of ostrich feathers" (146-47). In addition, the car appears out of nowhere: the driver of a buggy that has taken
Percy and John from the depot "hailed an opaque body somewhere ahead of them in the gloom" (146): it is the car. Finally,
like the eagle bearing Geffrey, the car bears the boys upward.
It ascends on the ground for a while; then workers attach four
huge cables to the vehicle, and it is lifted up high, beside a
huge perpendicular "knife-blade of stone" and then down the
other side of it (148). In short, the car indeed is much like a
golden, ornate, even feathered bird capable of traveling high

into the sky. Significantly, the description of the car's journey especially stresses up/down movements; and Barry Sanders has counted 70 occurrences of up/down images in *The House of Fame*. For Sanders, such movements emphasize instability (6; see also Steed). This trait marks the Washingtons' province as well.

After traveling by air to the general vicinities of their destinations, the protagonists continue the journeys by land. Geffrey walks to the House of Fame; John, along with Percy, continues in the car, back on the ground now. John and Percy pass objects similar to some items Geffrey sees during his flight with the eagle. Geffrey has seen "the ayerissh bestes, / Cloudes, mystes, and tempestes, / Snowes, hayles, reynes, wyndes" (965–67). John views "shreds and tatters of chinchilla, courtesy clouds in the green moon's heaven...passing the green moon like precious Eastern stuffs paraded for the inspection of some Tartar Khan" (149). He also imagines seeing

> some lads sailing above him in the air, showering down tracts and patent medicine circulars, with their messages of hope for despairing, rockbound hamlets. It seemed to him that he could see them look down out of the clouds and stare.... (149)

Critics have disagreed as to just what Chaucer means by "ayerissh bestes." The juxtaposition of this phrase with the mention of clouds perhaps suggests clouds shaped like animals—hence the reference to *airish* beasts, or beasts in the sky. Similarly, John sees animal-like—along with people-shaped—clouds. Both descriptions also emphasize downward movement: in Chaucer's, the rain, snow, and hail fall; in Fitzgerald's, boys seem to shower down pamphlets. Rain, snow, and hail provide water to nourish vegetation and are therefore connected to natural creativity; they perhaps show Geffrey's need for renewed creativity. In John's case, when he envisions the creative act of boys attempting to communicate with others through the written word, to bring hope to barren towns, he is perhaps projecting his desire to create. However, there is an irony to the boys' creativity: their pamphlets amount to mere advertisements designed to make a profit from the sale of medicine—and fraudulent medicine at that. Even as John imagines creative acts that would offer hope and nourishment, it

seems that he cannot help also thinking of using creative abilities to make money unscrupulously.

Having reached their destinations, Geffrey and John both
encounter buildings that contrast greatly with the first structures they visited. Geffrey reaches the House of Fame, located
on an ice mountain featuring the names of the famous. Those
of the shady northern side remain while those on the sunny
southern side soon melt away. Thus, the mountain suggests
the capricious, fleeting nature of fame. Similarly, John visits
the Washingtons' chateau, atop a solid diamond mountain. At
first glance, a hard diamond seems quite different from ice.
However, both substances are hard; and though a diamond
seems much more permanent than ice, in fact it is not. Near
the end of John's dream, the diamond blows up, destroyed just
as completely as melting destroys ice. Both materials, then,
represent the temporary, the uncertain. Wealth (a diamond),
like fame (ice), proves an unreliable foundation on which to
base one's creative efforts.

The beryl House of Fame features towers and pinnacles;
many windows; gold-plated walls, floors, and roofs set with
fine stones; and many minstrels, harpists, pipers, jugglers,
magicians, and other artists who perform and ask the grotesque, changeling goddess Fame to grant them renown. Altogether, the House of Fame conveys a sense of opulence, action,
and power, but at the same time a sense of the capricious nature of fame. Some of Fame's petitioners receive fame; others,
even if just as worthy, do not.

In comparison, seen from the outside, the Washingtons'
marble chateau features "many towers," "sloping parapets," "a
thousand yellow windows with their oblongs and hectagons
and triangles of golden light," "the faint acciaccare sound of
violins" (150). Touring the house, John encounters "a daze of
many colors, of quick sensory impressions, of music...of the
beauty of things, lights and shadows, and motions and faces"
(151); and he sees a room with walls of gold as well as one
lined with diamonds. In addition, floors "flame in brilliant
patterns from lighting below, patterns of barbaric clashing
colors, of pastel delicacy, of sheer whiteness, or of subtle and
intricate mosaic..." (151). At dinner, John eats from dishes
made of diamond and emerald. In short, like the House of
Fame, this place suggests opulence and power; even some
details indicative of these qualities are the same: the golden,

bejeweled walls; the towers; the many windows. Both places also contain signs of creativity: beautiful music emanates from both, and the very buildings themselves are products of creativity. Yet in each case the goal of the creativity is faulty. The artists in the House of Fame perform to receive fame from the goddess—a temporal, undependable entity. The Washingtons are concerned only with riches; all their activity occurs to ensure their continued wealth. John learns that some years ago Braddock Washington kidnapped artists of several types—a landscape gardener, an architect, a stage designer, a French decadent poet, and a "'moving-picture fella'" (171)—to design the chateau and its surroundings. But all of these artists except one proved useless and impractical for the Washingtons' purposes; no one but the movie director was, as Percy tells John, "'used to playing with an unlimited amount of money'" (172). In this instance, Braddock Washington parallels the goddess in that he judges artists, not on the basis of merit, but rather on the basis of something utterly divorced from that consideration—in his case, their acquaintance with spending lots of money. Braddock is like an emissary of the god Wealth. At this chateau, as in the House of Fame, there is no proper goal for creativity; here, only wealth, which like fame is temporal and undependable, is important.

At this point in "The Diamond as Big as the Ritz," Fitzgerald departs temporarily from his use of *The House of Fame* as primary model and interpolates a love story instead reminiscent of part of Chaucer's Prologue to *The Legend of Good Women*. Both Fitzgerald's depiction of John's relationship with Kismine Washington and Chaucer's description of his poet-persona's reactions to the daisy/Alceste exhibit a tension between the transcendent and the carnal aspects of courtly love and thus show Fitzgerald once again echoing Chaucer's concern with the conflict between the permanent, nonmaterial aspects of existence and the temporal, material ones.

In the opening frame of the Prologue, the poet-persona says,

> Of al the floures in the mede,
> Thanne love I most thise floures white and rede,
> Swiche as men callen daysyes in our toun.
> To hem have I so gret affeccioun,
> As I seyde erst, whanne comen is the May,
> That in my bed ther daweth me no day

That I nam up and walkyng in the mede
To seen this flour ayein the sonne sprede,
Whan it upryseth erly by the morwe.
That blisful sighte softneth al my sorwe,
So glad am I, whan that I have presence
Of it, to doon it alle reverence,
As she that is of alle floures flour,
Fulfilled of al vertu and honour,
And evere ilyke faire, and fressh of hewe;
And I love it, and ever ylike newe,
And evere shal, til that myn herte dye. (41–57 F)

Besides stressing the flower's freshness and beauty, the poet-persona calls her "the clernesse and the verray lyght / That in this derke world me wynt and ledeth" (84–85 F). In short, the poet-persona worships—not a courtly-love lady—but a lovely, natural, perennial daisy. The daisy seems worthy of his worship, a proper goal for the creative efforts that result in this lovely tribute to the flower.

Later, in the dream, the poet-persona meets a figure who seems to be the daisy personified: Alceste, queen of the god of Love, Cupid:

Me mette how I lay in the medewe thoo
To seen this flour that I so love and drede;
And from afer com walkyng in the mede
The god of Love, and in his hand a quene,
And she was clad in real habit grene.
A fret of gold she hadde next her heer,
And upon that a whit corowne she beer
With flourouns smale, and I shal nat lye;
For al the world, ryght as a dayesye
Ycorouned ys with white leves lyte,
So were the flowrouns of hir coroune white
For of o perle fyn, oriental,
Hire white coroune was ymaked al. (210–22 F)

Alceste, says the dreamer, is beautiful, meek, good, and faithful. In other words, he depicts Alceste in much the same way as he has depicted the daisy itself. Yet the daisy is a purely natural, organic object involving no costly ornaments and exacting no heavy toll from her worshiper. She is presented as truly possessing the traits assigned to her by the poet-persona and as truly worthy of his spontaneously creative efforts to praise her. In contrast, Alceste's beauty—and her resemblance to the daisy—results from her opulent trappings: the green clothing and pearl crown. Furthermore, whereas the daisy's power over the poet-persona is not by the flower's design—the poet-persona simply feels compelled by the daisy's freshness and beauty to praise her—Alceste's power may be seen as manipulative and calculated. And notably, hers is verbal manipulation; she creates a text with which to convince—seemingly Cupid, but really the dreamer—to follow her plans.

When Cupid berates the poet-persona for having created works featuring evil women—a suspect accusation considering the poet-persona's recent adoration of the daisy—and suggests that the poet-persona will have to repent cruelly of his deeds, Alceste seemingly urges the god to show mercy:

"Y aske yow this man, ryght of your grace,
That ye him never hurte in al his lyve;
And he shal sweren to yow, and that as blyve,
He shal no more agilten in this wyse,
But he shal maken, as ye wol devyse,
Of wommen trewe in lovyng al hire lyve,
Wherso ye wol, of mayden or of wyve,
And forthren yow, as muche as he mysseyde
Or in the Rose or elles in Creseyde." (433–41 F)

Her words seem to convince Cupid to relent; and, despite the dreamer's earlier protests that he was simply aiming to speak the truth in his earlier works, not maliciously to create evil characters, the dreamer agrees to do penance by now writing legends of good women.

Chaucer's intentions regarding Alceste's role in this interaction have been much debated. It is possible that Chaucer means her to be a negative figure. Elton Dale Higgs holds that Alceste deviously controls this situation all along. It is she who guides Cupid into taking the course of action she desires. "Cupid's queen," says Higgs, "has firmly entrenched herself in his court" (94). Unlike the quietly inspirational, natural daisy, Alceste is a product of a bookish imagination (she is a figure from mythology) and of beauty gained from clothing and jewels. Yet, despite her suspect nature, and despite all evidence to the contrary regarding the dreamer's past works, when she uses clever speeches that seemingly ask for mercy yet intimate that mercy is needed because of the dreamer's past books, she almost forces the dreamer into writing the book she desires. In other words, she creates her own "text" in which the poet-persona has written evil works and should be allowed to repent. In the tradition of the courtly-love lady, rich, powerful Alceste is rather coldly exacting devotion from her worshiper. In short, in Alceste and in the poet-persona's naive acceptance of her dictum is that blend of transcendent, idealized love and carnal love—with all its possibilities for being tainted with desire for material wealth and power—which is at the heart of the courtly-love system.

The love story in "The Diamond as Big as the Ritz" is much like the story of the daisy/Alceste and the poet-persona. Just as Chaucer's poet-persona travels one spring morning into a meadow, John walks past rosebushes and moss and trees. Just as the poet-persona meets the daisy and Alceste, John encounters Kismine, who seems to John a beautiful daisy but is actually more like Alceste. Upon first meeting her, John feels Kismine is "the incarnation of physical perfection" (161). She is "dressed in a white little gown that came just below her knees, and a wreath of mignonettes clasped with blue slices of sapphire bound up her hair. Her pink bare feet scattered the dew before them as she came" (160). Kismine herself says she is girlish and innocent. John and Kismine fall in love but must meet secretly because Kismine thinks her father will have John poisoned if he learns of their love.

This first meeting of John and Kismine significantly parallels the Chaucerian poet-persona's meetings with the daisy and Alceste. Both Kismine and Alceste appear fresh, innocent, and beautiful. And like Alceste, Kismine's colors are green and white. Alceste's dress is green and her crown white; Kismine's dress is white, and her "crown" consists of mignonettes, sometimes green, sweet-smelling, springtime flowers traditionally associated with courtship (Stevens 174; Daniel and Stephans 817). So far, Kismine seems as sweet and lovely as the daisy; and John's love for her seems transcendent. But like Alceste, Kismine is much associated with the earthly—that is, with power and wealth. Alceste's white crown consists not of flowers but of costly pearls; similarly, amid the mignonettes in Kismine's crown are precious blue sapphires. Further, Kismine possesses a measure of power. This quality becomes apparent when she tells of her father's murder of past visitors brought there by her sister, Jasmine. The killings have been necessary, she says, to protect the secret of the diamond mountain. But, Kismine says, the visitors

> "always had a very good time. She'd give them the nicest presents toward the last. I shall probably have visitors too—I'll harden up to it. We can't let such an inevitable thing as death stand in the way of enjoying life while we have it. Think how lonesome it'd be out here if we never had *any* one. Why, father and mother have sacrificed some of their best friends just as we have." (174; Fitzgerald's emphasis)

Kismine says that she feels sorry that John—who up to now has known nothing about the Washingtons' plans for him—must also be put to death: "'...I'm honestly sorry you're going to—going to be put away—though I'd rather you'd be put away than ever kiss another girl'" (175).

Subsequently, when John attempts to escape, Kismine redeems herself by wanting to go with him. But up to then, she is pictured as essentially cold-hearted—out to use John for her own enjoyment just as other members of her family have done with other guests before putting them to death. Her lack of conscience seems to stem from an amoral upbringing in which riches have been god. Alceste acts similarly: she manipulates the poet-persona to achieve her own ends. Alceste uses a combination of beauty, riches, and verbal power to achieve control over the poet-persona, and Kismine has the potential to have such power over John, though it would perhaps be a more limited power in that Kismine does not seem nearly so clever as Alceste. They are both mere parodies of the fresh, innocent, natural flowers they appear to be. These women are instead in a sense personifications of wealth and power and thus not worthy goals for the protagonists' creativity.

However, there is an important difference between Alceste and Kismine: in Chaucer's poem, Alceste's power over the poet-persona directly ruins his creativity, for she manipulates him into writing works usually called dull—the legends themselves. But in Fitzgerald's story, though Kismine's beauty and seeming sweetness attract John, she has had nothing to do with his having come to the Washington chateau; eager to hobnob with the wealthy, he arrived as Percy's friend and thereby became entrapped. Still, it is clear that John's relationship with Kismine has prompted no gain in imaginative insight for him; even though she does not cause his failed creativity, she does nothing to help prevent the negative outcome, either. In fact, her final action—mistaking worthless rhinestones for valuable diamonds—makes for a vacuum: John is bereft of the riches that he feels would give him impetus for action, yet he feels he has nothing else to substitute for them.

The next portion of "The Diamond as Big as the Ritz" echoes *The House of Fame*. In both works, the protagonists next encounter places that reveal explicitly the true nature of the opulent palaces they have recently visited. Geffrey goes to the whirling house of twigs, a labyrinthine shack swarming with people in chaos. This bird-cage-like structure (Braswell 111), located in a valley beneath the House of Fame, represents the extreme form of the essentially purposeless activity found in the House of Fame itself. Similarly, John sees places—two of them—somewhat like this whirling cage: the cage in which the kidnapped aviators live, and a mountain cavity that Percy and his parents enter via a trap door just before the mountain blows up. The aviators' cage is actually a "large cavity in the earth about the circumference of a merry-go-round and covered by a strong iron grating" (165). Its residents, flyers who have unfortunately discovered the Washingtons' secret, yell to John, "'Come on down to Hell!'" (165). John finds that the prison is bowl-shaped: "The sides were steep and apparently of polished glass, and on its slightly concave surface stood about two dozen men..." (166). When the men hear that someone has escaped from the chateau, they yell jubilantly; and "a pandemonium of joy ensued" (168). They dance, cheer, yodel, wrestle, and run up the sides of the bowl. But Braddock Washington comes to tell them that the escapee has been killed, whereupon he pushes "the button in the grass so that the picture below went out instantly, and there remained only that great dark mouth covered dismally with the black teeth of the grating" (169). In short, as does Chaucer in his picture of the house of twigs, Fitzgerald here creates a portrait of creativity gone completely awry. Consumed only with maintaining his wealth, Braddock Washington's creative powers have resulted in the building of an expensive prison whose "great dark mouth" represents silenced true creativity. Whatever light gets into the cavity does so only with his consent—by push button. Further, trapped as they are, the aviators can only spend time engaged in meaningless, chaotic activity. The place's similarity to the house of twigs is stressed when it is compared to a merry-go-round, which also whirls about. Also this place is beneath the diamond mountain, just as the house of twigs is in a valley beneath the ice mountain. But most of all, the cage-like house of twigs and the aviators' cage resemble each other in that both are scenes of much chaos—undirected creativity.

The Washingtons themselves are as much entrapped as the aviators. They therefore serve a dual role: they ensnare others, but they are also ensnared by the god Wealth. In a way, then, they are representatives of this god and also, like the petitioners in the House of Fame, his subjects. And when their diamond mountain is destroyed, symbolically doing away with the god Wealth, they become like the chaotic mob in a second version of the house of twigs—one that, like that structure, offers no goal at all. Near dream's end, as airplanes are about to descend upon the diamond mountain and end the Washingtons' secret existence, John, Kismine, and Jasmine escape. But looking back, John sees that Percy and his parents have gone through a trap door into the mountain. Kismine reveals that this is no way of escape; the mountain is wired to explode, so they have chosen to be blown up with it. It does explode, destroying diamond, Percy, his parents, and the aviators alike. Percy and his parents have deliberately trapped themselves just as Mr. Washington previously imprisoned the aviators. Just after the imprisonment, utter chaos ensues—the blowing up of the mountain. The Washingtons have all along been figuratively imprisoned in wealth as the purpose for their actions, just as the petitioners to the goddess Fame are imprisoned in a desire for renown. Now, literally, they are enveloped in the diamond mountain, which, at this point, like the house of twigs, offers no "god" at all.

Amid the chaos, however, a man of great authority does appear in each work. In *The House of Fame*, he appears in the house of twigs, perhaps to provide a goal for the chaotic activity, though his intended function will forever remain unclear. In "The Diamond as Big as the Ritz," the authority is God, a sign of whose control appears shortly before the mountain's destruction. Just after the airplanes arrive to attack the mountain, John sees Braddock Washington offer God a bribe: a huge diamond that Braddock offers to have hollowed out and made into a chapel complete with "an altar of iridescent, decomposing, ever-changing radium which would burn out the eyes of any worshipper who lifted up his head from prayer..."

(185). In return, Washington asks that the clock be turned back and the airplanes never have found his mountain. Washington's concept of the appropriate thing to create and the appropriate manner in which to worship God shows in full measure the perversity of his creativity founded on wealth. Notably, however, God will have none of Washington's attempts at bribery. John sees the sky darken for a moment, the birds become quiet, and the trees become still. Then,

> the dawn and the day resumed their place in a time, and the risen sun sent hot waves of yellow mist that made its path bright before it. The leaves laughed in the sun, and their laughter shook the trees until each bough was like a girl's school in fairyland. God had refused to accept the bribe.
>
> For another moment John watched the triumph of the day. (186-87)

God and natural creativity—the laughter of the trees, the rising of the sun—triumph; a man of great authority indeed has taken charge, providing order. Washington's efforts at control and the god of his devotion, the god Wealth, are nothing in comparison—at least in this one scene.

However, despite the insight John presumably should gain from this vision of God's triumph, he ends disillusioned. For John, the god of Wealth wins after all, as becomes clear when, at the end of the dream, John learns that Kismine, whom he directed to bring some jewels away with her, has mistakenly brought worthless rhinestones. He bitterly realizes that they will have to live in Hades and work for a living. When Kismine asks if her father will be there, John replies, "'Your father is dead.... Why should he go to Hades? You have it confused with another place that was abolished long ago'" (190). John's response indicates that, like the poet-persona of *The Parliament of Fowls*, he has learned nothing from his dream. He is sorry about the loss of the mountain, but not because he has realized the unworthiness of riches as a goal. Instead he is sad because he is not wealthy. Despite the Washingtons' amorality, he still desires what has made them that way. Also, his remark about the original Hades—Hell—having been destroyed long ago shows that for him, the god Wealth—the god the residents of the current Hades worship—is for him still in control while God, whom devils in the other Hades recognize, is rejected.

"'There are only diamonds in the world, diamonds and perhaps the shabby gift of disillusion. Well, I have that last and I will make the usual nothing of it,'" John concludes (191). He thereby underlines his failure to learn and predicts that any future creative efforts he will undertake will surely fail.

At the end of the story, John proclaims that he wants to lose consciousness, and he falls asleep. Rather paradoxically, he has been more awake in his dream—more awake, that is, to possible insights—than he is when literally awake. There is not much to the closing frame of the story—only the sentence saying that he has fallen asleep. His dream is at a dead end, and so is his creativity. His subsequent life will, presumably, be a blank about which no further comment is possible. The story's negative end thus continues the trend established in "The Offshore Pirate" and "The Ice Palace."

"The Diamond as Big as the Ritz" is intriguing in that, unlike Fitzgerald's earlier two stories, it more closely approximates the point of view of Chaucer's dream visions: Though still in third person, Fitzgerald's story features a dreamer who is a man. The potentially creative woman of "The Offshore Pirate" relinquishes her creativity to a man; the potentially creative woman of "The Ice Palace" could, it seems, be saved by a man (Roger) but instead chooses to return to the womb, in a sense, as she returns to a dream of the past, tied up with a maternal vision of Margery Lee. In both instances, women who do not achieve their identities as artists can either be placed into or can place themselves into "dreams" not of their own making, "dreams" of another artist's making. But in "The Diamond as Big as the Ritz," John's creative potential is destroyed solely by his own failure to recognize the implications of the scene in which God wins out over the Washingtons' temporal values. His disregard of this scene probably occurs because he has never had a personal dream to counter the one his culture has provided for him. A woman—namely, Kismine Washington—appears only as one of the attractions associated with the Washingtons' material paradise. Like the typical courtly-love lady in a medieval dream vision, she is an object of the dreamer's attention within the dream account rather than a dreamer herself. Notably, however, even though Kismine partially echoes Chaucer's Alceste, unlike Alceste, Kismine does not lead John away from positive creativity. John fails on his own; she is just ineffectual. Perhaps she is an Ardita or a Sally Carrol after a failed dream, stripped of her voice, stripped of even an artistic potential. In any case, in Fitzgerald's next use of the dream-vision genre, he would alter somewhat his treatment of female characters and also provide a more positive dream outcome than in any of his first three dream visions.

With *The Vegetable*, Fitzgerald created his only published explicit dream vision—as well as his only professional full-length play. On stage, the play proved a dismal failure. When it opened on November 19, 1923, at Nixon's Apollo Theater in Atlantic City, many people walked out during the second act; the play closed a week later (Sklar 131–32; Scribner xix). Referring to the last name of the play's protagonist, Fitzgerald called the play a "'colossal Frost'" (qtd. in Scribner xix). Several factors probably contributed to its failure. Charles Scribner III points out that the topic of satire, the corruption of American government officials, came at the wrong time; a year after the play was produced, the Teapot Dome scandal became known. "Fitzgerald's political fantasy," says Scribner, "contained far more truth than the audience was prepared to take in" (xx). In addition, the play may have failed because it is, as Henry Dan Piper points out, "dramatic only in a literary sense. It relied on words" and did not make good use of the "non-verbal elements" that are "as important to a play as language. The result was something that read much better than it acted" (97). In fact, in a letter of January 1923, Fitzgerald told Maxwell Perkins that the published play seemed "'rather as a book of humor...than like a play—because of course it is written to be read'" (qtd. in Scribner xvii).

Finally and perhaps most importantly, the theme of the play may have been misunderstood. For example, one reviewer of the published play comments that the Act II dream becomes "Jerry Frost's unconscious estimate of himself and his incompetence" and not a representation of the effects of the values of modern society upon Jerry (Rev. of *The Vegetable* 188). More recently, Sergio Perosa has said that "the subject of the play is...an indictment of the fallacy of dreaming, a denunciation of our irrational illusions" (52). Both the anonymous reviewer and Perosa miss the mark widely. The reviewer feels that Fitzgerald fails to satirize society since Jerry's dream represents the workings of only one man's mind. However, Jerry may be thought of as the archetypal American who shares commonly held assumptions about the American dream of wealth and political power yet may also have hidden dreams of another sort. The play is less about corruptions in American politics than it is about Americans' perceptions of that corruption, their tendency to see only the lovely surface of the American dream and not its nightmarish underside, its capacity to pervert creativity, and their tendency to give up or look down on any dreams that run counter to it. Perosa contends that the play concerns the fallacy of dreaming. And, to be sure, the usual dream of wealth and power is held up for ridicule; yet, Jerry Frost's dream in which he sees the nightmarishness of this particular dream helps him grow, gives him the impetus to follow his own dream.

To make clear such ideas, as in his previous dream visions, Fitzgerald provides structure and other elements similar to those in Chaucer's dream visions. However, in contrast to Fitzgerald's earlier dream visions, *The Vegetable* contains relatively few direct parallels to any one of Chaucer's dream visions. The work thus is important as an indication of Fitzgerald's growth as an artist, his increasingly evident attempt to use in his own divergent way principles derived from his reading of Chaucer's dream visions.

Like a Chaucerian dream vision, the play consists of three parts: Act I occurs in the waking world and establishes the protagonist as frustrated artist in need of a dream to renew creativity; Act II is a dream account in which protagonist meets "shadows"; and Act III, back in the waking world, reveals that the dreamer has found a measure of renewal.

Act I features several interrelated characteristics common in Chaucer's dream visions: mention of sleep and dreams, of various art forms, and of books as insufficient in prompting creativity. All of these reveal an artist-protagonist too dull and frustrated to create successfully; he needs to dream.

At the beginning of the play, stage directions say that the setting is a cold March day in a "small and stuffy" house in which "it's an awful bother to raise these old-fashioned windows; some of them stick...."[2] Springtime and windows usually symbolize growth and insight. However, here such details instead indicate lack of creativity. Though spring, it is still cold outside; inside, it is stuffy; and the windows here signify lack of insight in that they are hard to open. Having established initially an atmosphere of lack of creativity, Fitzgerald reinforces the idea through mention of books and other art forms. Jerry's living room features a bookcase that "held 'Ben Hur' when it was a best-seller, and it's now trying to digest 'A

Library of the World's Best Literature' and the 'Wit and Humor of the United States in Six Volumes'" (3). The Frosts are apparently enough interested in books to have collected these volumes; but the personification of the bookcase, as if it, not the Frosts, read the books, suggests that this inanimate object is getting more out of the books than they do. Additionally, the works mentioned suggest limitation and thus the stifling of creativity. *Ben Hur* seems to be there simply because it is a best seller. And is it not rather presumptuous to label any group of books "The World's Best Literature," as if the labeler had the final word on the subject, or as if the relative value of books were forever set? The Frosts also have not taken the time to decide upon which individual works they wish to read; in purchasing such a volume, they have allowed someone else to decide for them what the best books are. It seems equally brash of someone—again, not the Frosts—to try to subsume all the varied examples of American wit and humor under just one title. In short, it sounds as if the Frosts are members of a book club that focuses merely on pre-packaged, popular goods. Similar to Chaucer's negative view of pre-packaged courtly-love sentiments, Fitzgerald's attitude is that such "literary consumerism" surely ruins the "consumer's" creativity.

Subsequent references to books and other forms of reading material underscore Jerry's lack of creativity. When Jerry first appears, he "leans over a table...and turns the pages of a magazine, yawning meanwhile and tentatively beginning a slow clog step with his feet. Presently this distracts him from the magazine, and he looks apathetically at his feet" (7). Shortly thereafter, Jerry asks his wife, Charlotte, for the *Saturday Evening Post*. He has much trouble even getting Charlotte to reply to his query; and when he does, he finds he cannot interest Charlotte in reading a story he has found quite fascinating: that of "the fella who gets shipwrecked on the Buzzard Islands and meets the Chinese girl, only she isn't a Chinese girl at all" (10). Thus, Jerry is, on the one hand, easily distracted from his reading; and, on the other, when he *is* interested, the interest is in a banal story. His inability to communicate effectively his view of the story to his wife also indicates Jerry's deficient creative faculty. Jerry, however, does not recognize his own failure. In telling Charlotte about being analyzed at work, he reveals that he thinks he has learned a great deal from his reading about such testing processes. Feeling Charlotte does not understand the process, he disgustedly tells her, "A lot

you know about business methods. Don't you ever read 'Ef-
ficiency' or the 'Systematic Weekly'" (13). Of course, it de-
velops that Jerry himself does not understand the analysis he
has undergone. When the examiner asked him what sort of job
he would like, Jerry replied, "'Well, what have you got to offer?'" (14). Jerry was unable to comprehend that the question
was nonliteral. Also, he reveals to Charlotte his lack of understanding when he says of the test, "I think I got away with it
all right. At least he didn't give me any black marks on my
chart—just a lot of little circles" (15). He does not make the
logical connection of little circles with scores of zero—of failure. Jerry, in short, has learned little from his reading of business magazines.

In Act I, Dada, Jerry's senile father, is introduced as a man
who has "lately become absorbed in the Old Testament and in
all Old Testament literature, over which he burrows every day
in the Public Library..." (18). Almost blind and deaf, Dada
appears to have "something grave and thoughtful and important...going on back of those faded, vacant eyes," but actually
"half the time his mind is a vacuum, in which confused clots
of information and misinformation drift and stir..." (18). Dada's true condition is shown in several ways. When Jerry asks
him who he thinks will be nominated for President that night,
with stunning illogic, Dada replies, "I should say that Lincoln
was our greatest President" (19). Also, Dada's most characteristic action—his pulling the Bible off the bookshelf and in so
doing causing two or three other books to crash to the floor—
illustrates well the disarray of his mind. Dada's reading of the
Old Testament makes of him the only character at all well acquainted with Christianity—which, as in Chaucer's poems,
presumably could offer an alternative to materialistic values—
but he proves utterly ineffective at gaining knowledge from his
reading of sacred documents or at communicating messages
from them. As in "The Diamond as Big as the Ritz," religion
as the wellspring of a creativity expressed in the worship of
God is dead. Dada is also an extreme version of Jerry, a man
also given to reading yet unable to use constructively what he
has read.

Other art forms besides literature are mentioned in Act I.
Jerry has taken music lessons; but these, like his books, have
provided him with no effective creative expression. At one
point, Jerry

begins to sing, unmusically, and with faint interest, a piece which is possibly his own composition. The tune varies considerably, but the words have an indisputable consistency, as they are composed wholly of the phrase: "Everybody is there, everybody is there!" (7)

Shortly thereafter, Jerry "gives out a harsh, bark-like sound and raises his hand swiftly, as though he were addressing an audience" (7). These details emphasize both Jerry's desire to be creative and his utter failure to be creative. He can only sing out of tune a song with no meaningful lyrics and pretend to be giving to an imaginary audience a speech consisting only of an animal sound. In reality, his own wife will not even listen to him when he tries to tell her about the *Post* story.

Act I also reveals that Jerry does have creative potential thwarted by the opposing dream thrust upon him by American society. As Jerry tells Charlotte, he has taken an aptitude test at work, during which the analyst (who represents the traditional American dream) asked him about his ambitions. Revealing to the analyst that as a child he wanted to be a postman, Jerry cannot understand that the analyst wants to know only of his ambitions to rise to a higher position with the railroad, his current employer, not of his childhood dreams. Asked if he has studied at home for a higher position, Jerry replies that he has taken music lessons; but, again, the analyst is interested only in whether or not Jerry has studied anything to do with railroads. Jerry then tells Charlotte of his reply to the analyst: "I said they worked me so hard that when I got home at night I never want to hear about railroads again" (14).

Besides indicating Jerry's rather childish, unsophisticated storytelling strategy of stringing together many independent clauses with *ands*, Jerry's account of his conversation with the analyst shows that Jerry has an embryonic sort of creativity. He does like to tell a story, however poorly. And though he believes he has abandoned any ambitions, Jerry has had since childhood a goal indicative of his potential creativity. If Jerry had his way, he would be a messenger, a bringer of the written word to the public. Jerry is thus an artist-figure, albeit a highly frustrated one, surrounded as he is by people such as the analyst, whose concept of appropriate avenues of "creative" expression is decidedly limited. Jerry, in fact, appears quite untalented; though he certainly tries, he can neither sing nor speak well. But this lack of talent may indicate only that Jerry has sought creative expression in areas for which he is indeed unsuited. Jerry is no musician, no speechmaker, no storyteller. He is also no good at trying to accomplish something significant as a railway clerk. His special way of exercising creativity has been denied to him. Notably, Jerry's very name indicates the nature of his problem. Various names for which *Jerry* is a nickname (such as *Gerald*) mean "spear"; thus the name suggests power, the phallic, the naturally creative (just as the testicle images in "The Diamond as Big as the Ritz" suggest such forces). However, undercutting these suggestions, the word *frost* is associated with coldness and lack of movement. Jerry Frost's creative power is indeed buried within him, hidden by a covering of frost—of the cold, deadly, and inactive.

Society, largely in the persons of Jerry's wife and sister-in-law, has produced the "frost" that covers Jerry. Instead of a postman, Jerry is a railroad clerk far removed from any action suggestive of creativity. As a mere clerk, he neither journeys nor conducts others on their journeys. He is stationary; apparently, the only text he conveys is the words written on the tickets he issues to passengers. Jerry has allowed himself to be goaded into such a stultifying existence for years. Charlotte makes fun of his ambition to be a postman and instead wants only for Jerry to make more money at his present place of employment; Doris, Charlotte's sister, also proclaims the material American dream when she says of Jerry:

> He'd never be rich if you *gave* him the money. He hasn't got any *push*. I think a man's got to have *push*, don't you? I mean sort of *uh*! [She gives a little grunt to express indomitable energy, and makes a sharp gesture with her hand.] I saw in the paper about a fella that didn't have any legs or arms forty years old that was a millionaire. (31; Fitzgerald's brackets)

Doris goes on to suggest that the way to get rich is by inventing something like cold cream or an undetectable henna. Jerry, Charlotte counters, does not have the brains to come up with such a scheme. Besides considering such dreams of wealth significant, Charlotte and Doris seem to find a dream of political power agreeable, as becomes clear when Jerry, seemingly offering an insincere defense of himself in the face of Charlotte and Doris' disdain, proclaims that he at one time wanted to be President. He thus substitutes for his own dream—ridiculed by Charlotte—what he feels will be more acceptable to them: the dream of political power. Charlotte and Doris, in other words, believe in the American dream of wealth and power and show disgust toward Jerry for not living up to it. They are a bit like Chaucer's Alceste, who misunderstands (perhaps on purpose in her case) the dreamer's brand of creativity and manipulates him into following her opposing plans. Interestingly, in contrast to Alceste, Charlotte and Doris are right up to a point about Jerry: he does not have the sort of mind necessary for a creativity directed toward attaining huge profits. His creativity is of another sort altogether.

Unfortunately, Jerry himself has almost totally accepted the values of his society. Besides saying that he has always wanted to be President, Jerry tells Snooks, the bootlegger who comes to sell him liquor, that Snooks "ought to want to rise in the world," that "everybody ought to" because the Bible says so. "It's one of the commandments" (47). As in "The Diamond as Big as the Ritz," a twisted religion based upon worship of money—and of political power—has replaced worship of God— even for Jerry, though the nature of his dream shows that he is not without inner knowledge of the destructiveness of such a "religion."

Also in Act I, Jerry meets two people who have a creativity focused on attaining wealth and power. Doris' fiance, Joseph Fish of Fish, Idaho, and Jerry's bootlegger, Snooks, have committed themselves and their talents to this American dream. Members of Joseph's family have done so in a socially acceptable manner. They have been, according to Doris, "mayor a couple of times.... His [Joseph's] father's in business up there now" (25). The business is a funeral parlor; thus the family's money and power come from dealing in death. Snooks, too, has sought and found money and power—in his case through criminal activity. Fitzgerald describes Snooks as disreputable and filthy, a man who "speaks in a villainous whine" and has a missing tooth, a broken nose, a squint eye, and "three days' growth of beard" (32–33). Ironically, Snooks says of himself that "Sandy Claus is here" (33). Yet, Snooks is hardly to be identified with the familiar symbol of giving and sacrifice, of positive creativity; instead, Snooks is the American dream at its worst, bereft of any redeeming feature, replete with poor

vision, brokenness, and growth only of something as inconse-
quential as a beard. While Jerry Frost at least attempts to sing
well, Snooks speaks in a "villainous whine." Fitzgerald thus
underscores the contrast between a more positive sort of creativity and Snook's brand.

At the end of Act I, Jerry's thwarted creativity having been
established, Jerry's dream begins in much the way a Chaucerian dream vision does—with music. Jerry hears a loud
noise outside: "a mighty cheer goes up and there is the beating
of a bass drum" (54). A politician enters and proclaims that
Jerry has received the Republican nomination for President of
the United States. Interestingly, in an earlier draft of the play,
Jerry becomes not only President but also a millionaire. In any
case, Jerry's dream has begun, a dream in which he will learn
what would happen if a man who possessed a different sort of
creativity were to find himself called upon to use creativity to
gain and keep money and political power.

In the dream account, Jerry is revealed as indeed an inap-
propriate servant of the god of wealth and political power. As
in *The House of Fame*, the dream focuses in part on a building—in this case, the White House. As with the House of
Fame, all sorts of suggestions of creativity appear in this place;
in fact, in describing the White House, Fitzgerald uses what
Bennett calls "the dream-faculty of increasing and multiplying
figures [that] Chaucer exploits in all his dream-poems..." (123).
Specifically, Fitzgerald multiplies instances of whiteness,
somewhat as Chaucer does in *The Book of the Duchess*, where
the multiple connotations of the color white give Good Fair
White a multivalent symbolic value (Manning 99). Here, in
this dream White House, everything is white: not only the
exterior walls of the building, but also the wall surrounding
the grounds, the vines and flowers, Jerry's so-called Special
Tree, a sign with "Jerry Frost" spelled out in electric lights, the
kittens, the dog, even the parrot. White, as in Chaucer's
poem, takes on multiple meanings: usually white signifies purity, but here the color, a familiar identifying feature of a common symbol of political power, the White House, itself comes
to signify a deadly sort of power. Here, like white frost, the
color takes over, literally "coloring" (or "uncoloring") everything, including ordinarily naturally colorful objects such as
parrots and flowers. Notably, too, the color white takes over
Jerry Frost himself: he appears wearing "a loose-fitting white
flannel frock coat, a tall white stovepipe hat. His heavy gold

watch-chain would anchor a small yacht, and he carries a white stick, ringed with a gold band" (65). Also he smokes a white cigar. Significantly, Jerry's white trappings include several phallic symbols: the stovepipe hat, the stick, the cigar. Coupled with whiteness, these items symbolize the frosting-over of his creative power. Also significantly, two other white items are Jerry's own "creations": the sign spelling out his name, and the Special Tree, a gift that he has planted himself. Even these symbols associated with Jerry's creativity are frost-covered. In the best dreamlike fashion, Fitzgerald has created a palpable sense of distorted creativity through symbolically using color and objects, including buildings.

In earlier drafts of *The Vegetable*, Fitzgerald included in Act II an episode concerning Jerry Frost as millionaire. This scene has something in common with Chaucer's *The House of Fame*, in which many musicians come to Fame's castle and perform to receive fame. This episode, known in manuscript as "The Musicians," emphasizes the use of creativity to gain the similarly undependable and transitory wealth. Jerry tells a character named Horace,

> I got some private musicians, you know. (He makes a megaphone of his hands) Hey! Music! (Immediately three grotesque and preferably dwarfed musicians come running on the stage, instruments in hand)....
>
> I want to hear some music.... See? If I tell 'em to play they got to play. If I tell 'em to stop, they stop. (Appn. 1, 1–2)

Jerry then throws the musicians twenty-dollar gold pieces, the smallest change he has. Here, Jerry's slight musical talent—part of his waking personality—is transformed into the actions of these musicians, which are fixed only upon earning money, not satisfying any artistic impulse. Jerry becomes something like the goddess Fame, controlling these artists with promise of money instead of promise of fame.

In encountering four dream characters who are distortions of people Jerry has met in the waking world—Snooks, Joseph Fish, Dada, and Jerry himself—Jerry meets his shadows and thereby sees several variations on the theme of using creativity to seek riches and power. Snooks, a bootlegger in the waking world, sells countries, not liquor, in the dream. Snooks is now

called "the Honorable Snooks, or Snukes, Ambassador from
Irish Poland," a brand-new country in Europe that consists of
"three or four acres of Russia and a couple of mines in Austria
and a few lots in Bulgaria and Turkey" (79). Snooks tells Jerry
that Irish Poland wants to sell to the United States

> the Buzzard Islands.... Garden spots. Flowery para-
> dises ina middle of the Atlantic. Rainbow Islandsa
> milk an' honey, palms an' pines, smellin' with good-
> smellin' woods and high-priced spices. Fulla animals
> with million buck skins and with birds that's got
> feathers that the hat dives on Fifth Avenue would go
> nuts about. The folks in ee islands—swell-lookin'
> husky, square, rich, one hunerd per cent Buzzardites.
> (83)

Snooks' waking tendency to sell appears in exaggerated form
here as a propensity to sell an entire country. In speaking of
high-priced spices, the valuable animal skins, and the feathers
sought after by haberdashers, he makes clear that his main interest is financial. In fact, his words echo in hyperbolic form
some of the early accounts of the American continent sent back
to England (and other places) to "sell" people on settling there.
They mirror also the Biblical account in Numbers of Moses'
sending spies into the land of Canaan to see what kind of land
it is. Upon the spies' return to the wilderness in which the Israelites have been wandering, they tell Moses that the promised land "surely...floweth with milk and honey"; and they
show the Israelites the grapes, pomegranates, and figs they
have gathered in Canaan (Numbers 13:27). Snooks' account of
conditions on the Buzzard Islands is surely a parody of this
Biblical story, one that perverts the account, changing it into
an ad campaign. Snooks' account is a reminder of the material
nature of the American dream as opposed to the Biblical dream
of the promised land with which the American dream was
often linked (ironically, as it turns out). Snooks, the ultimate
in salesmen, shows the farthest extreme of the perverse use of
creativity in service of wealth and power.
    Joseph Fish, who in the waking world only *wishes* to be a
senator, appears in the dream as the senator from Idaho. He is
behind Idaho's move to have Jerry impeached. Thus, in the
dream, Fish's creativity is used to seek political power at the
expense of another person's well being. And, in a discarded

portion of Act II, Fish also uses his creativity to make money. In a scene called "The Coffin Corner," Fish explains about the recent boom in sales in his family business:

> We started out to put Fish coffins in every home, and we did it. We got people looking for the Fish labels on their coffins. We showed them a coffin needn't be an eyesore. We ran ads showing good-looking girls stepping into cheap but attractive coffins, and we got testimonials from spirits who had used Fish coffins. (Appn. 1, 3)

Paradoxically, Fish is excited about the growth of a business associated with lack of growth, with death: coffins. Like Snooks, Fish is but an advertising executive producing "copy" with which to sell his product. Perhaps a faint echo of Venus' temple in *The House of Fame* occurs in this scene. The artistic products are, in one sense, the coffins, and in another, the ads concerning the coffins. Coffins are art that houses only the motionless and unchanging; similarly, the ads concerning the coffins are also art that has as its actual subject only death and stasis. And both coffins and ads are produced solely for monetary gain. Somewhat similarly, Venus' temple features stillness instead of active creativity. But unlike in Fish's advertising ad, in Venus' temple, at least a remnant of a worthy goal for art exists—a picture of the goddess of Love—but here only the god Wealth oversees creative efforts.

As in the waking world, a confused Dada reads the Old Testament and ignores events around him; but, as with Fish and Snooks, his qualities appear in exaggerated form in Jerry's dream. Indeed, Dada becomes a false prophet who uses isolated Bible verses in a distorted, illogical way to justify misguided actions. In the published play, Dada is responsible for the move to impeach Jerry because of his (Dada's) rash actions as Secretary of the Treasury. As Dada explains, the United States

> was the wealthiest country in all the world. It's easier for a camel to pass through a needle's eye than for a wealthy man to enter heaven....
> So all the money in the Treasury I have had destroyed by fire, or dumped into the deep sea. We are all saved. (95)

While Fish and Snooks worship money, devoting their creative efforts to making it, Dada scorns such worship yet offers no positive alternative. He merely destroys the object of their worship, producing utter chaos in the land. He quotes a single verse from the Bible and then assumes that in destroying all the money, everyone has been ensured a place in heaven. Then, in a scene cut from the final version of the play entitled "The End of the World," Dada, speaking to a crowd, again uses an isolated Biblical passage. He says that "Gabriel's Trump will blow one week from today just at this hour.... I calculated it by the second letter in the third word of every fourth verse of Isaiah" (Appn. 1, 4). Instead, at the appointed time, the sun shines; and a band begins to play. While Dada believes the heavenly choir is about to sing, everyone else realizes that the end has not come. Ironically, Snoops and Fish, who have relatively good minds capable of formulating effective creative products, disregard the spiritual; in Fish's case, where the subject is death, the omission is particularly glaring. Dada, in contrast, dimly tries to worship the Judeo-Christian God, but he can neither reason properly nor transform the products of his imagination into effective messages.

As for Jerry Frost himself, besides showing that he cannot handle wealth, Jerry reveals the incompatibility of his kind of creativity and political power. Asked how he got to be President, Jerry replies, "I just made up my mind...and then I went ahead and did it. I've always been a very ambitious sort of—sort of domineerer" (66). This is surely an ironic statement: the dream Jerry may have been all this, but the waking Jerry of course never has been. Then, when his troubles with Idaho's threat of impeachment and Dada's burning of the money occur, Jerry explicitly indicates his inability to create an effective plan. When Idaho threatens him, Jerry can only say vaguely, "Maybe I'll get some idea how to fix it up. I'm a very resourceful man. I always think of something" (66). Ultimately, his only solution to the problem is to take Snooks up on his sales pitch about the Buzzard Islands and to offer to trade Idaho for the islands, a decision that will only ensure his impeachment and otherwise cause chaos by bringing on a war against Irish Poland. And, when Dada gives away the Treasury, Jerry's answer is to have the Treasury Department "strike off a couple billion dollars more," perhaps with Jerry's picture on them (98). This scheme to create new money never has a chance to cause trouble, for the Treasury Department will not go along with it. In short, all of Jerry's efforts to create as President prove dismal failures. Like Snooks and Fish, he has no appropriate goal for his efforts. And like Dada, he lacks the sort of intellect necessary to formulate effective plans.

Jerry's failure is related most clearly to creativity when, about to be impeached, he makes a very bad speech to the nation. He says to the radio audience,

> I want to tell you about a vision of mine that I seem to see. I seem to see Columbia—Columbia—ah—blind-folded—ah—covered with scales—driving the ship of state over the battle-fields of the republic in the heart of the golden West and the cotton-fields of the sunny South. (105)

Filled with hesitations that give way to nearly every banality imaginable, this speech surely indicates in full measure Jerry's incompetence at being creative in this fashion. And it is not just Jerry who is thus incompetent. Another governmental official, Judge Fossile, makes an equally bad speech:

> Now, gentlemen, the astronomers tell us that in the far heavens...there is a vast space called the hole in the sky.... In that dreary cold, dark region of space the Great Author of Celestial Mechanism has left the chaos which was in the beginning. If the earth beneath my feet were capable of expressing its emotions it would, with the energy of nature's elemental forces, heave, throw, and project this enemy of mankind [Jerry] into that vast region, there forever to exist in a solitude as eternal as—as eternity. (109–10)

Replete with high-flown phrases, excessively adjectival, and hyperbolic, this speech is an almost verbatim reproduction of a speech given by Congressman George Boutwell of Massachusetts at Andrew Johnson's impeachment hearing (Scribner xv–xvi). Presumably, for the fictional Judge Fossile and Jerry Frost and for the real-life Congressman Boutwell, when governmental power is the goal, the result is bad art.

During his Act-II dream, then, Jerry meets several shadows. Fish and Snooks possess imaginations—as does Jerry, deep inside—yet they accept society's view of what is a worthy goal to seek with that ability. Jerry, too, has a tendency to accept this same view. Dada represents a creativity pointed toward a more eternal goal—but pointed confusedly, illogically—also a tendency of Jerry's. Thus the dream-Jerry reflects all the worst possibilities inherent in Jerry Frost: an inept use of creativity for the wrong ends.

At the beginning of Act III, the dream has ended. In the Frost living room, "through the open windows the sun is shining in great, brave squares upon the carpet." Yet in the house is an "air of catastrophe, a profound gloom that seems to have settled even upon the 'Library of Wit and Humor' in the dingy bookcase" (114). Outside the house, then, there are signs of creativity; but inside, as at the start of the play, no such signs appear. Soon, the reason for the disparity becomes clear: Jerry has disappeared; he is outside in the sun, not inside amid the gloom. Charlotte explains to a detective that, a few nights before, after spending restless hours during which he talked in his sleep, Jerry left the house and has not been seen since. Jerry, so stationary in Act I (before the dream), has become active enough to alter his life by, first, leaving behind the stultifying atmosphere of his house.

In fact, Jerry has become creative enough to fulfill his dream of becoming a postman. For the first time in a Fitzgeraldian dream vision, a protagonist manages to renew creativity through a dream, much as the poet-persona in *The Book of the Duchess* does. The poet-persona creates *The Book of the Duchess* itself, thereby fulfilling the desire he speaks of in the opening frame to overcome his dull, sorrowful imagination. Similarly, whereas all his earlier attempts to create have been dismal failures, Jerry is a huge success as a postman. Carrying and using an unusual-sounding whistle symbolic of his newfound ability to communicate with people in his own special way, Jerry even looks different: "In the gray uniform his once flabby figure appears firm, erect—even defiant. His chin is up—the office stoop has gone. When he speaks his voice is full of confidence..." (132). Jerry has acquired the discipline and direction necessary to be effective. Now, he can both make music—with the whistle—and speak well whereas before, he could do neither. Most importantly, he now has a job which involves written communication. As a result, Jerry has gained much self confidence and feels he is the best postman in the world. "I just feel it," he says, "I know my job.... I'm just naturally *good*" (133).

However, Jerry also reveals the tenuous connection of this job to creativity when he says,

> I came near leaving that pink letter with a little girl
> down the street who looked as if she needed one
> pretty bad. I thought that maybe it was really meant
> for her, and just had the wrong name and address on
> by mistake.... I get tempted to leave mail where it re-
> ally ought to go instead of where it's addressed to.
> Mail ought to go to people who appreciate it. It's hard
> on a postman, especially when he's the best one they
> ever had. (135–36)

Hitherto inept, Jerry now has pride in his work and is active in disseminating messages to the public; but he is normally just a bringer of messages written by other persons and thus stands only on the periphery of creative endeavors. He shows frustration at not writing letters himself to people who need them— such as the little girl—and at having to deliver letters as addressed, not as he would like them addressed. In short, he still lacks creative control.

However, at the end of the play, Jerry becomes a writer himself—of a letter that effects a reconciliation with the previously critical Charlotte. The letter, Charlotte reveals, says that Jerry is "well and comfortable. And that he's doing what he wants to do and what he's got to do. And he says that doing his work makes him happy" (142). Charlotte shows that the letter has had a great effect upon her when she follows this account with the question: "If I wrote him a letter do you think you could find him with it, Mr. Postman?" and says that she would "be proud of him if he's a postman, because I know he always wanted to be one" (142). So, at the end of the play, though other things remain much as they were at the start—for example, Dada still lets several books tumble to the floor as he pulls out the Bible, Joseph Fish still has his mind on embalming fluid, and Jerry's boss still speaks of the scores of zero on Jerry's test—Jerry has changed for the better, and Charlotte approves of the change. Charlotte speaks the final line of the play. Upon hearing Jerry's whistle blowing and realizing he has returned home, she lifts her arms "rapturously" and says, "The best postman in the world!" (145). She has truly come to appreciate Jerry's sort of "creativity." At the same time, the recent storm having ended, the sun shines into the room once again. Even it reflects the sense of renewal; true reconciliation seems to have occurred.

The Vegetable, then, is the earliest example of a Fitzgeraldian dream vision with a positive ending. The play juxtaposes two types of dreams: a man's private dream of his own brand of creative endeavor, and a very material American dream that can destroy the private dream. Positive creativity wins out here, even making a convert of Jerry's major critic, Charlotte. In contrast, in "The Diamond as Big as the Ritz," the dreamer ends in despair, perhaps because he has never formulated any other dream for himself and thus has nothing to substitute for the material American dream. Thus, faced with a vision of nature's creative response to the majesty of God, he can only disregard any lesson it offers.

"The Diamond as Big as the Ritz" and *The Vegetable* are intriguing in a few other ways as well. For one thing, they reveal Fitzgerald's continual struggle with point of view. "The Diamond as Big as the Ritz," like the earlier two Fitzgeraldian dream visions, features a dreamer who can neither tell his own story nor have an explicit dream that he himself generates. But Jerry Frost at least is an actual dreamer. However, as protagonist of a play, he does not formulate his own dream account; the dream is of course simply presented on stage. He must instead become an artist by writing a letter to his wife alone, not a work designed for public consumption (within the plot of the play, that is). Because of the strictures of the play form, the letter cannot even be presented directly to the audience; it must be quoted by Charlotte. Fitzgerald had seemingly not yet hit upon a way to approximate the effect achieved in a medieval dream vision of having an artist tell his own dream.

Also, *The Vegetable*, like "The Diamond as Big as the Ritz," features a particular view of women. Charlotte, throughout Act I, plays the role of the destroyer of the private dream and propagator of the material national dream. Charlotte is less pliable and passive than Kismine, and thus a bit more like Alceste than is Kismine. But with the attention altogether on Jerry's dreams, Charlotte is never shown with any sort of dream of her own beyond the cultural dream of wealth. In Act III, after she starts seeing things Jerry's way, the issue is still *his* dream. In fact, Charlotte's prime function at this juncture is to serve as a mouthpiece for Jerry's creative output whereas previously she has at least spoken her mind about what she sees as her own dream. Perhaps in the end she is much like Ardita, willing to let her mate be the imaginative one.

Two years after *The Vegetable*, Fitzgerald was to produce his novel *The Great Gatsby*, by far his most complex dream vision, and one that, by focusing upon the ultimately successful artist Nick Carraway, continues the positive trend in endings begun in *The Vegetable* and also deals interestingly with the issues of point of view and gender raised so many times in Fitzgerald's earlier works.

CHAPTER FOUR

REVISING A TRIBUTE:
THE GREAT GATSBY

*"A slow sort of country!" said the Queen. "Now, here, you
see, it takes all the running you can do, to keep in the same
place. If you want to get somewhere else, you must run at
least twice as fast as that!"*
—*Lewis Carroll,* Through the Looking-Glass and
What Alice Found There

The Great Gatsby (1925) is the most complex—and the last—of F.
Scott Fitzgerald's dream visions. The work contains echoes of
all four of Geoffrey Chaucer's dream visions—echoes that, as
in Fitzgerald's earlier dream visions, revolve around the question of what it takes for the artist to be truly creative. The
novel's parallels with *The Book of the Duchess* are quite perva-
sive and reveal especially well the profound implications of
Fitzgerald's new adoption of the usual dream-vision point of
view: the first person. Also of especial interest in *Gatsby* is the
courtly-love-like relationship it portrays, a relationship with
echoes of those in *The Book of the Duchess,* the Prologue to *The
Legend of Good Women,* and *The Parliament of Fowls.*
　　The Great Gatsby and *The Book of the Duchess* both focus on a
hitherto unproductive dreamer who meets his shadow and his
anima in a dream and thereby regains his creativity. The opening part of each frame presents a narrator who is a currently
unimaginative artist, having relied too exclusively upon only a
part of what is needed for creativity. Two ingredients are
needed: those provided by the conscious mind—objectivity,
perspective, discipline—and those linked to the unconscious

mind—imagination, involvement, even chaos. In their dreams and in their accounts of those dreams, these narrators meet their shadows, who have confusing stories to tell of their timeless devotion to lovely ladies (anima figures). The dreamers must keep questioning and even editing the shadows' tributes to these ladies to arrive at the truth of the situations. In so doing, they formulate their own stories, which have far different focuses—and much more success artistically—than do the stories of their shadows. The closing frames reveal that the dreamers have learned from their dreams and have indeed been able to complete their own tributes, which exhibit both ingredients of creativity and thus indicate that the dreamers' problems have been resolved.

Both *The Great Gatsby* and all of Chaucer's dream visions, including *The Book of the Duchess*, feature a contrast between the waking world pictured in the frame sections and the dream world pictured in the core. In his important article, "Nick Carraway's Self-Introduction," A. E. Elmore emphasizes the presence of a frame in *The Great Gatsby*, theorizing in fact that the novel features two sorts of frames: 1) The opening section begins in the West, and Nick returns to the West in the final section. The middle section occurs in the East. Thus there is circular geographical movement. (See also Sklar 175–76.) 2) The events of 1922 fall between Nick's arrival in the East in the spring and his return to the West in the autumn. Thus spring and autumn, representing birth and death and preparation for rebirth respectively, frame a summertime sequence of events (Elmore 142–43). In short, the novel has both a spatial frame and a temporal frame set apart from the place and time of the middle section. The dream imagery of the core also sets it apart from the less dreamlike frame.

The opening frame of *The Great Gatsby* parallels the opening frame of most of Chaucer's dream visions. Like a typical Chaucerian opening section, the opening frame of *Gatsby*— along with a few other passages in other parts of the novel— emphasizes the novel as a self-conscious piece of art and thus Nick Carraway as artist. For one thing, the opening frame (paragraphs one through seventeen) begins with a prologue of four paragraphs in which Nick Carraway, in introducing himself and his subject, Jay Gatsby (Elmore 130–31), stresses these ideas. After these paragraphs, extra white space appears on the page (7), after which the subject shifts from Nick's opinion that Gatsby "turned out all right at the end" (6) to Nick's account of his own family history (7). These initial paragraphs are therefore set apart from the rest of the frame not only in content and logical sequence but also in physical space on the page.

In this prologue, Nick stresses his mixture of fascination with and repulsion to the texts of other people, and his tendency to examine and then apply such texts to his life. In the novel's second sentence, Nick quotes his father's most memorable words to him: "'Whenever you feel like criticizing anyone...just remember that all the people in this world haven't had the advantages that you've had'" (5). Nick then reveals that he has spent much time analyzing this text. He believes his father "meant a great deal more than that"—specifically, that "a sense of the fundamental decencies is parcelled out unequally at birth" (5–6). He says that he has been "turning [the advice] over in...[his] mind" (5) for years. Next, Nick shows that his attitudes and behavior have greatly affected by this text; as a result of it, he has been "inclined to reserve all judgements, a habit that has opened up many curious natures to me and also made me the victim of not a few veteran bores" (5). In other words, it has made Nick the audience to still other texts: "the secret griefs of wild, unknown men" (5). But the effect upon Nick has clearly been mixed: he derides these men's tales as "usually plagiaristic and marred by obvious suppressions" (6) and tells how he "feigned sleep, preoccupation or a hostile levity" (5) to avoid being told such tales; yet he also says that he is "a little afraid of missing something" (6) if he forgets the advice from his father that has led him into the role of audience to such stories.

Further, Nick has been influenced to come to the East by the texts of his relatives. When Nick consulted with his family about his proposed move, "all my aunts and uncles talked it over as if they were choosing a prep-school for me and finally said 'why—ye-es,' with very grave, hesitant faces" (7). Their communication of approval seems to have resulted in his making the move. Nick, therefore, concentrates very much on the texts of others, thereby revealing two things: his connection to art and also his initial limitations as an artist.

Nick also explicitly mentions that he is writing a novel. In introducing the reader to Jay Gatsby, Nick calls him "Gatsby, the man who gives his name to this book" (6). Later, within the dream account, Nick says, "Reading over what I have written so far I see I have given the impression that the events of three nights several weeks apart were all that absorbed me" (53). Moreover, the events of the novel occur in 1922, as becomes apparent when Nick mentions that he wrote Gatsby's guest list on a 1922 timetable. According to Matthew Bruccoli, Nick is supposedly telling of these events of 1922 sometime between autumn 1922 and autumn 1923; yet at one point Nick says, "After *two years* I remember the rest of that day..." (171; emphasis added). This comment puts his writing of the novel at 1924, the same year that Fitzgerald finished the novel. Perhaps, says Bruccoli, "...the extra year [1923–24] was deliberately built into the scheme of the novel to indicate that Nick has spent the year 1923–24 writing the book...to strengthen the impression that the narrator is the author" (*Apparatus* 118–19). Such evidence surely reveals art conscious of itself as art and shows that Nick is an artist.

What Elmore calls Nick's self-introduction (the prologue plus the next seven paragraphs) as well as the rest of the opening frame (paragraphs twelve through seventeen) is significant not only for introducing the reader to Nick and to his Middle-Western family but also for introducing various images that will be significant motifs in the dream account. Such linkage also occurs in a Chaucerian dream vision. For example, the opening frame of *The Book of the Duchess* mentions Alcyone's bereavement; then, the topic of bereavement recurs in the account of the dream, where it applies to the Man of Black. Such recurring images in *Gatsby* have been examined by John J. McNally and by Elmore, though they have not related the patterns to the idea of dream phenomena. McNally sees that in particular Nick's father's advice "forebodes significant events" such as the many occasions on which Nick reserves judgment on various characters (39). Elmore mentions a number of patterns established in the self-introduction. Several of them emanate from a single passage of the self-introduction in which Nick describes his early days in the East:

> ...I went out to the country alone. I had a dog, at least I had him for a few days until he ran away, and an old Dodge and a Finnish woman who made my bed and cooked breakfast and muttered Finnish wisdom to herself over the electric stove. (8)

Also, after giving directions to a stranger, Nick felt, he says, like "a guide, a pathfinder, an original settler" (8). The image patterns begun here include animals (Nick's dog, which reappears Myrtle Wilson's dog); cars (Nick's Dodge, transformed into Gatsby's resplendent auto); servants (Nick's Finn, who becomes the Buchanans' butler and/or Gatsby's servants); exploration (Nick's exploring the neighborhood, which becomes the various journeys to and from New York, as well as Nick's overall trip through a dream world toward self-knowledge) (Elmore 143–44).

Significantly, one of the image patterns established in the opening frame of *Gatsby* works at once to establish a waking world-dream world correspondence and to emphasize the novel as self-conscious art narrated by an artist. The pattern involves Nick's tendency to see life as if it were a movie. Nick closes his self-introduction with a brief paragraph (paragraph eleven) which reads, "And so with the sunshine and the great burst of leaves growing on the trees— just as things grow in *fast movies*—I had that familiar conviction that life was beginning over again with the summer" (8; emphasis added). Robert Emmet Long comments that this sentence suggests that "already time seems accelerated and dreamlike, like Gatsby's own time sense" (139). Here, in the waking world, Nick thinks of time in terms of movie time; but for him, the connection is a simile, a figure of speech. He knows the difference between the time it really takes for the leaves to grow on trees and the time they *seem* to take. In the dream, he will show this principle of wrenched chronology in operation, but within the dream as if really occurring (from Gatsby's vantage point at least), and in highly exaggerated form. Also the dream account will feature direct references to movies, as in Gatsby's guest list and in Nick's remark about a "scarcely human orchid of a woman" who turns out to be a movie star (111).

Nick—like Ardita in "The Offshore Pirate"—is thus a director. Edwin T. Arnold's statement about Fitzgerald's use of director figures applies not only to Ardita but also to Nick: Arnold says that Fitzgerald tends to use the movie metaphor to present two possible attitudes toward life: that of the actor, who "enters the illusion and is controlled by it," and that of the director, who "'dominates' the cheap and mundane around him" and is, for Fitzgerald, the real "artist" (44). Interestingly, Nick will be not only the writer-director of the dream account but also the actor involved in the dream itself, a situation made possible by the novel's first-person point of view.

Nick is a frustrated artist, much like the various frustrated artists of Chaucer's dream visions. Various passages in the opening frame indicate the source of the frustration. Nick states in the opening frame that he was "rather literary in college—one year I wrote a series of very solemn and obvious editorials for the 'Yale News'..." (8). Otherwise, most of the texts of interest to Nick are the solemn and obvious texts of other people. These suggestions of the nature of Nick's artistic identity show an artist in something of a straight jacket, whose imagination is not much engaged. In fact, Nick lacks much direct experience of life—particularly, of love. For instance, he reveals later that, before coming East, he was involved in a "tangle back home" with a girl:

> I'd been writing letters once a week and signing them
> 'Love, Nick,' and all I could think of was how, when
> that certain girl played tennis, a faint mustache of per-
> spiration appeared on her upper lip. Nevertheless
> there was a vague understanding that had to be tact-
> fully broken off before I was free. (64)

Like a Chaucerian poet-persona, Nick, to begin with, knows not love in deed. Thus Nick has a stagnant imagination—and all because of excess attention to outside texts. He is similar to the poet-persona of *The Book of the Duchess* in that both speak of love yet do not really know about the subject. In the case of this poet-persona, it might be said that attention to the courtly-love text has resulted in his bereft condition; in Nick's case, surrender to the solemn texts of other people (and of himself) is part of what has stymied him.

However, interspersed among all these hints of Nick's enjoyment of solemn texts are seemingly contradictory indications of Nick as an imaginative artist. For one thing, however disdainful he may be about the wild tales of his associates, he has often listened to them anyway. Even his ways of avoiding such storytellers shows imagination: he has "*feigned* sleep, preoccupation, or a hostile levity..." (5; emphasis added). Also, as Elmore points out, Nick's very style in this opening section contains "incantory, ritualistic elements," "hyperbolic and antithetical elements," and "reference to the mysterious and supernatural" that betray that Nick is hardly utterly solemn and nonimaginative (139). For example, in the opening frame, Nick's ability to create effective similes and metaphors shines, as in the description of the way leaves grow on trees, and even more markedly in his report of the appearance of East and West Egg. Long Island Sound, says Nick, is "the great wet barnyard" into which "a pair of enormous eggs" jut, to the confusion of birds flying overhead (9). This particular comparison requires Nick to shift points of view—to that of birds—since the land formations appear as eggs only to someone far above them. In short, Nick's style in the opening frame, along with his interest in listening to the wild stories of other people (even if reluctantly), reveals an imaginative side.

Most examples of Nick's imaginative talk in the opening frame occur when Nick speaks of his attitude *after* having had this dreamlike experience, not *before*. But, significantly, *before* the dream, Nick shows imagination about one thing: earning money. In speaking of the books he planned to read upon moving to the East, Nick says that he had "a dozen volumes on banking and credit and investment securities" that promised "to unfold the shining secrets that only Midas and Morgan and Maecenas knew." And, he adds, he "had the high intention of reading many other books besides." After all, he was "rather literary in college" (8–9), implying that the other books will be literary rather than financial. Here Nick indicates his much more imaginative response to the financial texts than to any other texts. After all, he has fancied the information that bankers and investors have to offer him as being "shining secrets"—surely a phrase indicating his imaginative investment in the subject. On the other hand, when Nick starts to think about books with literary merit instead of usefulness as money-making aids, he immediately summons up thoughts of the "very solemn and obvious editorials" he once wrote. Seemingly he equates his dull, uninventive productions with the literature he intends to read. In short, it seems that, for Nick, before his dreamlike experience, only the notion of making money can lead him to use imaginative language whereas the idea of any other goal for creative efforts renders him quite dull.

Yet, in the opening part of the frame, Nick also reveals a pre-dream tension between his attraction to wealth and the pull of something more lasting. Nick says that while growing up in the Middle West, he considered the place "a country of wide lawns and friendly trees" (7). He thus establishes the link of the Middle West to Nature. Even more importantly, he says that upon first coming to the East, he thought of his *new* home as offering "so much fine health to be pulled down out of the young breath-giving air" (9). He took the bungalow at West Egg because it seemed a shame to be practical and find rooms in the city when he could take a place that reminded him of the lawn- and tree-filled Middle West. The tension in Nick becomes apparent when he says that he came East because the Middle West no longer seemed like the "warm center of the world" but rather like "the ragged edge of the universe" (9). The phrase "warm center of the world" hints of several notions: of Nature as nurturing and life-giving; of the warmth of mother love; of a central being in the universe—a god. Yet this same place became for him worn and worthless, one to be described with a word for clothes worn by the poor: "ragged." It is as if Nick is really saying that his new values are material ones, that the Middle West, in representing Nature, God, and Love, is something he wished to reject—but could not quite reject. The tension is most clearly disclosed when Nick speaks of the view he has from his West Egg house: "...I had a view of the water, a partial view of my neighbor's [Gatsby's] lawn and the consoling proximity of millionaires—all for eighty dollars a month" (10). Nick lists water and lawn, parts of Nature, in such a way as to confuse even them with the notion of Wealth. The well-manicured forty acres of lawn is Nature purchased by Nick's millionaire neighbors; and even the ocean has seemingly been leased for the eighty-dollar rent.

Thus, for Nick, juxtaposed against undependable Wealth, which tends to distort and destroy, is Nature. This emphasis upon the conflict between a temporal and therefore negative creative goal and Nature is quite Chaucerian. In *The Parliament of Fowls*, for instance, the artificial code of courtly love— which is tied up with notions of high social standing—is set against the promptings of Nature, presented as knowing best about the love-match appropriate to the formel eagle. The situation is not so different from that of *The Book of the Duchess*, where the same artificial code helps the Man in Black avoid the world of Nature around him—including the natural death of his wife. In *The House of Fame*, the goddess Fame is highly unnatural and therefore set against not only the goddess of Love, Venus, but also Nature, just as in the Prologue to *The Legend of Good Women*, the unnatural Alceste, with her manipulations, is in opposition to the natural, fresh daisy. In all these works, there is also a Christian element: to follow God is to follow Love is to follow Nature. All three are as one, and all three are eternal. Anything unnatural (and thus fleeting and undependable)—courtly love, fame, and, wealth—is set against this eternal trio.

Therefore, Nick needs a dream, not only because to begin with he needs to balance the excessive perspective that he has about most things with a greater degree of imagination, but also because what imagination he does have before the dream seems largely focused upon money—that unworthy, fleeting entity. He must reevaluate his priorities, decide what the "warm center of the world"—that is, what the eternal—really involves and how he can focus upon it. And Nick needs not only to have a dream but to tell it, and to tell it effectively. As Elmore states, Nick's "understanding is not entirely complete as he sits down to recount the story. The recounting, the sorting out of the story, will itself be the final stage of the initiation ceremony" (13). By the closing frame, the reader thus expects to see further change in Nick—a further indication of his ability to balance his excess perspective with imagination and to recognize what values he wishes to commit himself to. But whatever the exact stance of Nick's artistic understanding at any given point, clearly he begins as a frustrated artist who needs a significant dream for renewal.

In another way Nick is ripe for a significant dream. Carl Jung speaks of the usual nature of such dreams:

> They reveal their significance...by their plastic form, which often has a poetic force and beauty. Such dreams occur mostly during the critical phases of life, in early youth, puberty, at the onset of middle age (thirty-six to forty), and within sight of death. ("On the Nature of Dreams" 77)

Nick Carraway is approaching a benchmark age—not one mentioned by Jung but certainly one Fitzgerald considered critical. At one point, Nick reveals that his thirtieth birthday has come:

> I was thirty. Before me stretched the portentous menacing road of a new decade....
> Thirty—the promise of a decade of loneliness, a thinning list of single men to know, a thinning briefcase of enthusiasm, thinning hair. (143)

According to Richard Lehan, "Thirty became for Fitzgerald the tragic age—the day of reckoning..." (53). At this age, Nick is indeed feeling a sense of decay and danger; he therefore is ready to dream, to find fresh insight into his life and art.

Fitzgerald's choice to use in this novel the first-person narrator Nick has received much critical attention—though no one has previously linked it to Chaucer's use of the first-person point of view in his dream visions. Remarkably, however, critics of each author have spoken in similar ways about each author's use of this point of view. Chaucer's poets-personae have been variously described as naive, experience, rigidly commonsensical, astute at psychology. Nick has been described in much the same ways. A particular point of comparison is the double vision spoken of regarding each author. J. Stephen Russell applies to Chaucer a statement by A. C. Spearing in Spearing's *The Gawain-Poet: A Critical Study* to explain what Russell calls the "peculiar double perspective of the dreamer" in Chaucer's dream visions (Russell, "Meaningless Dreams" 23):

> "Two states of consciousness are presented to us in an alternation so rapid that it feels like simultaneity; that of the Dreamer who naively experiences the successive phases of his adventure, and that of the narrator who has already learned of the vision, and who is telling the story with the benefit of that wisdom." (qtd. in Russell "Meaningless Dreams" 23)

The situation in the dream visions may be a bit more complex than Spearing describes; for, as Chaucer's poets-personae begin telling of their dreams, they (like Nick) may not have completely learned all they can from their dreams. But they are on the way toward gaining fully "the benefit of that wisdom."

Fitzgerald's effect in *The Great Gatsby* has been similarly described by Malcolm Cowley, who in what has become a commonplace of Fitzgerald criticism states that Fitzgerald himself "cultivated a sort of double vision," that he described in his novels "a big dance to which he had taken...the prettiest girl...and...at the same time he stood outside the ballroom, a little Midwestern boy with his nose to the glass, wondering how much the tickets cost and who paid for the music" (66). The use of the first-person narrator Nick Carraway proves

Fitzgerald's most significant expression of his own complex
way of looking at life, as is evident in particular in the following passage from Nick's account of the party at Tom and
Myrtle's apartment:

> I wanted to get out and walk eastward toward the park
> through the soft twilight but each time I tried to go I
> became entangled in some wild, strident argument
> which pulled me back, as if with ropes, into my chair.
> Yet high over the city our line of yellow windows
> must have contributed their share of human secrecy to
> the casual watcher in the darkening streets, and I was
> him too, looking up and wondering. I was within and
> without, simultaneously enchanted and repelled by
> the inexhaustible variety of life. (36)

The casual watcher, like the narrator of Spearing's formulation,
can rather objectively digest the material from the dream for
later telling. He is "without," "repelled by the inexhaustible
variety of life," able thus to stand apart from it and seek understanding of it. But the entangled partygoer Nick, like
Spearing's Dreamer, actually experiences the dream, becoming
imaginatively involved as a character in it. He is "within,"
"enchanted...by the inexhaustible variety of life." In renewing
creativity, both the poet-persona and Nick must learn to amal-
gamate the two roles that their dreaming entails: the detached
narrator and the involved dreamer. Nick achieves this blend
just as the poet-persona of *The Book of the Duchess* does: by
viewing and then reviewing (that is, telling about) his shadow's confrontation with the same dilemma.

In *The Book of the Duchess*, the poet-persona marks his transition from the waking world to the dream world by speaking
of hearing birds sing in harmony and of a bit later going forth
out of his chamber on a horse that has suddenly appeared
there. He then follows hunters into a forest, where eventually
he meets the Man in Black. The dream vision thus serves as
an interior journey. The mention of the singing of birds at the
outset of the journey hints at the inspirational nature of the
dream; the trip by horse into the forest, a place suggestive of
natural creativity, further suggests the interrelated ideas of the
journey and the renewal of creativity.

The first sentence of paragraph eighteen marks the transfer
of Nick Carraway from the waking world to the dream world:

"And so it happened that on a warm windy evening I drove over to East Egg to see two old friends whom I scarcely knew at all" (11). Nick, like the Chaucerian poet-persona, emphasizes travel to otherworld (driving from West Egg to East Egg across a body of water) and inspiration (the wind). In addition, Nick's statement stresses the transformations of identity that are about to occur in the dream world. The people Nick barely knows in the waking world—Tom, Daisy, and Gatsby—are rather suddenly transformed into significant parts of his experience.

That the bulk of *Gatsby* may be considered a dream has been hinted at by various critics. Thomas Caldecot Chubb, a reviewer of the novel, is perhaps the first to have done so; but his remarks about the dreamlike quality are scornful rather than laudatory. He comments that the novel is "a hasheesh dream for a romantic minded inhabitant of Nassau County" (238). In a more positive tone, Long speaks of the novel's "dreamlike and expressionistic atmosphere" (155). And John F. Callahan speaks of Nick as concerned about the contrast between East and West, defined by Callahan as the difference between "nightmare" and "reverie" (40). But Nick himself provides the best evidence of the novel's dreamlike nature when near the end of it, he talks about a dream he has had about West Egg:

> West Egg especially still figures in my more fantastic dreams. I see it as a night scene from El Greco: a hundred houses, at once conventional and grotesque, crouching under a sullen, overhanging sky and a lustreless moon. In the foreground four solemn men in dress suits are walking along the sidewalk with a stretcher on which lies a drunken woman in a white evening dress. Her hand, which dangles over the side, sparkles cold with jewels. Gravely the men turn in at a house—the wrong house. But no one knows the woman's name, and no one cares. (185)

Here Nick recounts an explicit dream; and his account is filled with many dreamlike qualities, particularly distortions and unnatural transformations and fuzzy identity. The houses seem to have been unnaturally transformed into crouching animals and to have been, in an equally unnatural way, multiplied in number beyond what the eye could see and still be able to make out in such detail a single woman and her jewels. The sky and moon are distorted, seeming to be merely parts of a painting. The drunken woman has no known identity. This brief explicit dream account bears much resemblance to Nick's entire account of his experience in the East, as William A. Fahey has noted. Fahey explains this passage as a fusion of the significant elements from the larger account: Gatsby's parties and their "indifferent" guests; a drunken Daisy wearing the "pearls that have bought her" and being "poured into her wedding dress for delivery to the wrong man" (Tom Buchanan); Myrtle "laid out on the garbage bench, her indifferent slayer driving on; Tom going to buy another pearl necklace" for his next mistress (84–85). Indeed, Nick implies that the short dream has been but *one* of his "more fantastic dreams"; might not his larger account of his experience be considered *another* of his fantastic dreams?

The dream account in *The Book of the Duchess* reflects the features of a natural dream. These characteristics include reports of spatial and temporal distortion, such as sudden appearances and disappearances of both people and places, and lack of logical sequence of events and ideas. These same qualities begin to appear in *The Great Gatsby* when Nick goes across the bay to visit Tom and Daisy at their East Egg mansion. This scene contrasts rather sharply with what precedes it: Nick's account of his family background, his move to the East, and, finally, his trip across water into this other realm, that of the old-moneyed East Eggers. This trip thus marks the beginning of the dream account. The visit with the Buchanans also illustrates the dreamlike qualities found in the entire core of the novel (extending into the last chapter, near the end of the novel).

Perhaps the most glaring of the dreamlike qualities is the distortion of time. In "Gatsby and the Hole in Time," Robert W. Stallman says that *Gatsby* "gets its time-theme summed up in the words...'In the meantime / In between time—.' What is defined here is a hole in time" (3–4). Stallman refers to the song "Ain't We Got Fun," part of which is quoted in the novel (100–01). He has rightly observed a treatment of time set apart from the ordinary notion of it operative in everyday (waking) life. It is indeed as if the events of the core of the novel (Stallman would say, of the whole novel) occur in a time warp. In this scene alone, examples abound: The *Post* story that Jordan is reading breaks off—to be continued. The conversation

about plans to be made for the longest day is never completed.
Jordan says she has been lying on the couch for an impossibly
long time, as if time has been utterly suspended. A certain
five-minute period is recalled by Nick as mere "broken fragments." It is not the right time for candles (perhaps it is still
light outside), yet they are lit. Stallman states that in fact almost every scene in the novel is rather like Jordan's story—to
be continued, "not finished but disrupted" (11).

Spatial distortions are also striking throughout the dream
account; an example from the Buchanan dinner-party scene is
Nick's description of the appearance of the Buchanan living
room as he enters it. Daisy and Jordan seem to him to have
been flying around the room—like witches, he perhaps implies—and not only the curtains but also the rugs appear to
Nick to have been doing the same. To be sure, Nick uses similes in most of the passage to create these distortions of space,
so that it is only *as if* such things were occurring. However,
significantly, at the end of the passage, Nick calls into question the basic reality of the situation: "...the curtains and the
rugs and the two young women ballooned slowly to the floor"
(12). Here, he switches from similes to a plain metaphor. It is
as if Nick is saying that the women and objects really have
been flying.

Distortions of identity also occur in the dream account. In
this scene, Nick takes a long time to recognize Jordan Baker for
who she is—a sports champion: "'Oh—you're *Jor*dan Baker,'"
he exclaims rather late in the evening (23). Nick then recalls
thinking about having once heard "some story of her too, a
critical, unpleasant story, but what it was I had forgotten long
ago" (23). So Nick does not recognize Jordan after all for who
she is; the unpleasant story must have been accurate about this
selfish, careless woman, but he cannot remember it. Further,
there is the story of the butler's nose, part of which Daisy tells
Nick: "'Well, he wasn't always a butler; he used to be the silver polisher for some people in New York that had a silver
service for two hundred people'" (18).

Finally, distortions of logic occur. In this scene, there are
many non sequiturs—for example, Daisy's talk of planning
something for the longest day of the year being followed immediately by her talk of Tom's having injured her little finger.
Candles are lit, then snuffed out, and then lit again—all
"pointlessly" (20). In short, filled as it is with uncertainly
identified figures floating illogically in a time warp, this scene

provides a good example of the dream qualities of the core of *Gatsby*.[1]

A significant portion of Nick's dream account consists of his reporting conversations he had with Gatsby about Gatsby's past. These reports parallel those of the poet-persona concerning his talks with the Man in Black. In each case, the interchanges center on a relationship with a woman—for the Man in Black, Good Fair White; and for Gatsby, Daisy Fay Buchanan. In *The Book of the Duchess*, the reader meets Good Fair White only through the words of the Man in Black; the conversations about her constitute the bulk of the dream account. Such is not the case with *Gatsby*, of course, which consists of much more besides these conversations. The reader knows of Daisy not only through Gatsby's tales but also through Nick's direct observations of her (and through Jordan Baker, who tells Nick of part of Daisy's past). Nick's view of Daisy is therefore more complex than the poet-persona's of Good Fair White. Seemingly, as Nick experienced the dream, he tended to be caught up in it, to share partly in Gatsby's naive, dreamy view of Daisy; yet even then he was also able to stand back and see her for who she really was. Even more so, in telling the dream, Nick can have perspective on the experience. Nick's attitude toward Daisy thus serves, paradoxically, as both a counterpart and a foil to Gatsby's image of her; it both mirrors and balances. It is as if for Nick there are two Daisys: the idealized Daisy of Gatsby's (and his own) dream world, and the "real" Daisy, on the one hand corrupt but on the other simply a real human being (real within the world of the novel) who cannot live up to Gatsby's idealization of her. Indeed, Daisy bears resemblance not just to Good Fair White of *The Book of the Duchess*. She is also much like three other figures from Chaucer's dream visions: from the Prologue to *The Legend of Good Women*, the actual daisy of the waking world, as well as the daisy-like Alceste of the dream world; and from *The Parliament of Fowls*, the formel eagle.

In the opening frame of the Prologue to *The Legend of Good Women*, the poet-persona—very much awake—goes out to a meadow to see the daisy, of which he speaks words of adoration. In his description of the daisy, he emphasizes both physical and nonphysical traits, focusing especially upon the daisy's love of light—both literal light and the figurative light of virtue. Additionally, he emphasizes the flower's beautiful appearance—particularly its red-and-white color and its sweet smell. According to Beryl Rowland, Chaucer intends here the short-stemmed meadow daisy (*Bellis perennis*). Such a daisy, also called the English daisy, is common in England but not in America. It has a pleasant odor similar to that of newly cut grass (210), comes in colors of pink or white, and (as is evidently the case in Chaucer's poem) may be tipped in crimson (Stevens 79). This yellow-centered flower is a perennial and therefore associated with the ever-recurring annual cycle of life, death, and rebirth.

In merely using the term *daisy*, Chaucer was calling up certain images in the minds of his medieval readers. During the Middle Ages, various French poems (and, later, English poems) in praise of the daisy, or *marguerite*, were composed. According to John L. Lowes, in these works, "the *marguerite* fell in large measure heir to the possessions of the Rose" (629). Thus, the daisy was associated with the love and beauty of the rose and with the danger signified by the rose's thorns and (sometimes) red color. Red, of course, can stand for life and passion as well as for danger and violence; so it may be negative, but need not necessarily be so. In itself, apart from the link to the rose, the daisy is also associated with both the positive and the negative: sweetness, prettiness, and brightness, but also redness, possibly suggestive of potential violence, and the yellow center, which, relative to the (sometimes) whiteness of the petals, suggests corruption. The daisy differs from the rose in part in being less "cultivated": people cultivate roses, not content to let nature do all the work, but—at least traditionally—daisies simply grow naturally. This naturalness of the daisy is also two-sided: being natural can mean being naturally good, sweet, and pretty; but it can also mean being wild and untamed.

The poet-persona's description of the daisy, while definitely sounding positive overall, exhibits balance and perspective. The poet-persona is able to see the daisy for what it is: a real flower growing wild in an actual meadow, full of positive qualities, but also "rede" as well as white (42 F). Neither the wildness nor the redness is hidden away—repressed—as they might be in an account more idealized. Indeed, perhaps "redness" becomes truly dangerous—exhibiting its negative qualities—precisely when it is unrecognized; conversely, when admitted as part of life, perhaps it instead is diffused, taking on its more positive meaning—of life and passion. In any case, it seems that the poet-persona's balanced view of the daisy enables him to create successfully; for his tribute to the daisy is beautiful indeed and has been termed by many critics a resounding artistic success.   The passage is a triumph of "realism," not of the artifice of derivative courtly-love literature.

The poet-persona next falls asleep and meets a daisy-like figure, Alceste.   He pays tribute to her, too, focusing on her lovely green, white, and golden accouterments.   Significantly, however, he does not mention that red is among Alceste's colors; it is her consort, the god of Love, who must tell the poet-persona that "'Mars yaf to hire corowne reed, pardee, / In stede of rubyes, sette among the white'" (533–34 F).   Alceste exacts devotion from the dreamer, who stands accused by Cupid of having written evil works about evil women.   Alceste, seemingly merciful, steps in and says that the dreamer should pay the penance of writing legends of good women.   She appears to save him from worse punishment at the hands of Cupid.   But Elton Dale Higgs holds that Alceste really manipulatively imposes her will on the dreamer (89–94)—no matter that the accusation against the dreamer is suspect in the first place.   As he tries to tell the royal pair, he has simply attempted to give a balanced picture of women (Higgs 87–88)—and, after all, as the reader can attest, his recent tribute to the feminine daisy is balanced.   However, naively assuming that Alceste knows best, that she is thoroughly the daisy personified, he lets himself be convinced that she is right and agrees to the penance.   His penance, the writing of legends of good women, results in tributes (namely, the legends) that many readers have found dull and artistically unsuccessful—much in contrast to the usual enthusiastic response to the pre-Alceste, pre-dream tribute to the daisy.

There are differences between the daisy and Alceste, differences the dreamer cannot see, precisely because he is the dreamer, not the awake poet-persona.   In appearance, the Alceste at first glance seems as beautiful as the daisy; and in character, as sweet, good, and honorable.   But the dreamer fails to see that Alceste's appearance is artificial.   In contrast to the natural daisy, Alceste's lovely, daisy-like colors of white, yellow, green, and red are purchasable rather than natural to her, resulting from green clothing and costly white pearls and gold.   The red in her crown—which the dreamer does not notice at all—comes not from rubies, which, even if expensive, at least are traditionally associated with love, honor, and renown

(Patch 317), but from Mars, the god of war, thus suggesting Alceste's love of power and dominance. But it is most significant that the dreamer does not even see the red; he, unlike his waking self, does not integrate this potentially negative trait into his overall picture of Alceste. In Alceste's case, if seen, the redness should signify to the dreamer Alceste's dual nature, her potential for evil; but it remains hidden, just as her costly white and green ornaments cover who she really is, making her seem a daisy when she is not.

Alceste may be considered a fay, a figure defined by Robert J. Ewald in his dissertation, "The Jungian Archetype of the Fairy Mistress in Medieval Romance," as "a woman of great beauty with supernatural powers who comes from an 'other world' where the ordinary laws of space and time do not apply" (4). The fay can heal, prophesy, shift shapes at will, and prompt a knight to perform chivalric deeds. She has an entourage of maidens (comparable to the nineteen ladies who accompany Alceste) with whose help she can carry off a knight to her home in fairyland. More than anything else, she is inconsistent: "in one role, she is the helpful and maternal Dame du Lac, yet in another, the sinister and scheming Morgain la Fee" (2). In the Middle Ages, Ewald adds, the fay was often blended with the courtly lady.

Ewald further contends that the fay is an anima figure. The word *anima* means soul, but Carl Jung has appropriated the term to refer to soul in a special way: as the "chaotic urge to life, " or the "archetype of life itself" within the personality. The anima capriciously "lures into life the inertness of matter that does not want to live..." ("Archetypes" 27). Only by confronting his anima can a man experience another archetype that hides behind the anima: the "archetype of meaning"— often manifesting itself as the "wise old man" ("Archetypes" 32). In other words, a man reaches a state of meaning and order through chaos. The anima is experienced by a man as feminine, since, as Jung explains, a man thinks of this chaotic principle as coming from outside himself, as not part of himself. "What is not-I [for a man], not masculine, is most probably feminine, and because the not-I is felt as not belonging to me and therefore as outside of me, the anima-image is usually projected upon women" ("Archetypes" 27).

In past eras, says Jung, it was possible for men to project the anima onto cultural figures such as goddesses or other religious figures. Since in the modern world people often no longer have access to such figures, the anima-images and other archetypal images "lapse into unconsciousness again and hence are unconsciously projected upon more or less suitable human personalities" ("Psychological Aspects" 200). Thus, Chaucer depicts a goddess, Alceste, while Fitzgerald depicts a human being, Daisy.

The anima is ambivalent—that is, her projection can be positive, negative, or some combination thereof. Jung sees special danger in a situation in which this or any other archetype of the collective unconscious takes over: "If," he says, "the activation [of the archetype] is due to the collapse of the individual's hopes and expectations, there is a danger that the collective unconscious may take the place of reality" ("Psychological Foundations" 314). However, "if the translation of the unconscious into a communicable language proves successful, it has a redeeming effect. The driving forces locked up in the unconscious are canalized into consciousness and form a new source of power..." ("Psychological Foundations" 315). The anima, he seems to be saying, must find its proper "place," must be recognized and controlled by the conscious mind.

Both the daisy and Alceste are anima-images. For the poet-persona, the daisy possesses life and light—that "chaotic urge to life" that inspires the poet-persona to create a lovely tribute to her. In this instance, the poet-persona seems to work his way beyond the imaginative, emotional chaos to let this force form "a new source of power" and to find meaning and order. Thus the poet-persona sees the daisy with balance: as both white and pretty but also wild and red. Notably, the poet-persona meets the daisy and composes his tribute to her while he is awake—that is, while his conscious mind is in control; yet he is also able to be imaginatively inspired by the daisy. Interestingly, here, before his dream, this poet-persona has the necessary blend of imagination and perspective; the dream seems to upset the balance. It is as if in this poem, his apparent farewell to the dream-vision genre, Chaucer turns around his earlier dream-vision message about the potential of dreams to restore creativity; here, he instead reveals the danger of their "taking over," upsetting the balance in the opposite way.

In his dream of Alceste, the dreamer lets the forces of the unconscious—personified in the dream-figure Alceste—scize power. Alceste, as anima-image, impels the dreamer to write— but unsuccessfully and destructively. Here, he lacks the blend of imagination and perspective he has had when awake; only the involved dreamer, imaginatively idealizing Alceste, is present. Interestingly, in the F manuscript of the Prologue, this dreamer never does wake up; he presumably creates the legends while he is still asleep, still dominated by the chaotic unconscious, still without perspective.

Nick's and Gatsby's depictions of Daisy Fay Buchanan in *The Great Gatsby* resemble the poet-persona's of the daisy and Alceste. First, of course, the names are the same. Critics have frequently delved into the symbolic value of the daisy to try to understand all that Fitzgerald intended in giving the character this name; most commonly, they have related the white petals and yellow center of the daisy to the seemingly pure surface yet really corrupt inner nature of Daisy. (See, for instance, Crim and Houston 115–16.) In so doing, critics have been thinking only of the type of daisy most familiar to Americans, the shasta daisy, or Chrysanthemum maximum. (See Seymour, et al 422–23.) But, given the Chaucerian connection, it seems important also to consider Daisy's links to the English daisy. The most notable difference between the two flowers lies in their possible colors: the English daisy, like the shasta, may be white; but it also may be pink or tinged in crimson. Certainly, the opposition between Daisy's pure appearance, largely the product of a life of wealthy ease, and her corrupt soul is significantly expressed in the shasta daisy's contrasting white petals and yellow center; the contrast is quite reminiscent of the expensively clothed Alceste, in appearance a daisy, but corrupt inwardly. This idea is not lost with the English daisy, which also may be white and also features a yellow center. But perhaps as significant is the fact that the English daisy may be pink or red-tinged: goodness (white) may be either blended with or tinged with danger and violence (pink or red). Both the daisy and Alceste are partly red; the redness becomes a danger only in the case of Alceste, for the dreamer does not recognize this quality in her. The redness signals Alceste's manipulative nature, which she uses to destroy the dreamer's artistry, but only if he will let it. Daisy Buchanan's redness becomes evident to Nick when she kills Myrtle Wilson and Myrtle blends "her thick, dark blood with the dust" on the road where she has fallen (145), and when Daisy indirectly causes other deaths. However, this redness remains hidden to illusion-bound Gatsby; so he lets her destroy him.

Like the daisy and Alceste, Daisy is a fay. Her maiden name is Fay. And, as William Bysshe Stein comments, the references to chivalry in the novel (such as Nick's calling Daisy "the king's daughter" high up in a castle [127]) are all connected to Daisy, who can thus be seen as the "evil queen of the modern land of Faerie." Gatsby becomes a "mock redeemer knight," and Daisy is a "reincarnation of Morgan le Fay. As the latter was wont to deceive all her lovers, so is Daisy" (67). Daisy's connection to the fay is clearly not in name only.

For Nick, depending upon his status as detached narrator or involved dreamer at a given point, Daisy is both an idealized product of his unconscious urgings and a "real" woman possessing both positive and negative aspects, as any real person does. That is, at times, Nick is like the sleeping dreamer of the Prologue; at other times, like the waking poet-persona. These two attitudes result from Nick's double vision: as he has the dream, he is utterly involved in it; as he tells of his dream, he is both recalling how he felt when he was caught up in the illusion and relating how he feels now that he is recounting it. For example, Nick sometimes is caught up in Daisy's alluring voice. "...A stirring warmth flowed from her [Daisy]," he says, "as if her heart was trying to come out to you concealed in one of those breathless, thrilling words" (19). Also he says that "Daisy began to sing with the music in a husky, rhythmic whisper, bringing out a meaning in each word that it had never had before and would never have again" (114–15). Daisy's voice, Nick also states, "couldn't be overdreamed—that voice was a deathless song" (101). Nick also at times is impressed with Daisy's association with light and with her loveliness: she has, he says, face that is "sad and lovely with bright things in it, bright eyes and a bright passionate mouth" (13–14). Even the light of day hates to leave her (just as the light loves the daisy of the Prologue): "...the glow [in the room] faded, each light deserting her with lingering regret like children leaving a pleasant street at dusk" (18). Some of these emphases are much like those of the Prologue's dreamer, who also stresses beauty and light. (The other—the attractive voice—is a prime ingredient in the Man in Black's catalogue of his lady's outstanding features.) In terms of genre, these are sentimental/romantic responses, that, according to modernists, were suspect, but according to Fitzgerald (echoing Chaucer's stance), simply need to be balanced with perspective.

So far, Nick has been shown to see Daisy just as Gatsby does—without perspective, as an ideal. This "involved-dreamer Nick" is indeed much like Gatsby—and in turn both are much like the dreamer of the Chaucer's Prologue. But that is not all there is to Nick. He also in many instances adds to his involvement the same sense of perspective found in the waking poet-persona of the Prologue. In an early part of his dream, set at the Buchanan mansion, Nick describes Daisy as wearing white and looking as if she has just flown about the room. Later in the dream, back again at the Buchanan mansion, Nick again describes Daisy's appearance: "The room, shadowed well with awnings, was dark and cool. Daisy and Jordan lay upon an enormous couch, like silver idols, weighing down their own white dresses against the singing breeze of the fans. 'We can't move,' they said together" (121–22). Earlier, Nick the involved dreamer primarily idealizes Daisy, taking her whiteness at face value. At this point he seems to assign no negative value to her appearing to have flown around the room. It is only the subsequent picture he paints of Daisy that leads to the connection of flying with witches. But in the second description the detached narrator Nick sees Daisy as a real person with varied facets. Her whiteness has become silver, a shiny, beautiful, precious substance, but one also heavy and hard. Before, her dress was white; now, she herself is a silver idol wearing a white dress.

Other examples of Nick's balanced treatment of Daisy abound. While at times Nick idealizes Daisy's lovely bright face and alluring voice, Nick also says that although Daisy's look promises "that there was no one in the world she so much wanted to see," actually the look is calculated; it is "a way she had" (13). And he even recognizes the truth behind Daisy's voice. When Daisy tells him of her troubled marriage, he realizes that "the instant her voice broke off, ceasing to compel my fascination, my belief, I felt the basic insincerity of what she had said" (22). Later, at the Plaza Hotel, when Tom has revealed that Gatsby is a bootlegger and Gatsby tries to talk to Daisy, "the voice begged again to go" (142). Nick can see that the thrilling voice can cover insincerity and can speak words damaging to Gatsby. It is hardly the perfect and thoroughly positive entity that Gatsby has always and Nick has sometimes made of it. In short, Nick can see that the notion that Daisy is utterly pure, lovely, and good is specious, a matter of surfaces.

As the silver idol image indicates, as with Alceste, the beautiful surface is mainly the product of riches.

Daisy is really a mix of positive and negative—that is, she is, within the novel, really a real human being. Nick emphasizes Daisy's humanity most of all when he comments on Gatsby's first meeting with Daisy after their five-year separation: "There must have been moments even that afternoon when Daisy tumbled short of his dreams—*not through her own fault* but because of the colossal vitality of his illusion. It had gone beyond her, beyond everything" (101, emphasis added). For Gatsby, Daisy remains only an anima-image, someone on whom he has projected his chaotic, urgent illusion. (See Person.) Gatsby is always like the sleeping dreamer of Chaucer's Prologue, and perhaps Daisy is as dangerous as she is (even more dangerous than Alceste is to the Chaucer's dreamer) because of Gatsby's utter disregard for her humanity, for the possibility that like anyone else she has a dark side. If Nick—who sees both sides of Daisy—mainly emphasizes her negative qualities in much of the novel, perhaps it is partly as a corrective for Gatsby's failure to see this side of her at all. Nick wants to cut Daisy down to size. The situation is somewhat different for the waking poet-persona of the Prologue: he indicates his balanced view of the daisy before starting to dream and therefore does not face the same need to correct another's limited vision; but, in *The Book of the Duchess*, the Chaucerian dreamer will, like Nick, face this need. Also, Chaucer's daisy comes across in the end as an essentially positive figure, with a few potentially negative qualities being mentioned. Daisy seems much more negative, but again, two factors may be responsible for this impression: Daisy's "redness" becomes so destructive because it remains hidden, especially to Gatsby, so that it can do more damage than it otherwise would; and Nick, to correct Gatsby's excessively positive impression of her, speaks more of the negative than of anything else about her.

Nick and Gatsby, then, are, paradoxically, both doubles and opposites. A look at their conversations as compared to those of the dreamer and the Man in Black from *The Book of the Duchess* indicates much more about these functions. In these conversations, Nick meets his shadow, Gatsby, just as the Chaucerian dream meets his, the Man in Black. Charles P. Tisdale states that *The Book of the Duchess* has three main characters "or one central character (the narrator) whose psyche, through the dream medium, divides into two personified faculties within him...." These characters converge in the poem's resolution (368–69). In similar fashion, according to Arthur Mizener, Fitzgerald's

> use of a narrator [in *Gatsby*] allowed Fitzgerald to keep clearly separated for the first time in his career the two sides of his nature, the middle-western Trimalchio [Gatsby] and the spoiled priest [Nick] who disapproved of but grudgingly admired him. (*Far Side* 185)

Accordingly, as E. Fred Carlisle maintains, the novel contains three Nicks. $Nick_1$ is the "detached moralist" who "retains his double view of Gatsby." $Nick_2$ and $Nick_3$ both participate in the dream events, with $Nick_2$ being "an agent in the action...[who] maintains a limited perspective as an observer..." and $Nick_3$ being the Nick with "the most limited perspective." He "maintains *no* perspective as an observer" and "participates fully in the action." This third Nick "fools himself, as he lives in an illusion" (352). Tisdale's and Carlisle's formulations are remarkably similar, revealing the similar set of relationships among the main figures in the two works.

Thus, like *The Book of the Duchess*, *Gatsby* features two sorts of character splittings. Just as the poet-persona is both involved and detached, Nick is split into two figures in that he is both the involved dreamer Nick and the detached narrator Nick; sometimes the two identities seem to overlap since while telling the dream, Nick captures both how he felt during the experience and how he feels as he tells about it. The detached narrator is a particularly dynamic figure in that the amount of perspective he has alters as he gains more and more insight from telling the dream. But Tisdale, Mizener, and Carlyle also speak of a slightly different sort of double vision shared by the two works, one resulting in another split: of the dreamer (either the Chaucerian dreamer or Nick) into a character resembling himself, and a character who is his shadow, who manifests those personal attributes that the dreamer would prefer to hide from his conscious self. Outside the dream looking in, the narrator has perspective upon the experience of his dream counterparts, both his dreaming self and his shadow. Totally within the dream, the dreamer having split in two, the dreaming self lacks much perspective on his own dreaming actions but does have perspective on his shadow's acts. In his psychologically complex picture of his poet-persona, Chaucer shows an almost modern awareness of the significance of the individual's inner being, of the role of that individual's imagination in making him an artist—and this within a culture that promoted reliance on models and tended to disregard the very qualities Chaucer stresses.   Coming at the matter from the other side of the romantic period, Fitzgerald shows a similar awareness—of the importance of the individual and his inner being, and of the difficulties, from the modernist perspective, of such personal expression.

Both the poet-persona in *The Book of the Duchess* and Nick in *The Great Gatsby* describe similar initial meetings with their shadows.   In *The Book of the Duchess*, the dreamer goes through a green wood filled with animals and arrives at a huge oak tree where

> I was war of a man in blak,
> That sat and had yturned his bak
> To an ook, an huge tree.
>   "Lord," thoght I, "who may that bes
> What ayleth hym to sitten her?" (445–49)

The young man is a "wel-farynge knyght" (452), yet green and pale; but the man does not notice the dreamer, so caught up is he in his sorrow.   As the dreamer stands there, the Man in Black sings the following lay, or "complaynte" (487):

> "I have of sorwe so gret won
> That joye gete I never non,
> Now that I see my lady bryght,
> Which I have loved with al my myght,
> Is fro me ded and ys agoon.
>   Allas, deth, what ayleth the,
> That thou noldest have taken me,
> Whan thou toke my lady swete,
> That was so fair, so fresh, so fre,
> So good, that men may wel se
> Of al goodnesse she had no mete!" (475–86)

Next, the dreamer

> went and stood ryght at his fet,
> And grette hym, but he spak noght,

But argued with his owne thoght,
And in hys wyt disputed faste
Why and how hys lyf myght laste. (502–06)

Thus, the dreamer, having traveled through an area suggestive
of fertility and creativity, comes to the center of that area, only
to find a person whose isolation and creation of a song about
sorrow and death indicate a creativity gone awry. As the narrator tells about this event, he manifests the double vision just
described: he is both inside and outside the action, observing
the Man of Black from a distance yet speaking as though he
were a part of the man's psyche, with the ability to discern
what is happening in the man's heart. He says, for example,
that the man has almost lost his mind (511), something that, as
one who has simply met the man, he could not normally know.
Also, the man, he says, "argued with his owne thoght" (504)—
again, a piece of information an on-looker should not ordinarily have access to. In a way, then, the dreamer *is* the Man in
Black—at least a part of him is.

In *The Great Gatsby*, Nick describes his first glimpse of Jay
Gatsby as occurring on a "loud bright night" complete with
birds, frogs, and cats. Nick notices a figure whom he assumes
must be Gatsby emerge "from the shadow of my neighbor's
mansion" and regard the stars. Nick feels that Gatsby is
"content to be alone—he stretched out his arms toward the
dark water in a curious way." Nick, though far from him,
"could have sworn he was trembling"; yet, looking toward the
water, Nick sees only a green light (23–24).

This passage from *Gatsby* is comparable in several ways to
the description of the dreamer's meeting with the Man in
Black. Just as Chaucer's dreamer travels through a green place
filled with animals, Nick journeys through a place full of trees,
birds, frogs, and cats, all suggestive of natural creativity. Just
as the Man in Black is isolated and sorrowful, so is Gatsby. In
one way or another, each shadow is creating a tribute to his
lady. The Man in Black yearns for his lady in song; Gatsby
reaches out, an action symbolizing his creation of a whole
identity and lifestyle with which he hopes to attract his beloved. In each instance, the unnaturalness of the man's conduct—standing in much contrast to the natural greenness of
the scene—is symbolized by an unnatural type of green: the
green face of the Man in Black, suggesting the sickness of his
obsession with his dead wife; and the green light to which

Gatsby stretches his arms, suggesting the sickness of his obsession with Daisy. In each instance, too, the dreamer has special knowledge of the shadow's emotional state: Chaucer's dreamer knows that the Man in Black feels he is losing his mind; Nick senses that Gatsby is trembling, something Nick is too far away to see. Also, in contrast to the insights of their counterparts, each shadow does not note the presence of the other man, so caught up is he in his own affairs. Already, each dreamer manifests a double vision while each shadow decidedly does not. However, though each dreamer realizes some things about his shadow, such as the fact that he is bereft, each dreamer continues to see the shadow as an enigma.

Significantly, though *Gatsby* in its published form features no close parallel to the Man in Black's lay, the manuscript of the novel does, though the parallel episode does not occur at the point of Nick's first seeing Gatsby. The section of the manuscript in which the song occurs corresponds to the last part of novel chapter six, in which, following Gatsby's party that Daisy and Tom attend, Gatsby speaks to Nick about his commitment to repeating the past. This section of the novel also contains the flashback to Daisy's incarnation. Nick ends the *novel* chapter by reporting his own reaction to Gatsby's tale: "Through all he said, even through his appalling sentimentality, I was reminded of something—an elusive rhythm, a fragment of lost words..." (118). In the manuscript, a song was part of the "appalling sentimentality" of which Nick speaks. (In his corresponding comments in the manuscript, Nick refers specifically to the song, calling it "doggerel" [163].) The lyrics of Gatsby's song are as follows:

"We hear the tinkle of the gay guitars
   We see the shining Southern moon;
     Where the fire-flies flit
 And the june bugs sit
 Drones the crickets single tune.
We hear the lapping of the wavelets
   Where the lonesome nightbirds sing
And the soft warm breeze
Tell the tall palm trees
   The Dreamy Song of Spring." (163)

Gatsby tells Nick that he made up the song when he was fourteen, that "the sound of it always makes me perfectly happy"

(163). While the song of the Man in Black speaks in indirect terms of the death of his lady, Gatsby's song points back to the time before Gatsby met Daisy, a time of adolescent happiness when his dream was still directed toward the universal. It therefore points back to a time before the death of his dream, just as the Man in Black's song concerns the period before his lady's death. Interestingly, Gatsby's song is permeated with references to Nature. It, like the Man in Black's song, shows confusion of past and present: with the temporal Daisy as his focus, Gatsby cannot hope for this sort of happiness borne of attention to the universal; but he believes that it is still possible. In addition, both the Man in Black's lay and Gatsby's song are poor art: the lay proves confusing to the dreamer; it is mere courtly-love convention. And Gatsby's song is, says Nick in the manuscript, "terrible stuff" (177) reminiscent of many of the popular songs of the era. Interestingly, for Chaucer, the pre-packaged sentiments of typical (perhaps, of lesser) courtly-love poetry is to be scorned as incapable of communicating realistically and understandably to an audience; for Fitzgerald, it is the pre-packaged, commercialized sentiments of popular music that should be scorned—but for much the same reasons. Both the hackneyed courtly-love poetry and the popular songs of romantic love are bad art.

That the Man in Black and Gatsby are shadow figures for these two dreamers is apparent from these initial encounters. Both the Man in Black and the dreamer are having problems with creativity; so are Gatsby and Nick. Both the Man in Black and the dreamer are polite young men suffering from an excess of sorrowful emotional involvement to the exclusion of perspective, though perhaps the dreamer instead lacks the ingredient he at first glance seems to have—that is, he only seems to have imaginative involvement. Both Nick and Gatsby are polite ("formal") young men (Nick is twenty-nine; Gatsby appears to be in his early thirties) whose problems with creativity partially match each other. Nick has emphasized detachment and perspective almost to the exclusion of imagination, yet, like Gatsby, he has emphasized imaginative involvement with the goddess Wealth (in Gatsby's case, that is, with Daisy).

The dream account of *The Book of the Duchess* largely consists of the poet-persona's reporting the Man in Black's story of his relationship with Good Fair White. The work is indeed self-conscious art: a poem about a dream about a story. Likewise, the dream account in *The Great Gatsby* includes the report of Gatsby's story about his relationship with Daisy. Thus the novel is also self-conscious art: a novel about a "dream" about a story. In each case, the shadow's tale becomes known because of the dreamer's efforts to extract from the shadow information about the shadow's puzzling behavior. In Chaucer's poem, the story is reported in the order in which the Man in Black has told it to the dreamer—that is, not in chronological order, and from a very limited point of view. Similarly, in *The Great Gatsby*, except in one instance, Gatsby's story is reported in the order in which Nick has heard it. So this story is not reported in chronological order; and it features a severely limited point of view.

In *The Book of the Duchess*, the Man in Black first notices the dreamer after the dreamer has stood in the green, animal-filled woods for a while listening to the man's woeful song:

> But at the last, to sayn ryght soth,
> He was war of me, how y stood
> Before hym, and did of myn hood,
> And has ygret hym as I best koude,
> Debonayrly, and nothing lowde. (514–18)

The Man in Black apologizes for having failed to notice his new companion, at which point the dreamer begs his pardon for disturbing him. In *Gatsby*, Nick and Gatsby meet at a party—notably set in Gatsby's garden, where Nick, some days earlier, first saw Gatsby. This time, the area is not filled with cats, frogs, and birds; but it is filled with animal-like guests, as the animal names on Gatsby's guest list make clear. In this instance, instead of the dreamer's approaching the shadow, the reverse occurs. A man Nick does not recognize tells Nick he looks familiar, and they find they both were in the Third Division during the war. When Nick tells the man that he has not yet met the host of the party and explains that he (Nick) lives next door,

> "I'm Gatsby," he said suddenly.
> "What!" I exclaimed. "Oh, I beg your pardon."
> "I thought you knew, old sport." (52)

Gatsby's smile, Nick finds, has the "quality of eternal reassurance in it" (52). In his early thirties, Gatsby speaks with "elaborate formality" and picks his words carefully (53). And he does not drink, causing Nick to wonder at the time "if the fact...helped to set him off from his guests, for it seemed to me that he grew more correct as the fraternal hilarity increased" (54). In short, initially, the Man in Black and Jay Gatsby seem similar to their counterparts. Both men appear sober, courteous, and above all isolated and mysterious.

Both the poet-persona and Nick tell next about their initial questions concerning their shadows' strange behavior. The dreamer asks the Man in Black what is troubling him but receives no understandable answer. The Man in Black merely speaks of how "fals Fortune hath pleyd a game / Atte ches with me, allas the while!" (618–19), causing the man to lose his "fers," or pawn. (See 655–82.) Because Gatsby merely smiles his understanding smile and disappears, having bowed, Nick must ask Jordan Baker, not Gatsby himself, about Gatsby: "'He's just a man named Gatsby,'" she says; but then she adds, "'Well,—he told me once he was an Oxford man.'" Nick says that "a dim background started to take shape behind him [Gatsby] but at her next remark it faded away. 'However, I don't believe it'" (53). Thus, just as the Man in Black is an enigma to the dreamer, Gatsby is a puzzle to Nick. At the end of the party, Nick views Gatsby much as he did when he first saw him—as an isolated mystery man: "A sudden emptiness seemed to flow now from the windows and the great doors, endowing with complete isolation the figure of the host who stood on the porch, his hand up in a formal gesture of farewell" (60). In short, these two polite, enigmatic, isolated young men pique the curiosity of their counterparts, leading them to ask all manner of questions to fit together the puzzle pieces, to make sense of their fragmented stories, a process that helps them overcome their own problems as artists. What Letha Audhuy says of Nick Carraway applies to Chaucer's dreamer, too: Nick, she says, is much like a Grail Knight "who must ask the meaning of the various symbols displayed in the castle"; therefore, "he makes guesses, suppositions; he asks questions, listens, and learns" (50–51).

The tales of the shadows heard by the dreamer and Nick are failed art, according to Chaucer's and Fitzgerald's notions of what failed art is: they are too fragmented, sentimental, hard to make sense of. In particular, they have in common a lack of attention to what past tense really means. R. A. Shoaf provides a crucial key to the understanding of both *The Book of the Duchess* and *The Great Gatsby* when he states that the Man in Black "writes" a romance that is "bad literature because it rejects the intrinsic preterite of a story" (167). He is "lost in a false present tense" (164). His

> most serious error is to try to live *in* the past—not *with* it—by stopping the present and finally preventing the future. To stop the present he sits apart and alone in a dark forest where he repeats to himself the love po- ems he has written...while to prevent the future he contemplates suicide.... He is an archetypal *fin 'amour* [that is, courtly] lover, and, therefore, "according to the code," he must be ever constant in love. (164)

In other words, the Man in Black has created only that which preserves, freezes in time, his past love affair and his lost Good Fair White, as though both are eternal, not temporal. He fully identifies Good Fair White with his anima, which exists timelessly, apart from the actual life or death of the human be- ing onto which it is projected. Thus he identifies the lady completely with the contents of his unconscious mind and fails to see her as a multi-faceted mortal being. As Shoaf says, the Man in Black truly lives in the past—that is to say, in his dream, in his unconscious—instead of with the past, as just one part of life. Gatsby, too, errs in the same way: he creates his story in a false tense. He may say that he and Daisy *met* in 1917 Louisville and *kissed* under the stars, but the past tense of these words is meaningless to him. For him, his past love af- fair and the Daisy of 1917 are just as eternal—just as real in the present—as are the love and the lady of the Man in Black. Both figures saturate themselves in a dream of the past instead of simply looking back at the past, or simply having a dream, and realizing that the dream is just one part of their present lives, to be seen with perspective.

The Man in Black tells his story to the dreamer in a series of flashbacks which concern five stages of his life:

A	His life before meeting Good Fair White
B	His first meeting with Good Fair White and failure to win her
C	His proclamation of love to Good Fair White, her rejection, and his subse- quent one-year mourning period

D   Good Fair White's having mercy on him
            and their subsequent seven-year happy
            life together
E   Good Fair White's death and his subse-
            quent mourning period

These flashbacks appear in mixed order; and interspersed in
the telling are the comments and inquiries of the dreamer,
who, because of the confusing order and terminology, has to
ask questions to untangle the tale. The order of the flashbacks
is as follows:[2]

    E E A E A D A B E B C D E

Jay Gatsby tells Nick a story of love and loss and indeed
creates an entire life and identity. In content and structure,
his text bears much similarity to the tale of the Man in Black.
Amid the flashbacks, Nick, like the dreamer, keeps asking
questions to get at the truth of the confusing, fragmented tale.
The major parts of Gatsby's tale may be labeled as follows:

A   pre-1917: Gatsby's life prior to meeting
            Daisy
B   1917: Gatsby's first meeting Daisy and
            making her the embodiment of his dream
C   1917-22: Gatsby's period of mourning
            (and amassing of wealth) upon learning
            that Daisy has thrown him over for Tom
            following Gatsby's return to the war
D   1922 (summer): Gatsby's reemerging as a
            nouveau riche who has big, gaudy par-
            ties—and his having a renewed relation-
            ship with Daisy
E   summer's end 1922: Daisy's rejection of
            Gatsby at the Plaza; his refusal to mourn
            except as before; his death

The last two parts are, of course, not parts of Gatsby's tale told
to Nick; they are Gatsby's tale as lived out by him and as
vicariously experienced by Nick. Chapters one and two of the
novel consist solely of Nick's talk about his background and
Nick's trip to see the Buchanans; he meets Gatsby at the end of

chapter two. Gatsby's "tale" starts at the end of chapter two, when he is seen stretching out his arms toward the green light. The order of its telling is as follows:[3]

C B D A C D B D E E A B C E E C A E C E C

In comparing these two lists, one does not see total correspondence, but instead a similarly mixed chronology, and a similar effort on each dreamer's part to comment on the tale. For the Man in Black, the chief problem that results in such a muddled tale is that he confuses two periods of mourning, preferring to live in the past, where the loss of Good Fair White was temporary. Similarly, Gatsby tells a muddled story because he confuses two affairs with Daisy, preferring to pretend that the past relationship, with its possibility of succeeding, is in the present. Of course a person can repeat the past, Gatsby actually says to Nick. Even when Daisy rejects him outright at the Plaza Hotel, an event which by all rights should plunge Gatsby into a period of mourning for the death of his dream of Daisy, Gatsby still regards his loss as at most temporary, just like the first one was. That very evening, for instance, he keeps vigil in front of her house. Likewise, the Man in Black mistakenly regards his second mourning period as being for a temporary loss, like the first one was. Both shadows have confounded the temporary with the eternal.

It is intriguing to examine some of the corresponding parts of the tales told by the Man in Black and Gatsby. Chronologically (in terms of occurrence, not of telling), the first part of each tale pertains to the shadow's life before meeting his beloved—that is, before he fixed his creative efforts on that one limited goal (or, in Jungian terms, before he projected the anima onto a particular human figure). The Man in Black tells the dreamer that before first seeing his lady he was devoted to Love:

"I have ever yit
Be tributarye and yiven rente
To Love, hooly with good entente,
And throgh plesaunce become his thral
With good wille, body, hert, and al." (764–68)

Here, the Man in Black stresses that prior to knowing Good

Fair White, he devoted himself to an eternal figure, the god of
Love ("I have *ever* yit"), expending all his creative efforts in his
worship of this god.

Similarly, before meeting Daisy, Gatsby devoted himself to
the universal and eternal. In his imagination, Gatsby felt he
was not the child of his parents (of the temporal); instead, he
was "a son of God" whose

> heart was in a constant, turbulent riot. The most gro-
> tesque and fantastic conceits haunted him in his bed
> at night. A universe of ineffable gaudiness spun itself
> out in his brain while the clock ticked on the wash-
> stand and the moon soaked with wet light his tangled
> clothes upon the floor. Each night he added to the
> pattern of his fancies until drowsiness closed down
> upon some vivid scene with an oblivious embrace.
> (105)

As elsewhere, here Nick retells a part of Gatsby's story that he
has heard from Gatsby. (In earlier stages of its composition,
the novel contained much more material in Gatsby's own voice,
just as Chaucer's poem contains numerous of the Man in
Black's speeches.) Like the Man in Black, Gatsby early on
showed devotion to something universal, something above and
beyond the mundane earth. Later, just before Gatsby focuses
his devotion on Daisy—on something "perishable" instead of
eternal—he thinks that "...the blocks of the sidewalk really
formed a ladder and mounted to a secret place above the
trees—he could climb to it, if he climbed alone, and once there
he could suck on the pap of life, gulp down the incomparable
milk of wonder" (117). Such is the nature of the object of his
early devotion. This early stage is creative, as is apparent from
the description of Gatsby's having "added to the pattern of his
fancies" as one would intricately structure a story, and his
imagining that the sidewalk blocks form a ladder to the stars.
In short, both men manifested early on a "chaotic urge to life"
as yet unfocused on a single temporal object.

Next the Man in Black and Gatsby zero in on specific ob-
jects. The Man in Black meets Good Fair White; Gatsby, Dan
Cody and then Daisy Fay. Like the dreamer in the Prologue to
The Legend of Good Women, the Man in Black in *The Book of the
Duchess* has a severely limited perspective on his relationship
with a lady. Good Fair White is for him what Alceste is for the

dreamer of the Prologue: an idealized creature. Describing their first meeting, the Man in Black stresses

> "That as the someres sonne bryght
> Ys fairer, clerer, and hath more lyght
> Than any other planete in heven,
> The moone, or the sterres seven,
> For al the world so hadde she
> Surmounted hem alle of beaute,
> Of maner, and of comlynesse,
> Of stature, and of wel set gladnesse,
> Of goodlyhede so wel beseye—
> Shortly, what shal y more seyes" (821–30)

The man also emphasizes that Good Fair White is a "golden girl" with a beautiful voice. She, he says, can

> "Carole and synge so swetely,
> Laughe and pley so womanly,
> And loke so debonairly,
> So goodly speke and so frendly
> That, certes, y trowe that evermor
> Nas seyn so blysful a tresor
> For every heer on hir hed,
> Soth to seyne, hyt was not red,
> Ne nouther yelowe, ne broun hyt nas,
> Me thoghte most lyk gold hyt was." (849–58)

His lady, he adds, "hadde not hir name wrong" (951); *Good Fair White* is appropriate in view of this lady's "ryght faire shuldres" (952) and body. She is "lyk to torch bryght / That every man may take of lyght / Ynogh, and hyt hath never the lesse" (963b–65). This golden girl with a sweet voice is also associated with whiteness and brightness.

Good Fair White is for the Man in Black an idealized figure, not the human being she really must have been (within the plot of the poem, that is). However beautiful and good Good Fair White was, surely, like any other human being, she was not perfect; and most definitely she was mortal—that is, even if she were a wonderful person, that wonderful person is alive no longer. But the Man in Black does not recognize these shortcomings. She is a perfect creature in his eyes; and he thinks of her as immortal, not mortal. His idealization of her

in this manner makes of her actually a dangerous creature to
him; for his image of her has the power to bind him to her forever, to exact a devotion that renders him unable to get on
with his life. The Man in Black is indeed caught in a false past
tense. As an artist, he can focus his creative efforts only on
constructing a "text" meant to keep alive his hope of a future
with this lady. He is, in other words, trying to preserve her in
a "story." Specifically, he does so by using ambiguous courtly-
love terms to talk about a "loss."

Gatsby's story includes talk of his meeting with Dan Cody,
the point at which Gatsby begins to project his anima onto a
single goal—the goddess Wealth, one might call it. Cody is "a
product of the Nevada silver fields, of the Yukon, of every
rush for metal since Seventy-five" (105). To Gatsby, Cody's
yacht represents "all the beauty and glamour in the world"
(106); and, apparently, while working for Cody for five years,
Gatsby picks up Cody's very material values. As Nick says,
when Cody dies, Gatsby is "left with his singularly appropriate
education; the vague contour of Jay Gatsby had filled out to
the substantiality of a man" (107). Gatsby has therefore associated his universal dreams with something more specific—with
temporal riches—even before meeting Daisy; and he has had a
creative response to this "god": he has "fleshed out" the "character" he made up as a boy: Jay Gatsby.

Sometimes Nick and always Gatsby sees Daisy much as the
Man in Black sees Good Fair White. Nick Carraway characterizes Daisy as a golden girl with an alluring voice and an association with whiteness and brightness. Nick, however, also
sees the other side of Daisy and realizes that the whiteness is
really hard silver and that there is redness—violence—inherent
in her. But Jay Gatsby, like the Man in Black and his attitude
toward Good Fair White, sees only the whiteness and the
brightness, and thus Daisy becomes more dangerous to him
than her negative qualities alone could ever have made her.
Gatsby comments to Nick that Daisy has a "curious and lovely
mouth" and a "voice huskier and more charming than ever."
He sees Daisy as "gleaming like silver" (157). Notably, both
Nick and Gatsby compare Daisy to silver; but Gatsby emphasizes the metal's brightness alone, not its hardness, whereas
earlier, Nick has stressed both positive brightness and negative
heaviness and hardness ("a silver idol" weighed down). In
addition, Gatsby, like the Man in Black, does not see that however wonderful Daisy might be, and however lovely their past

relationship might have been, it was fleeting, incapable of re-establishing in the present. To keep the dream alive, Gatsby creates a "text"—not just stories he tells, but a life and identity—all to, in Gatsby's own words, "'fix everything just the way it was before'" (117). His words fit the Man in Black's attitude, too.

Gatsby's mistaken view of Daisy also bears resemblance to the courtly-love relationship in Chaucer's *The Parliament of Fowls*. There, Nature tells a formel eagle to choose among three suitors, one of whom is obviously the best choice. This most appropriate suitor is of higher birth and of gentler heart than are the other prospective mates. Yet, despite the clear difference, and despite Nature's urging that the eagle make the proper choice, the formel eagle decides not to decide; and Nature is forced to give her a year before she need select. For the sake of the courtly-love game she is playing, this "lady" keeps many other birds of lower degree waiting for her to make up her mind so they can have their turn at mating. It is a foolish game, of course; for there is no question whom she will eventually choose. Nature, in contrast to the artificial code, would have her choose now.

Willard Edward Farnham links this episode to an ancient folk-tale called *The Contending Lovers*, in which love-pleadings are held before a judge who fails to reach a decision. So the female is supposed to decide among the contenders, all of whom are of noble rank. Each contender must perform an important service for the maiden. The author never tells what the woman's decision is (501–02). One version of the tale, *The Caste Type*, has a lady's four lovers presenting "in turn before her father claims based on unapplied accomplishments, comeliness, and general excellence. The caste of the suitors is important when merit comes to be considered. Neither father nor daughter is able to choose the most deserving" (508–09). Such a tale is a "problem tale" or "hoax tale" (501). It builds suspense, promises a decision, and then fails to deliver. The incident in the tale is a game played by courtly lovers in which the lady keeps the gentlemen waiting and serving and pining for her, when all along she knows whom she will choose. Moreover, since the tale itself ends with the audience not being shown the decision, the story is also a hoax.

Gatsby contains just such a hoax tale, but in a sense Gatsby, not Daisy, is its primary author—that is, he fools himself, becoming so enmeshed in his tale of a wonderful relationship

with Daisy that it seems to him to be reality.   The triangle of
Gatsby, Daisy, and Tom bears certain resemblances to the
"rectangle" of the four eagles.   Obviously, Daisy is going to
choose Tom over Gatsby—in their world his "noble birth"
means everything.   Tom, of course, does not also have a gentle
heart, but a certain gentility and ability to behave in public as
if one did are part of Tom's social class.   Ironically, it is Gatsby
who has the gentle heart; so Fitzgerald is here commenting on
conditions within twentieth-century society, where nominal instead of real "nobility" is all that counts.   As in certain of the
Contending Lover tales, caste indeed proves the deciding factor.
But despite the sure choice of Tom, Gatsby creates—indeed
lives in as protagonist—a hoax tale in which Daisy has not
made such a decision, in which she may choose—and even appears to have chosen—Gatsby instead.   Daisy serves as willing
co-author to this hoax tale, playing to the hilt her role of the
lady who may have decided upon Gatsby, or who at least is
undecided.   In the Plaza Hotel scene, it is revealed that Daisy
has been toying with Gatsby, probably in an attempt to get
back at Tom for his philandering.   Daisy and Tom's dual indis-
cretions seem curiously a part of what is perhaps an established pattern of theirs by which they gain each other's attention—and perhaps also a pattern common in their social class,
much as the medieval courtly-love game was a marker of the
upper class and not understood by other classes, especially the
bourgeoisie who wished to infiltrate courtly ranks.   Such a pattern is implied when Tom says that

> "the trouble is that sometimes she [Daisy] gets foolish
> ideas in her head and doesn't know what she is do-
> ing.... And what's more, I love Daisy too.   Once in a
> while I go off on a spree and make a fool of myself,
> but I always come back, and in my heart I love her all
> the time." (138)

Both Tom and Daisy, then, seem to "write" the courtly-
love text by whose rules they both operate—a text that helps
them maintain the distinctiveness of their social class.   In the
end, Gatsby does not write the tale that will be played out ultimately; they have written it.   He becomes one of their pup-
pets, or characters (and in a way always has been).   For when
Daisy rejects Gatsby at the Plaza, she reveals quite directly that
Gatsby's dream is—and has been—dead.   She, says Nick, "was

drawing further and further into herself" in response to Gatsby's defense of Tom's charges against him, so "only the dead dream fought on as the afternoon slipped away," struggling to reach "that lost voice across the room" (142). As Nick puts it a bit later, on this occasion, the text entitled "'Jay Gatsby' had broken up like glass against Tom's hard malice and the long *secret* extravaganza was played out" (155; emphasis added). But, even after this episode, Gatsby still tries to enact his story of Daisy as the ideal lady, now in need of his rescue because she has committed manslaughter in running down Myrtle Wilson. He will say he was driving, he tells Nick, little realizing that even now, Daisy has turned to Tom, not to him, and the two are apparently "conspiring together," according to Nick (153), formulating their own text. In other words, Daisy and Tom take over Gatsby's tale, deciding to let him be sacrificial courtly hero. Therefore, when Wilson comes to see Tom, Tom tells Wilson a story: that it is Gatsby whom the deranged man is looking for. To be sure, Nick could be mistaken in his conspiracy theory; but if so, it is just Daisy alone constructing a new tale in which Tom, instead of being her co-author, is a character she manipulates along with Gatsby. In this sense, Daisy is not only like the formel eagle but also like Alceste in yet another way: Daisy, too, is creator of a manipulative "text." Ironically, finally, after the failures of such artist figures as Ardita and Sally Carrol, and after the non-artistic characters Kismine and Charlotte, a female character in one of Fitzgerald's works emerges as creator of a text, but she is a successful artist only in terms of her ability to preserve her own life and social standing, at other people's expense.

The unsatisfactory tales of Daisy and Tom and of Gatsby are not the only tales available in *Gatsby*, just as the Man in Black's unsatisfactory tale is not the only one heard in *The Book of the Duchess*. In questioning and editing the tales of their shadows, the Chaucerian dreamer and Nick create their own, more successful stories. The dreamer in *The Book of the Duchess* keeps probing critically the Man in Black's cryptic comments about such matters as the loss of a chess piece. For instance, at one point, the dreamer says to the man:

"What los ys thats" quod I thoo;
"Nyl she not love yows ys hyt soos
Or have ye oght doon amys,
That she hath left yows ys hyt thiss

For Goddes love, telle me al." (1139–43)

At another point, having already heard the story of how and where the Man in Black and Good Fair White met, the dreamer tells the man, "'Ye han wel told me herebefore, / Hyt ys no nede to reherse it more'" (1127–28). He desires fresh details instead. These two examples illustrate a gain in perspective for the dreamer: he critically examines the tale of the Man in Black, learning from it enough to enable him to write, presumably, *The Book of the Duchess* itself.

Likewise, Nick attempts to interpret and edit his shadow's story. For example, the day after the party at which Gatsby and Nick meet, they go into New York for lunch. On the way, Gatsby tells part of his story—which turns out later to have concerned his life soon after his 1917 affair with Daisy in Louisville. Gatsby says that he

> "lived like a young rajah in all the capitals of Europe—
> Paris, Venice, Rome—collecting jewels, chiefly rubies,
> hunting big game, painting a little, things for myself
> only, and trying to forget something very sad that had
> happened to me long ago." (70)

Nick first responds to Gatsby's tale by questioning its credibility and scorning its style as reminiscent of a B-movie plot:

> With an effort I managed to restrain my incredulous
> laughter. The very phrases were worn so threadbare
> that they evoked no image except that of a turbaned
> "character" leaking sawdust at every pore as he pur-
> sued a tiger through the Bois de Boulogne. (70)

Yet later in the same interchange, after Gatsby has delightedly told Nick of the medals he won during the war—"'even [from] Montenegro, little Montenegro down on the Adriatic Sea!'" (70)—Nick's reaction changes: Gatsby, Nick says,

> lifted up the words and nodded with them—with his
> smile. The smile comprehended Montenegro's trou-
> bled history and sympathized with the brave struggles
> of the Montenegrin people. It appreciated fully the
> chain of national circumstances which had elicited this
> tribute from Montenegro's warm little heart. My

incredulity was submerged in fascination now; it was like skimming hastily through a dozen magazines. (70–71)

Here, Nick emphasizes that Gatsby's words are a creative text in his comparing them to the contents of a "dozen magazines." And, as when he criticizes Gatsby's song for being like popular songs, here, he is equally concerned with appropriate genre. Is Gatsby's story a B-movie plot, a glossy magazine tale, or autobiography? Nick is not certain of the answer, but by the end of this single interchange, he *is* starting to interpret Gatsby's tale differently than before—with fascination at the imaginative vitality and variety of Gatsby's story submerging his scorn at how untrue and poorly told it is.

Other examples of Nick's editorial and critical activities occur when Gatsby talks about Daisy's reaction to his party, and when Gatsby tells him (near the opening of chapter eight) of a part of his 1917 relationship with Daisy. Of the reaction to the party, Gatsby says,

"I feel far away from her.... It's hard to make her understand."
"You mean about the dance?"
"The dance?" He dismissed all the dances he had given with a snap of his fingers. "Old sport, the dance is unimportant." (116)

What Gatsby really wants is for Daisy to say she never loved Tom, divorce him, and marry Gatsby in her childhood home in Louisville, as if were 1917 again. "'I wouldn't ask too much of her,'" Nick says, trying to "edit" Gatsby's story. "'You can't repeat the past'" (116). Gatsby, of course, believes that he can do just that, and he keeps talking about (creating his story of) that past, including the occasion in 1917 when he kissed Daisy and "wed his unutterable visions to her perishable breath" (117). Nick's response to this part of his tale (which in manuscript included Gatsby's song) involves further interpretation: "Through all he said, even through his appalling sentimentality, I was reminded of something—an elusive rhythm, a fragment of lost words, that I had heard somewhere a long time ago" (118). Though Nick cannot recall these words, his statements bespeak his identity as editor/interpreter of Gatsby's story. And he is a certain kind of editor: one who prefers initially the objective and realistic to the sentimental, but who eventually desires a balance of these two trends.

Such encounters occur all along as Nick hears other portions of Gatsby's story—and as he views the "text" that is Gatsby's house, parties, and entire existence—until, by the end of their relationship, Nick has formed a balanced picture of this man and has learned much about himself, too. At that point, Nick's efforts to edit and interpret start to extend to the texts of people other than Gatsby. Nick erases an obscenity that has been written on Gatsby's sidewalk. He recognizes—as "editor" of Gatsby's story—that this sort of word will not do as a "text" about Gatsby. Gatsby's life story, however poorly told and lacking in perspective it was as Gatsby himself told it, deserves a better telling than either Gatsby or the obscene vandal has provided. In writing about his own dreamlike experience in the East, Nick fills with something far more fitting the gap left when he erased the obscenity: he composes an artistically successful work in tribute—not to Daisy, but to Gatsby. He is indeed similar to the poet-persona who creates *The Book of the Duchess*, a work that improves upon the tale of the Man in Black. He is also much like the waking poet-persona in Chaucer's Prologue, whose tribute to the daisy succeeds while the dreamer's legends, written in tribute to Alceste, fail.

For, as mistaken as Jay Gatsby is about many things, both he and the equally muddled Man in Black have one characteristic to their credit: their huge urge to create imaginatively, to become involved in a glorious dream. The problem is that their imaginative urges are all-consuming, unbalanced by any perspective furnished by their conscious minds. They live in the sort of dream also experienced by the dreamer in the Prologue to *The Legend of Good Women*, the Man in Black in *The Book of the Duchess*, and any unwary knight fooled by the hoax tale of the formel eagle in *The Parliament of Fowls*. These are all dangerous dreams because they envelop the dreamers completely, cutting them off from consciously discerned reality. At the end of the F version of the Prologue, the dreamer never even awakens; while still dreaming, he composes the relatively unsuccessful legends. For Chaucer, without balance, effective creativity simply is not possible.

The creative efforts of the Man in Black and Gatsby are nonetheless highly attractive to their counterparts. So they listen, keep trying to sort out all the confusing signals by asking questions, and ultimately write down their own versions of the tales. They shift points of view and focus markedly in their new versions. They indicate all along, too, how hard they tried to lead the shadows to have more perspective. The dreamer of *The Book of the Duchess* succeeds; for he gets the Man in Black to admit in plain terms that Good Fair White is dead, thereby clearing the way for him to resume his life. The poet-persona awakens able to create a work that indicates his balance of imagination and perspective, his ability to live with, not in, a dream—*The Book of the Duchess* itself. Notably, this poem, like the story told by the Man of Black, is a tribute, but to a different person. The poet-persona focuses on the Man of Black as "protagonist," not Good Fair White.

According to Nick, Gatsby may also ultimately realize that the Daisy he thought he knew is dead to him. Nick says that, shortly before his death, as Gatsby sat in the pool awaiting a phone call:

> I have an idea that Gatsby himself didn't believe it [the phone call from Daisy] would come and perhaps he no longer cared. If that was true he must have felt that he had lost the old warm world, paid a high price for living too long with a single dream. (169)

Two possibilities exist here: either the reader is meant to think Nick is correct, and just as the Man in Black learns to speak the truth about Good Fair White, Gatsby finally learns the truth about Daisy; or else one is to believe Nick is wrong and Gatsby learns nothing. It is, rather, only Nick who has been educated. In support of the latter interpretation, Nick's statement is, after all, filled with "ifs." It sounds as though he merely hopes that Gatsby died thus enlightened about Daisy. The fact is that, just before going to the pool, Gatsby asked the butler to bring any phone messages to him there—as if he very much still expected Daisy to come to him. In this case, Gatsby's resemblance to the Man in Black does not extend to their final circumstances. But if Gatsby does at the last minute learn, there is an irony in the novel that does not exist in the poem: unlike the Man in Black, he cannot act upon his new-found knowledge and take up his life anew.

Whichever the case, Nick, like Chaucer's dreamer, does learn. Through vicariously experiencing the dream-events, the poet-persona and Nick learn through their shadows that utter submission to the imagination leads to the sort of confused, chaotic art produced by the shadows. Yet they also learn that such an imagination is important. Having learned to live with instead of in a dream, they are able to create works that combine the imaginative involvement of a Gatsby and a Man in Black with detachment and perspective. Nick and the poet-persona are also able to pay tribute in their works to different figures from those in the poor tales of their shadows: instead of Daisy and Good Fair White, Jay Gatsby and the Man in Black are the focuses, worthy of praise for imaginative devotion to their dreams.

CHAPTER FIVE

SEEKING AN ETERNAL PLACE: *THE GREAT GATSBY*

> As imagination bodies forth
> The form of things unknown, the poet's pen
> Turns them to shapes, and gives to airy nothing
> A local habitation and a name.
> —*Shakespeare*, A Midsummer Night's Dream

For F. Scott Fitzgerald, the house is a significant symbol. One of his sorrows was that as a child he lived, as he once told his friend Adila Bigelow, "in a house below the average / of a street above the average."[1] Critic Barry Edward Gross explains that for Fitzgerald, "the house is the concrete symbol for many ineffable dreams" (130). A house "above the average" is apparently for Fitzgerald a symbol of security, of firm foundations (Gross 130–31), and the end product of a creative effort directed toward a well-defined goal: both the goal represented by the blueprint—the architectural goal; and the goal of the people who will live in the house of providing a comfortable, pleasant shelter for themselves. It is therefore not surprising that houses should play an important part in Fitzgerald's works. Though this emphasis is found also in such works as "The Ice Palace" and *The Vegetable*, *The Great Gatsby* especially exemplifies it.[2] The novel features numerous dwellings, three of which mirror the three buildings depicted in Chaucer's equally architectonic *The House of Fame*: the Wilson garage in the valley of ashes resembles the desert-surrounded temple of Venus; Gatsby's house in West Egg, New York, is similar to

the House of Fame; and Myrtle Wilson and Tom Buchanan's
New York City apartment is reminiscent of the house of twigs.
Each edifice fails to offer an eternal goal for the artist and thus
reveals to him the need to search in other places for such a
goal. The novel also features a place that mirrors a setting in
Chaucer's *The Parliament of Fowls*: the "place above the trees"
to which Jay Gatsby wishes to go resembles the "starry place"
to which Scipio travels. However, while Scipio's starry place
indeed contains an eternal goal, Gatsby's starry place does not,
though Gatsby cannot see this fact.

Thus, no place in *Gatsby* contains the goal needed for full
creativity. Nick Carraway—much like Geffrey in *The House of
Fame*—travels in his dream to the various locales, observes the
strengths and weaknesses inherent in each place, and gains insight into a way he can become fully creative. He learns from
what he views in these places in much the same way as he
learns much from hearing and "editing" his shadow's poor
story. In fact, his listening and revising duties overlap his
travel to places: when he visits Gatsby's house, he is in effect
"hearing" a significant part of Gatsby's tale, the part Gatsby
creates, not just tells.

In *The House of Fame*, Geffrey awakens in his dream to find
himself within the glass temple of Venus, which features images of gold, tents, pinnacles, and portraits, including a picture of Venus, who has one her head "hir rose garlond whit
and red" (135). The temple also contains a table of brass on
which part of the *Aeneid* has been engraved. Going outside, he
finds himself in a large field that is

> As fer as that I myghte see,
> Withouten toun, or hous, or tree,
> Or bush, or grass, or eryd lond;
> For al the feld nas but of sond
> As smal as man may se yet lye
> In the desert of Lybye;
> Ne no maner creature
> That ys yformed be Nature
> Ne sawgh I, me to rede or wisse.
>   "O Crist!" thoughte I, "that art in blysse,
> Fro fantome and illusion
> Me save!" and with devocion
> Myn eyen to hevene I caste. (483–95)

Just after calling to God for help, Geffrey sees the eagle, which will soon take him to another place, the House of Fame. Geffrey's description emphasizes the absence of Venus from her own temple, the pervading sense of inactivity, the lack of worshipers of the goddess of Love. In the shrine, Geffrey sees only art long since completed, not current creativity. Conditions are even worse outside the temple, where Geffrey sees an unusual sight: a desert. The locale is unusual in that in typical French and English dream visions, Venus' temple is in a lush garden (Sanders 5). Though a desert is indeed a part of Nature, symbolically, it is Nature stripped of its usual vegetation and growth; it thus becomes anti-Nature. By summoning up in his readers thoughts of such a contrast, Chaucer surely underscores the arid, still, lifeless conditions rife in this locality and implies that at one time, the real Venus existed here in what was then a lovely, fresh garden and that at one time, worshipers paid tribute to her by producing the golden images that now sit within the temple. To its credit, at least the vestige of a goal for creative efforts appears in this realm: the picture of the goddess of Love—but no real Love, and no real Nature.

In *The Great Gatsby*, Nick travels to a similar locale: the Wilson garage in the valley of ashes. In chapter two of the novel, Nick tells of his first trip there on his way into New York City with Tom Buchanan. In the valley is a building of "yellow brick sitting on the edge of the waste land, a sort of compact Main Street ministering to it and contiguous to absolutely nothing" (28). The building contains three shops: one currently empty; one an "all-night restaurant approached by a trail of ashes"; and the last George Wilson's garage, described by Nick as "unprosperous and bare; the only car visible was the dust-covered wreck of a Ford which crouched in a dim corner" (29). As Nick also observes, the walls are colorless, and dust covers everything. It is indeed a place suggestive of inaction, of lack of creativity. Nick can find only a few words indicative of action to use in describing it: "ministering," "approached," "bought," "sold," "covered," and "crouched"; but he uses these words in a manner that reverses the usual implications. The Main Street is said to "minister," but to nothing. The restaurant can be "approached," but only by traveling through "a trail of dust." That this eatery features such a sooty, grimy front yard does not bode well for what sort of food customers are likely to encounter inside—surely not

anything very appetizing. The garage owner (Wilson) supposedly buys and sells vehicles and makes repairs; but inside the
garage only a "dust-covered wreck of a Ford...crouched" in a
corner. It seems laughable to consider that much buying, sell-
ing, or repairing would actually occur here. The verb *crouch* in
itself signals only suspended action; and the notion that in the
future the car could spring to action seems ludicrous, since the
vehicle is in disrepair.

The valley of ashes in which this building sits parallels the
desert in which the temple of Venus is situated. The area is,
says Nick,

> a fantastic farm where ashes grow like wheat into
> ridges and hills and grotesque gardens, where ashes
> take the form of houses and chimneys and rising
> smoke and finally, with a transcendent effort, of men
> who move dimly and already crumbling through the
> powdery air. Occasionally a line of grey cars crawls
> along an invisible track, gives out a ghastly creak and
> comes to rest, and immediately the ash-grey men
> swarm up with leaden spades and stir up an impene-
> trable cloud which screens their obscure operations
> from your sight. (27)

Just as the temple of Venus as pictured in Chaucer's poem may
at one time have stood in a green garden, this area seems at
one time to have featured green farms and gardens—Nature.
Now, however, it is anti-Nature, full of distortions of Nature.
It is anti-Nature in that the ashes and dust are the waste products of industry and therefore represent the attempts of industry and technology to control and overcome Nature. It is also
full of anti-action, just as the Wilson garage is: here, men
move, but dimly and crumbling; and their actions are thoroughly negative: they act only to bring industrial wastes to the
area, and they often hidden from view by a cloud of dust.

Nick meets four characters who exist in this environment:
George Wilson; Myrtle Wilson; Doctor T. J. Eckleburg (actually,
of course, only a picture on a billboard, but nonetheless a
"character" of sorts); and Michaelis, the restaurant manager.
Nick meets George and Myrtle on his initial trip through the
valley with Tom. Nick portrays George as follows: "...the
proprietor himself appeared in the door of an office, wiping his
hands on a piece of waste. He was a blond, spiritless man,

anaemic, and faintly handsome. When he saw us a damp gleam of hope sprang into his light blue eyes" (29). Also, "a white ashen dust veiled his dark suit and his pale hair as it veiled everything in the vicinity—except his wife..." (30). Asked to get chairs for the visitors, George goes "toward the little office, mingling immediately with the cement color of the walls" (30). Nick sees that George is so marginally alive that Myrtle can walk through him "as if he were a ghost" (30). "'He's so dumb he doesn't know he's alive'" (30), says Tom to Nick in regard to Wilson's ignorance of his and Myrtle's affair, and perhaps also in reference to George's shortcomings as a businessman. Tom, Nick says, has gone to the garage on the pretext of making a deal with George for the sale of Tom's car; when George complains faintly about how long the sale is taking and Tom threatens to take his business elsewhere, George is reduced to explaining himself embarrassedly as his voice fades off. In short, for Nick, George personifies the essence of this place—its inaction, its lack of creativity. To describe George, Nick uses only a few words that would ordinarily signify action; but in this case the terms ultimately denote inaction instead. For instance, even the most active verb, "sprang," refers merely to George's mistaken hope about the sale of the car. His hope is, in fact, utterly misplaced; Tom, not he, is doing the buying—and of George's own wife, not of a car.

In contrast, Myrtle seems to Nick out of place in this ashen world. Nick says she is "faintly stout" but able to carry

> her surplus flesh sensuously as some women can. Her face...contained no facet or gleam of beauty but there was an immediately perceptible vitality about her as if the nerves of her body were continually smouldering. She smiled slowly and walking through her husband as if he were a ghost shook hands with Tom, looking him flush in the eye. Then she wet her lips and without turning around spoke to her husband in a soft, coarse voice:
> "Get some chairs, why don't you, so somebody can sit down." (29–30)

For Nick, this woman manifests all the action and all the signs of Nature otherwise absent in this locale. For instance, he says that her figure *blocks out* light. Further, Nick states that she *carries* her flesh; her nerves *smoulder*; she *smiles* at Tom and *shakes* hands with him, *looking* at him "flush in the eye"; she *orders* her husband around; and she *makes plans* with Tom almost before George's very eyes. Her actions are direct and deliberate; her vitality and fertility, unmistakable. Importantly, myrtle, according to Lottie R. Crim and Neal B. Houston, is "an herb that was held sacred to Venus and accepted as an emblem of love, was also used in civic and religious ceremonies by the ancient Greeks. The herb also symbolized victory or triumph" (116). However, though she is linked to the goddess of Love, she is not the goddess herself but instead an *emblem* of love, much as the portrait in Venus' temple is. Moreover, Myrtle's fertility and vitality—her connections both to Love and to Nature—are threatened with destruction from either of two sources: the dust of the valley of ashes could overcome her, choking out this last sign of Nature, just as it has the farms and the gardens of the area; or her own desire to be something other than she is may destroy her. For Myrtle longs to be like Daisy, the goddess Wealth; she seeks to move away from her connections with Love and Nature and toward material goals. Thus, as with Geffrey and the temple of Venus, Nick finds in Wilson's garage a mere sign of Venus—of Love. And soon, even this remnant will be gone.

The third "character" to appear in this place is described by Nick as follows:

> The eyes of Doctor T. J. Eckleburg are blue and gigantic—their retinas are one yard high. They look out of no face, but, instead, from a pair of enormous yellow spectacles which pass over a non-existent nose. Evidently some wild wag of an oculist set them there to fatten his practice in the borough of Queens and then sank down himself into eternal blindness or forgot them and moved away. But his eyes, dimmed a little by many paintless days under sun and rain, brood on over the solemn dumping ground. (27–28)

More than Myrtle Wilson, Doctor T. J. Eckleburg's dim eyes are the remnant of a deity in the valley of ashes—and how strangely appropriate for the god of a place that owes its ash-ridden condition to industrial wastes to be an advertisement, a symbol of commercialism. Notably, Doctor T. J. Eckleburg himself is nowhere to be found; the oculist has disappeared for some unknown reason. The name of this oculist is significant: Crim and Houston point out that in German, "Eckle" and "burg" would combine to mean "loathsome town" (117). This appellation becomes oddly fitting when combined with the title "doctor"—suggestive of knowing, healing, and serving—and with the idea that the real Eckleburg was an oculist, a doctor skilled at making people see well. By implication, the oculist should see well, too. Taken together, the name means seer and healer of the loathsome town. But the healer of the loathsome town is gone; only a sign, which can neither see nor heal anything, remains. However, for one resident of the valley of ashes, the sign does have god-like power; and because George Wilson believes that it does, it does. Indeed, Nick eventually learns that, paradoxically, despite its utter lack of vitality, this sign turns out to wield more power than does the vital Myrtle.

Nick depicts a fourth character associated with this locale, Michaelis, the restaurant manager. Michaelis introduces another possible god for the valley: the Christian God whom Michaelis worships and represents. Nick does not mention Michaelis by name until near the end of the novel, when he talks about Michaelis' role in the aftermath of Myrtle's death. Initially, Nick mentions only that a restaurant manager lives in the valley and that the man's cafe has a front yard covered in ashes—a detail that shows Nick's less-than-positive impression of this man. Michaelis, though associated with the Christian God, is unable to keep the negative consequences of industrialization away from himself or his customers, who come to him seeking nourishment. However, to his credit, as restaurant manager, he at least keeps trying to provide such nourishment.

Later, in Nick's report of the events surrounding Myrtle's death, Michaelis puts in a significant appearance; and Myrtle's, George's, and the billboard's functions are further delineated. Michaelis, Nick says, finds George ill in the garage office and learns that George has locked up Myrtle in the couple's apartment above the garage. Michaelis is surprised at this news because he has thought of Wilson as incapable of such a thing, as "his wife's man and not his own" (144). Michaelis tries to find out what has happened but leaves when he sees he has customers going into his restaurant; after serving them, he simply forgets to return to see how George is doing. Later, he hears Myrtle's cries and then the car crash that kills her. He and another man go to the body and see Myrtle's "left breast...swinging loose like a flap," and "mouth...wide open and ripped at the corners as though she had choked a little in giving up the tremendous vitality she had stored so long" (145). Nick's description of Myrtle's death indicates his realization of Myrtle's role as remnant of Love and Nature; for he stresses that in dying, she gives up "tremendous vitality," a remark associated with his earlier description of her sensuality. The Wilson garage and valley of ashes thus prove even more barren than the temple of Venus. This area is now bereft of even a remnant of Venus. Ultimately only a lifeless advertisement remains to suggest a deity toward whom any creative efforts could be directed.

Nick then recounts the events occurring in the valley following the accident. Just after the wreck, George screams, "'Oh, my God!'" (145) over and over. Michaelis and some other men stay with George; but soon, Michaelis is the only one left to watch over him. Michaelis asks George about George's church membership and about whether he can call a priest for him. "'You ought to have a church, George, for times like this'" (165), he tells him. But George does not have one. A bit later, George begins to look out the window at the eyes of Doctor T. J. Eckleburg; he says that he (George) told Myrtle "'she might fool me but she couldn't fool God. I took her to the window...and I said "God knows what you've been doing...."'" Michaelis, shocked, says, "'That's an advertisement,'" but George does not reply (167). Later, when Michaelis goes home to get some sleep, George leaves to find his wife's killer. Finally, George Wilson shows a commitment to action, but of what sort? He intends only to destroy his wife's supposed killer, an action he apparently thinks has been ordained by the "god" of the valley of ashes. Doctor T. J. Eckleburg is only a portrait, just as the portrait in the temple of Venus is not the actual goddess; but at least there the portrait is of a goddess of Love—not of hatred and revenge.

As Nick depicts him, Michaelis points, though weakly, to an alternative to the anti-god Eckleburg. As Alexander R. Tamke explains, Michaelis, whose name connects him with the archangel St. Michael (Michaelis is a Latin form of Michael), serves as the "lone spokesman for religion" in the novel (305). When Michaelis first sees George following Myrtle's death, George is calling out to God, much as Geffrey calls to God in the desert; but as it turns out, George thinks of the billboard of Dr. T. J. Eckleburg as this God to whom he calls. When Michaelis tries to get George to contact a minister and to stop thinking of the billboard as a god, Michaelis, says Tamke, is providing "an admonishment against following Satan in the form of crass commercialism and materialism represented by the advertising sign...." The meeting between Michaelis and Wilson therefore becomes "an almost allegorical struggle between the forces of evil and those of God or good" (304). In Christian tradition, adds Tamke, St. Michael fights Satan, rescues the faithful from the devil, serves as the champion of God's people, and calls souls to Judgment; in short, St. Michael is an "intercessor and mediator" (305).

Michaelis tries but fails to fulfill offices like those of St. Michael. He tries to get George to realize who God is and who He is not. But because he is a mere human being, subject to normal biological drives, such as the need to sleep, he fails. He also fails earlier to stay with George and perhaps stop this whole chain of events because, seeing potential customers enter his cafe, he leaves George to serve them—to make some money—and, subsequently, he is subject to another common human failing—forgetfulness. Michaelis, says Tamke, "is unsuccessful, for he is but the twentieth-century common-man counterpart of the archangel and cannot triumph over the materialism and irreligion of modern society" (305). The Christian God, who could serve as goal for worshipful creativity, does not do so. Instead, George Wilson continues to think of the billboard as his god and undertakes a quest to destroy. Conversely, in *The House of Fame*, the Christian God is called upon and does seem to answer. When Geffrey, disturbed about being in the barren desert and having seen an empty temple of Venus, calls upon God, soon, as if in answer, the eagle appears to take him elsewhere, as if God were overseeing this quest for creative renewal. Despite troubled times, then, for Chaucer's era, there is felt to be an ultimate refuge in one's religious faith, a permanent refuge that leads one away from the temporal and unworthy. For Fitzgerald's era, such religious faith is not so easy to come by. False gods of the temporal and the commercial masquerade as the real thing for hapless folk such as George Wilson.

In short, then, Nick sees that no fit goal for creativity exists in the valley of ashes. Myrtle is only a temporal remnant of Love and Nature; Dr. Eckleburg's inert sign, an anti-god connected with the unnatural ashen condition of the valley in that both are results of commercial enterprises, provides George with the desire to destroy, not create; and Michaelis'

God is unrecognized by anyone but Michaelis, who is ineffectual at calling George's attention to Him.

Next in *The House of Fame*, Geffrey meets his guide, the
golden eagle, who takes him to his next destination, the House
of Fame. This ornately eloquent eagle—which is "of gold, and
shon so bryghte" (503b) bears the dreamer high and fast to
Fame's palace. Notably, however, the eagle is not with the
dreamer throughout his travels; later, he leaves Geffrey to his
own devices, one of various guides in the poem who provide
no ultimate answers. In *Gatsby*, as in "The Diamond as Big as
the Ritz," a car is somewhat parallel to the golden eagle. It is
Gatsby's resplendent vehicle, described by Nick as follows: "It
was a rich cream color, bright with nickel, swollen here and
there in its monstrous length with triumphant hatboxes and
supper-boxes and tool-boxes, and terraced with a labyrinth of
windshields that mirrored a dozen suns" (68). Later, the car is
called "'this circus wagon'" (128); and, according to the person
who witnesses it hit Myrtle Wilson, it is a "'big yellow car'"
(147). In short, the car—somewhat like the eagle—is golden
and ornate. Also somewhat like the eagle, it bears Nick on
some parts of his travels, as when he and Gatsby converse on
their way into New York in the car. Later on, like the eagle,
the car ceases to be any sort of "guide" for Nick's travels; but
unlike the eagle, it does not disappear. Instead it becomes an
agent of destruction, as Daisy kills Myrtle with it.

In *The House of Fame*, Geffrey is carried next to the House
of Fame, a place full of all the activity and movement so lacking in the temple and desert. The intricately designed beryl
palace full of pinnacles, images, tents, and windows has also a
golden gate carved with almost indescribable images. Every
wall of the palace is "plated half a foote thikke / Of gold..."
(1345b–46a) and is set with "the fynest stones faire" (1351b).
The place epitomizes opulence; it is a richly imagined piece of
art. However, the very opulence, the very multiplicity of objects suggests also the unnaturalness of the place. As Julius
maintains, the house is "not only fantastic and unnatural but
excessively so" (148). Geffrey sees that only the goddess Fame
serves as a goal for the creative action that has resulted in this
building; as an object of worship and adoration, this inconstant
creature can but inspire such an overdone place.

Geffrey also sees the people within the House of Fame, as
well as the names of famous and once-famous people written

on the rock of ice on which the castle sits. Both people and names are marked by suggestions of the multifarious, the inharmonious, the incongruous, and the impermanent. Commendably, the House of Fame features much activity, many people, much ornamentation, many jewels, and—above all—much sound. These are signs that people are currently creating; not all is still, complete, and silent as it is in the temple of Venus. The list of names written on the rock of ice bespeaks creativity in that it not only memorializes many creative people but also is itself a piece of art. Geffrey lists in his poem the names and vocations of some of the artists who have come to the House of Fame, thereby underscoring the large number involved. In particular, he seems interested in the musicians and their instruments, as when he speaks of the

> Many thousand tymes twelve,
> That maden lowde mynstralcies
> In cornemuse and shalemyes,
> And many other maner pipe,
> That craftely begunne to pipe,
> Bothe in doucet and in rede,
> That ben at festes with the brede;
> And many flowte and liltyng horn,
> And pipes made of grene corn. (1216–24)

Geffrey further lists the names of specific musicians: the famous Dutch piper Messenus, Joab, Theodomas, and others—in short, "moo than sterres ben in hevene" (1254). This catalogue of musicians, says J. A. W. Bennett, illustrates the emphasis throughout Chaucer's poem on "the multifarious multitudes." It is an example of Chaucer's use of "the dream-faculty of increasing and multiplying figures" (123).

In addition to musicians, Geffrey sees and hears

> jugelours,
> Magiciens, and tregetours,
> And Phitonesses, charmeresses,
> Olde wicches, sorceresses,
> That use exorsisacions,
> And eke these fumygacions;
> And clerkes eke, which konne wel
> Al this magik naturel. (1259b–66)

He also sees Medea, Circes, Calipso, Hermes, Ballenus, Limote, Simon Magus, Colle, and many other people. The sheer number involved implies that much is occurring in this place. And the mix of people—from various social classes and professions—indicates Chaucer's awareness of the upheavals in his day of the once-rigid class structure. It is an awareness certainly not limited to these listings in *The House of Fame*. Of all the dream visions, it is perhaps conveyed the most clearly in *The Parliament of Fowls*, where all "stations" of birds come before Nature, showing in their interchanges with birds of other classes what Derek Brewer terms the "mutual hostility and incomprehension between the classes" (137).

Initially, the golden eagle in *The House of Fame* directs Geffrey's attention to the cacophony inherent in the place by commenting that

> "The grete soun,"
> Quod he, "that rumbleth up and doun
> In Fames Hous, full of tydynges
> Bothe of feir speche and chidynges,
> And of fals and soth compouned." (1025b–29)

Geffrey's use and quotation of such up/down imagery to describe the House of Fame and its surroundings (such as in the depiction of Geffrey and the eagle's trip through the air to the castle) show his impression of the instability and, when used to describe sounds, the disharmony of this place. (See Steed; Sanders.) Later, in his description of the sounds made by the goddess Fame's petitioners, Geffrey further emphasizes cacophony. To be sure, Geffrey at one isolated point hears a "hevenyssh melodye / Of songes, ful of armonye" (1395b–96) sung about the throne of the goddess; however, both before and after hearing this harmonious sound, Geffrey witnesses much noisy commotion. Besides the initial rumbling, Geffrey hears the "confus matere" (1517b) of the writers who are all trying to tell their tales simultaneously; and he listens to

> a noyse aprochen blyve,
> That ferde as been don in a hive
> Ayen her tyme of out-fleynge;
> Ryght such a maner murmurynge,
> For al the world, hyt semed me. (1521b–25)

Notably, this transformation of sound and music into mere noise such as swarming bees would make occurs as the people approach the goddess Fame to ask her to grant them renown.

Geffrey also notices that the House of Fame and its environs contain many signs of impermanence. Geffrey says that the rock of ice on which the palace rests features on its sunny south side unreadable names of the once-famous while the shady northern side lists still-readable names. Geffrey is seeing that renown is undependable.

All these attributes—the multiplicity that suggests much creative action, the impermanence, and the cacophony—come together in Geffrey's depiction of the goddess Fame, who personifies the only goal for the creative efforts of the petitioners. As she sits on high upon her ruby throne, Geffrey sees that this figure is

> A femynyne creature,
> That never formed by Nature
> Nas such another thing yseye,
> For alther-first, soth for to seye,
> Me thoughte that she was so lyte
> That the lengthe of a cubite
> Was lengere than she semed be.
> But thus sone, in a whyle, she
> Hir tho so wonderliche streight
> That with hir fet she erthe reighte,
> And with hir hed she touched hevene,
> Ther as shynen sterres sevene. (1365–76)

This "lady" has as many eyes "as fetheres upon foules be, / Or weren on the bestes foure" (1382–83); curly hair of burnished gold; ears that stand up; tongues like those on beasts; and winged feet. Bennett points out that this picture of the goddess Fame inverts the conventional medieval portrait of a beautiful woman as Nature's handiwork: "Of the typical attributes of feminine beauty only one feature is allowed her—the bright blonde hair.... But otherwise, it is the grotesque and strange unnaturalness of her figure that is stressed" (128–29). In addition, Francis P. Magoun, Jr., and Tauno F. Mustanoja point out that Geffrey's portrait of the goddess Fame is surrealistic, "a real dream vision," for it is a "flexible, irrational picture" full of incongruities (53). These critics recognize the unnatural, incongruous, changeable qualities that mark the goddess Fame as viewed by Geffrey.

Despite possessing such horrific features, the goddess Fame nevertheless has a positive side: she represents the live- liness, the movement, the sheer multiplicity that constitute the only benefit of the House of Fame. Her most representative ac- tion is her expansion and contraction, which bring together both the negative and the positive qualities. Geffrey watches as, unnaturally and incongruously, she alters her size; but in so doing, she is at least acting, moving, affecting the world about her. She stands in much contrast to the immobile por- trait of Venus. However, the size changes also show Geffrey her undependability, similarly illustrated in her capricious be- havior toward her petitioners. While some order exists inas- much as organized companies of petitioners appear before her, wild vacillation reigns as the goddess grants and denies fame, regardless of the merit or lack of merit of a given petitioner.

The actions of the goddess Fame and her petitioners also reveal to Geffrey the essential nature of the creative efforts of these people. They desperately long for recognition. As Patri- cia Ward Julius explains, these are people whose

> vision is flawed, who scramble desperately for the re- nown which they think will *make them matter*.... That desperation is epitomized by the eighth and ninth companies who seek disrepute, the greatest infamy, to escape the terrible knowledge of their own unimpor- tance. (227; emphasis added)

In short, as Geffrey sees, the goddess Fame is the only goal for creativity, the only one who her petitioners feel can make them feel significant, provide them with a sense of identity. Julius' phrase "make them matter" perhaps best sums up their needs. But, as Geffrey has also seen, such an essentially undepend- able entity as Fame is a slippery objective. Its attainment can have little or no relation to one's merit; and once gained, such a goal is capable of slipping out of one's grasp at any time. It is a goal not connected to the eternal.

In *The Great Gatsby*, Nick visits a place resembling the House of Fame: Gatsby's house,[3] where he observes fantastic, chaotic parties attended by guests who, like the petitioners to Fame, want to matter. Nick says that the house itself makes a "*feudal* silhouette against the sky" (96; emphasis added)—a phrase that possibly links the building to the medieval House of Fame. The evidence of a connection becomes insistent in other passages. Initially, Nick describes the house as featuring "a tower on one side, spanking new under a thin beard of raw ivy, and a marble swimming pool and more than forty acres of lawn and garden" (9). The marble pool and lavish grounds indicate an opulence equal to that of the House of Fame— notably, an opulence that seems to be greater than Nature, represented by the water and garden greenery. The tower, reminiscent of the tower of the House of Fame, signifies the phallic, creative power associated with this place; that it is covered with a sign of fertility—ivy—increases the impression of such power. Other details add to this impression: at one point, Nick finds the house "lit from tower to cellar" and the "whole corner of the peninsula...blazing with light which fell unreal on the shrubbery and made thin elongating glints upon the roadside wires" (86). The brightness again is reminiscent of Fame's beryl palace. Inside, Nick sees all manner of richly adorned rooms: "Marie Antoinette music-rooms and Restoration salons"; Gatsby's library with its many uncut books; "period bedrooms swathed in rose and lavender silk and vivid with new flowers...dressingrooms and poolrooms, and bathrooms, with sunken baths...." There are also "Gatsby's own apartment, a bedroom and a bath and an Adam study..." (96). There, Gatsby shows Daisy

> shirts of sheer linen and thick silk and fine flannel which lost their folds as they fell and covered the table in many-colored disarray. While we admired [the shirts] he brought more and the soft rich heap mounted higher—shirts with stripes and scrolls and plaids in coral and apple green and lavender and faint orange with monograms of Indian blue. (97–98)

Nick's listings of the ornate rooms; expensive, colorful shirts; and the many party guests' names are similar both in content and style to Geffrey's catalogues that name the ornate designs and furnishings and many guests in the House of Fame. Just as Geffrey emphasizes that the House of Fame contains many windows, rooms, and cubicles, so does Nick stress such features of Gatsby's house. And just as the House of Fame is marked by much color and much ornamentation, so are Gatsby's house and shirts.

Stylistically, both Geffrey and Nick use the catalogue as a device to underscore the manifold contents of these places, the sheer plenty. One thing such lists do is to make use of what Bennett calls the "dream-faculty of increasing and multiplying figures [that] Chaucer exploits in all his dream-poems" (123)— that is, they simply make the scenes seem dreamlike. But the lists serve another purpose, one delineated by Stephen A. Barney in his discussion of the lists in *The House of Fame* and *The Parliament of Fowls*:

> Both poems exploit the sense lists give of plenitude
> and complete enumeration, and both poems are aware,
> with an essentially Chaucerian awareness, that the
> appearance of plenitude is specious, that abundance
> cannot substitute for perfection, that lists need imply
> no order or end.... (221)

Through listing, Geffrey not only shows the abundance available in the House of Fame but also sees the problem there is with sheer number. One can create, and create, and create; but what of the quality of what is created? Its quality would depend upon the goal, the center, that a creative project has to invest it with meaning and direction. As Barney states, "Abundance cannot substitute for perfection...." Similarly, Nick sees, through his listings, a problem with sheer abundance of material goods.

As Geffrey depicts with the House of Fame, Nick stresses the atmosphere of disharmony, impermanence, and incongruity at Gatsby's mansion—at the same time picturing a place brimming with many people engaged in much creative action. Nick suggests multiplicity when he describes there having been at Gatsby's party "enough colored lights to make a Christmas tree of Gatsby's enormous garden" and the many "glistening" hors d'oeuvre; the various salads; and the plentiful pastry pigs and chickens "bewitched to a dark gold" (44). Many musicians make music; countless bright colors and lights, odd hair styles, and striking clothes appear; the air is filled with floating cocktails and with cocktail music; much laughter and talk permeate the air, too; groups momentarily grow large with people. In short, much is happening. Nick enhances the impression of immediacy by using present tense in his initial description of the atmosphere. Particularly in emphasizing musicians and their many instruments, Nick's description echoes the multiplicity stressed in Geffrey's description of the House of Fame and its denizens.

Nick stresses that this is a place of creativity. Nick can see that Gatsby has created this gaudy, busy atmosphere, much as a stage or movie director would create a scene, and much as Gatsby has recreated for Nick the various components of his life story. Owl Eyes, one of Gatsby's guests, exhibits that he, too, recognizes Gatsby's creative feat when he comments to Nick that one of the books in Gatsby's huge library is "'a bona fide piece of printed matter. It fooled me. This fella's a regular Belasco'" (50). Edwin T. Arnold points out that Owl Eyes is referring to David Belasco, an American actor, playwright, and producer. Owl Eyes, says Arnold, has "grasped the essence of Gatsby.... James Gatz is playing the role of Jay Gatsby, but...he goes beyond the pose, and in doing so becomes not just the actor, but also the artist, the director" (49–50). And Gatsby has created not only a library but also an opulent palace and parties that bear the marks of a vivid but chaotic imagination. As Nick remarks later of Gatsby's dream, Gatsby has "thrown himself into it with a creative passion, adding to it all the time, decking it out with every bright feather that drifted his way" (101). Gatsby's mansion and parties are the palpable symbols—the bright feathers—of that dream. And Gatsby is not the only artist portrayed by Nick: the partygoers help create the atmosphere at the party, in their own attempts to create lives and identities for themselves.

As with the House of Fame, the activity that Nick observes in Gatsby's mansion has little direction. It, too, is marked by signs of incongruity, disharmony, and impermanence. The voluminous amount of food will ultimately be reduced to a pittance to include the "desolate path of fruit rinds" (116) that Nick speaks of regarding the aftermath of another of Gatsby's parties. The many musical instruments will play "'Vladimir Tostoff's Jazz History of the World'" (54), a piece suggestive of discord in several ways: the composer's name, "Tostoff," hints that the man merely "tossed off" the piece without much thought (Crim and Houston 116); jazz by definition implies a deviation from melody; and the history of the world is certainly replete with wars, fights, and other forms of disharmony. The many rooms are indeed filled with colors, hairdos, and clothing; but these things are gaudy and unnatural. The many cocktails eventually lead to drunkenness and the discord it brings—such as the wreck Owl Eyes has at party's end and the arguments that often break out.   The groups that swell with new members do so only for an instant and then dissolve; as Mary Kathryn Grant explains, "*The Great Gatsby* implicitly describes a masquerade where identities are never discovered, real relationships are never formed.... Any experience of community is undercut by anonymity and the possibility of change in partner" (191).   Perhaps nowhere is this sense of masquerade more prevalent than in the party scenes at Gatsby's place. Furthermore, as Nick discovers, the plentiful talk consists largely of rash rumors about Gatsby's background, forgotten introductions, and the "gasping broken sobs" (56) of a red-haired songstress.   In fact, by the end of the evening, Nick has viewed discussions that have turned into fights and chatter that has become muted thanks to the drunken vagueness that has overtaken many people in the crowd.

Nick's guest list encapsulates all these characteristics. Nick composes the list on the basis of two things: the names he can still see on a faded timetable on which he wrote down what he could recall of the names of the partygoers, and his memory of other names of partygoers.   In that this part of Nick's dream account is not a retelling of a single dream-event but rather a compilation that Nick makes as he writes his dream account, the guest list is especially significant in indicating what Nick has learned from his observation of the doings at Gatsby's mansion.   Nick uses this catalogue much as Geffrey uses his lists: not only to list names of people (just as Geffrey lists names of petitioners), but also, as Barney says, to picture a plenitude that is not as positive as it first might seem.   Nick suggests plenitude by making the list a very long one; he first suggests that it is ultimately negative by stressing that a *faded* timetable bears the almost *indecipherable* names of many of the guests: "It is an old time-table now," Nick says, "disintegrating at the folds and headed, 'This schedule in effect July 5th, 1922.' But I can still read the grey names..." (65). The names are much like the melting names engraved on the sunny southern side of the rock of ice that Geffrey speaks of in *The House of Fame*.   They bear witness to the impermanence associated with Gatsby's guests.   Whatever they are using as a goal for their creativity is not a lasting entity.

Nick remembers, reconstructs, and juxtaposes names that have much symbolic significance in indicating the multiplicity of action and yet the impermanence and the incongruity associated with Gatsby's party guests.   Two critics, Howard S.

Babb and Robert W. Stallman, have in separate studies commented upon such characteristics of the guest list. Babb calls the guest list "the passage coming nearer than anything else in *The Great Gatsby* to pure grotesque art...." It manifests the mixtures of realm of being (i.e., animal world and vegetable world), the juxtaposition of incongruous elements, and the combination of comedy and violence that are characteristic of the grotesque (341). Stallman, pointing out the strange mixture of realms of being, calls the list "a forest-preserve of crossed identities," such as the various names containing the word *buck*, Edgar Beaver's having white hair more suggestive of a rabbit than a beaver, and Francis Bull and the Hornbeams' sharing the attribute of horns (9–10). Thus the list shows how unnatural these parties are, containing such a mix of the natural order. Even a partial look at the list confirms the impressions of these critics; it further reveals a list that includes many names and descriptions of people with rather direct links to creativity: movie and theatrical people, literary figures, inventors, founders, builders, performers, and communicators. But though creativity is abundantly found, so are signs that the creativity has gone awry.

Nick lists the names of various movie people. Newton Orchid, "who controlled Films Par Excellence" (66), shares one name with Sir Isaac Newton, famed physicist who discovered the law of gravity, a man for whom a unit used in measuring force is named; and he shares his surname with the term for a flamboyant, brightly colored tropical flower used mainly as an ornament. Altogether, this name suggests the forcefulness of Orchid's control over his films, which are probably just ornamentative—spectacles with no deep value. The other movie people—Eckhaust, Clyde Cohen, Don S. Schwartze (the son), and Arthur McCarty—are simply "connected with the movies in one way or another" (66). Their identities and the exact nature of their creative activities are left hazy. The name *Eckhaust* suggests *exhaust*, a verb meaning "to deplete of resources" or "to wear out," or a noun referring to the escape of vaporous waste material. As an artist, then, Mr. Eckhaust is possibly the worn-out producer of vapid, wasteful movies. Clyde Cohen's first name is the slang term for a worker with no imagination, a simpleton (Crim and Houston 124); his surname calls to mind the surname of George M. Cohan, the noted American singer, playwright, and songwriter. Together, Cohen's names signify the man's lack of imagination, much in contrast to

Cohan. Don S. Schwartze (the son) bears a name combining the Spanish word for "sir" with the German word for "black," an incongruous union of languages and meanings suggesting that only in the beginning does the man seem a gentleman; on closer inspection, he has darker traits. Arthur McCarty's first name is that of the legendary British hero and that of the twenty-first President of the United States, Chester A. Arthur. Perhaps his last name is based upon that of Richard D'lyly *Carte,* a British theatrical producer. Ironically, Nick places McCarty's name last in the list of movie people, among those whose connection with the industry is indistinct to Nick, as if McCarty were the least important of them; but his name is suggestive of leadership. Perhaps Nick wishes to indicate that McCarty's abilities have gone unrecognized while the questionable talents of the other movie people have gained them a fame they do not fully deserve. In any case, Nick's inclusion of these particular names of movie people who came to Gatsby's parties, as well as the order in which he lists them, indicates Nick's recognition of creativity gone awry.

Nick also catalogues names of theatrical people. Gus Waize bears as his first name the shortened form of *Gustavus,* which in Old German means "to meditate" (Crim and Houston 125), and a last name that sounds like *waste.* Waize's creative meditations are probably wasted ones. Horace O'Donovan's name is an incongruous combination of the appellation of the famed Latin poet and a fairly common Irish surname with no evident connection with creativity; perhaps the man seems creative only at first glance. Lester Myer has a name suggestive of the word *less* and the prefix *my,* which indicates "muscle." This man is probably a weakling—one with "less muscle" than is normal. *George Duckwood* means, respectively, "farmer" and "stemless aquatic plant." As Crim and Houston suggest, perhaps "as an actor, Duckwood makes a good farmer" (125). Finally, Francis Bull has quite an incongruous name: *Francis* suggests either St. Francis of Assisi or St. Francis of Sales, a French bishop and devotional author; *Bull* is the name for the large, strong, aggressive male animal or for foolish talk. Mr. Bull apparently only seems saintly and capable of sensitive writing; underneath, he is aggressive and "full of bull." In short, Nick reveals theatrical people who also possess creativity gone awry.

Nick also catalogues names associated with literature or music. The first two parts of Dr. Webster Civet's name point to him as a learned man: *doctor* calls to mind a learned healer; *Webster*, the names of three talented and famous men. Daniel Webster was an American political leader; John Webster, an English dramatist; and Noah Webster, an American lexicographer. But in contrast, this man's last name is that of a catlike mammal that secretes an unpleasant defensive odor (Crim and Houston 119). Perhaps Dr. Civet is not so positive—so creative—a figure as he first appears. The Willie Voltaires bear a first name meaning "feelings of uneasiness" (as in having the "willies") and a surname they share with the French author Voltaire. Their creative abilities must make them uneasy. The bum Etty, who fights with Clarence Endive in Gatsby's garden, shares his name with a nineteenth-century painter, William Etty (Prigozy 103). It is ironic that the name of an artist should be applied to a bum whose highlighted action is a fight with a man whose name is that of a sharp-tasting plant. Mrs. Ulysses Swett's first name is that of James Joyce's novel and of President Ulysses S. Grant; her last name means, of course, "to perspire," or "to work long and hard," or "to vex," or "drudgery." Taken together, her names suggest someone for whom attempts to be creative are mere drudgery. Seen another way, her names may refer to the banning of Joyce's *Ulysses* during the 1920s. James Joyce's long, hard creative work may have seemed to be for naught (Crim and Houston 121); perhaps Mrs. Swett's labors to create have been similarly undercut. That Mrs. Swett is said to have run over another guest's hand with her car further indicates the ineptitude and carelessness of her actions. The Bembergs have the name of a nineteenth-century French composer (Crim and Houston 124). On either side of this name on the list are the gossipy Catlips and G. Earl Muldoon, whose brother is a murderer; Nick may be implying that the artistic Bembergs are not keeping very good company. *Backhysson* calls to mind Backhuysen, a seventeenth-century Dutch painter (Prigozy 104). As with the Bembergs, Nick surrounds Backhysson with less acceptable-sounding people: the Chromes (whose name is associated with the hard and metallic) and the Dennickers. The first part of the latter name—*den*—means "lair," as in the phrase "den of thieves"; the last part, *ker*, sounds like the word *cur*, which refers to either a mongrel dog or a cowardly person. The name thus suggests the lair of a mongrel or a coward—surely not a vicinity satisfactory for the artistic Backhysson. *Gloria*, which is perhaps the name of one of Benny McClenahan's girls (Nick does not remember for sure), is the name for a Christian doxology; this woman has a "melodious" last name that Nick also cannot exactly recall. Obviously, this woman's singing is not very memorable. Thus, as with the movie and theatrical people, Nick mentions names associated with literature and music that manifest only tenuous or somehow negative connections with creativity.

Other characters mentioned by Nick bear names associated with founders, builders, and performers of various kinds. Bunsen, whom Nick knew at Yale, shares his name with Robert W. Bunsen, inventor of the Bunsen burner, which produces an extremely hot flame. On the list, Bunsen is next to the blood-sucking Leeches and the odorous Dr. Civet—again, not very good company. Mrs. Chrystie, who has come with a man other than her husband, bears the name of a ski turn. The "christy" (formally, "christiania") is a turn in which the skier swings his or her body from a crouching position to change direction or to stop. This sportswoman may need to stop or change direction morally; perhaps she should at least receive a demerit for unsportsmanlike conduct in cheating on her husband. The Ripley Snells bear the name of George Ripley, an American Unitarian minister and literary critic who founded the Brook Farm Community, and of a "leader" of a very different and much less consequential sort: a snell is a threadlike material (such as gut) that connects a fishhook to a heavier line. A play on the word "leader" occurs here, one revealing the negligible talents of these people as leaders. The Dancies may be dancers, but they may also be mean, sharp-tongued people; for *dancie* is an obsolete term meaning "toothed" (Crim and Houston 121). Finally, Faustina O'Brien's first name suggests Faust, the magician and alchemist who sold his soul to the devil in exchange for worldly power (Crim and Houston 127). O'Brien's brand of creativity is obviously ill-directed. With these names, then, Nick continues the emphasis upon creativity gone wrong.

Nick lists certain other names that signify communication of various sorts. The name *Hornbeam* calls to mind the horns whose cacophonous sounds disturb Nick at the end of Gatsby's party. Besides being a strange amalgamation of the name of a famous Southern general and a rather common Jewish surname, *Stonewall Jackson Abrams* includes the term *stonewall*, which can mean "to refuse to answer." Such a man must be uncommunicative. The Catlips are probably gossipy, for a gossipy person can be called a "cat." The Belchers must belch; and the Smirkes must smirk, preferring to communicate only through unpleasant nonverbal expressions. Like all the others, these names help Nick stress the incongruous, negative creativity present among the partygoers. By the time he recomposes this list for his dream account, Nick has realized that the creativity featured at these parties is simply not directed toward an eternal goal; hence, it goes awry.

Another source of this impression of creativity gone awry is the ethnic parody that Fitzgerald includes in the guest list. For example, *Clyde Cohen* is an Anglo Saxon name combined with a Jewish name signifying the priestly tribe (as well as the name of George Cohan); *Stonewall Jackson Abrams* (as already mentioned) is the name of a Southern general combined with a Jewish surname. *Don S. Schwartze* mixes a Spanish-sounding first name signifying gentle birth with a Yiddish word meaning "black." Arthur McCarty and Benny McClenahan have Scottish last names; and O'Donovan and Faustina O'Brien, Irish. *Mrs. Ulysses Swett*, whatever else its significance, sounds like a parody of a Scandinavian name. *Eckhaust* is German; *Voltaire*, French. The idea that in modern society a mix of ethnicities is chaotically searching for some sort of recognition echoes somewhat Chaucer's recognition of the upheaval in the social class structure of his day—though, of course, the details differ.

Amid all the signs of a confused yet active creativity, Nick notices a goal of sorts. Like the petitioners to the goddess Fame, these Jazz Age partygoers are looking for something—for a sign that they matter, that they belong somewhere and have meaningful identities—something to give direction to all their chaotic action. They have come to Gatsby's house—with all its wealth—to seek that something; however, they have apparently chosen the goddess Wealth—and the warmth, comfort, and identity that they believe Wealth will bring to them—as their goal, as the goddess to whom they pay tribute, even though this goddess will fail them.

Likewise, Nick sees that his shadow, Jay Gatsby, is looking for the sense that he matters. In a way, the goals of Gatsby and his guests are much alike. Like them, Gatsby serves someone whom he considers a goddess, one who is actually (though Gatsby does not fully realize it) thoroughly linked to wealth. But the guests serve an amorphous, ill-defined entity; Gatsby serves Daisy Fay Buchanan, his goddess who for him is the personification of wealth. Daisy is an undependable being;

in fact, she is rather like the goddess Fame in this regard. Nick notices many signs of Daisy's changeable character. During his first meeting with her in the Buchanan mansion, Nick sees her being "buoyed up as though upon an anchored balloon," with her white dress "rippling and fluttering" as though she "had just been blown back in after a short flight around the house" (12). Then, when Tom Buchanan shuts the window, she balloons to the floor. Later, in the same room, she and Jordan look to Nick like "silver idols, weighing down their own white dresses against the singing breeze of the fans" (122). A bit like the expanding and contracting goddess Fame, Daisy changes—in her case, weight and buoyancy. But above all, Nick emphasizes Daisy's changeable voice. One moment, Daisy is speaking "breathless, thrilling words" (19) and the next is throwing her napkin down and leaving the room silently. Elsewhere, Nick describes Daisy's voice as a fluctuating thing: "The exhilarating ripple of her voice was a wild tonic in the rain. I had to follow the sound of it for a moment, *up and down*, with my ear alone before any words came through" (90; emphasis added). Further, says Nick at another point, Daisy's voice is "full of money—that was the inexhaustible charm that *rose and fell* in it, the jingle of it.... *High* in the white palace the king's daughter, the golden girl...."[4] In these passages, Nick emphasizes the up-and-down quality of Daisy's voice and thus her instability. Geffrey uses similar imagery to describe the unstable realm of the House of Fame and its inconstant goddess. The second passage also suggests Daisy as the goddess Wealth in that Gatsby, Nick realizes, sees her as royalty, set apart from humanity; and like the goddess Fame, she is golden. To further stress Daisy's goddess-like quality, Nick elsewhere terms her a silver idol.

Daisy's similarity to the goddess Fame becomes even more apparent when Nick reports on her visits to his bungalow and to Gatsby's house. Because Gatsby knows that Daisy is coming to tea at Nick's house, Gatsby tries to make of Nick's humble cottage an imitation of his own opulent palace. He has Nick's lawn mowed; then, as Nick reveals, "...at two o'clock a greenhouse arrived from Gatsby's, with innumerable receptacles to contain it" (89). Paradoxically, Gatsby uses even natural objects to create an atmosphere of unnatural plenitude with which to honor and attract Daisy. It is when Daisy arrives for the tea that her voice strikes Nick as consisting of the "exhilarating ripple" that one must "follow up and down" (89).

After tea, Nick, Daisy, and Gatsby go over to see Gatsby's mansion; as Gatsby shows the place to Daisy, Nick takes note of the many period rooms and many colorful shirts that Gatsby owns. Clearly all of Gatsby's creative efforts—including his making-over of Nick's house—have occurred with Daisy in mind. Her power over Gatsby becomes obvious when Daisy speaks of the "pink and golden billow of foamy clouds" that she has seen upon looking out of a window. She says to Gatsby, "'I'd like to just get one of those pink clouds and put you in it and push you around'" (99)—which, of course, symbolizes well just what she does to Gatsby. She is indeed for Gatsby powerful and capricious, a goddess Wealth, an impression that becomes even stronger when Nick sees Myrtle imitating Daisy in behaving like a whirling, changeable, and wealthy goddess.

Daisy attends the second of Gatsby's parties described by Nick, and Nick reports being aware that her presence makes a difference in the atmosphere, that it has resulted in "a pervading harshness that hadn't been there before.... Now I was looking at it [West Egg] again, through Daisy's eyes" (110). Here, Daisy's eyes become a bit like Dr. T. J. Eckleburg's. Just as his eyes seem to oversee the happenings in the valley of ashes, she looks the party over, judging it.[5] She is also no more able to understand the events than the billboard could ever be; yet, like the sign and also like the goddess Fame, she wields power over the events. Nick reveals that most of what she sees at Gatsby's party offends Daisy—"and inarguably, because it wasn't a gesture but an emotion. She was appalled by West Egg, this unprecedented 'place' that Broadway had begotten upon a Long Island fishing village—appalled by its raw vigor..." (113–14). Because Daisy does not like the party, Gatsby simply stops having parties; also for her sake, he fires all his servants. As Nick says, as quickly as it had begun, Gatsby's "career as Trimalchio was over" (119); "...the whole caravansary had fallen in like a card house at the disapproval in her eyes" (120). Daisy thus grants none of the wishes of her petitioners; even though the partygoers do not even know who she is, she exerts power over them when she shuts down the parties to which they have come seeking that mysterious "something" to give their actions meaning.

Later in his dream account, Nick reveals that at the Plaza Hotel, Daisy similarly fails to grant Gatsby's wish. Interestingly, Nick describes her rejection of Gatsby by speaking of the actions of her voice: Gatsby, he says, kept trying to "touch

what was no longer tangible, struggling unhappily, undespair-
ingly, toward that lost voice across the room" (142).   Nick
knows that the voice that moves up and down and all around
has moved as far away as it can.   Again, Daisy is much like the
capriciously shifting goddess Fame.

Daisy is also like the goddess Fame in that she is linked to
the unnatural instead of to Nature (or to God or to Love—in
short, to the eternal).   Daisy apparently cannot understand the
guests at Gatsby's parties because she is offended by natural
emotions—by the "raw vigor" the guests exhibit.   She prefers
"gestures"—counterfeit Nature, or the empty courtly-love-like
formulas associated with her high social stratum, as opposed
to anything natural.   In addition, Nick sees her as someone
who will not allow things to be natural; she seeks control instead.   Instead of obeying the law of gravity, she seems to float
about her house.   In a further departure from natural laws, she
wants to control the pink cloud in which she wishes to put
Gatsby—and, symbolically, she indeed does control it, and
him.   Finally, as indicated by the traits shared by Daisy and
the formel eagle of *The Parliament of Fowls*, Daisy (and perhaps
Tom along with her) creates a "courtly-love text" involving
Gatsby's sacrificing himself for her.   Her action runs counter to
the action Nature—or God or Love—would advocate.

Through observing the actions at the House of Fame, Geffrey sees liveliness and imagination but lack of an eternal goal
toward which artists can direct their efforts.   At the end of his
account of his trip to this edifice, Geffrey reports his dissatisfaction with it because of his failure to find the sort of tidings,
or message, he has been seeking—tidings of Love, of the eternal.   Similarly, Nick gains insight into the positive and negative qualities of Gatsby's domain.   He makes it clear in the end
that although Gatsby's mansion has featured "gleaming, dazzling parties" that long afterwards stay with Nick "so vividly
that I could still hear the music and the laughter...from his
garden and the cars going up and down his drive," the house
is for him essentially a "huge incoherent failure" (188), a card
house apt to cave in at any time (120).   Nick has realized that
however opulent, busy, and dazzling, it, along with the dream
of which it is a manifestation, has a fatal flaw as art: it boasts
no eternal goal that would lend coherence to it.

In *The House of Fame*, Geffrey visits a third place, the
whirling, labyrinthine house of twigs, the farthest extreme of
what he has found in the House of Fame.   Bennett calls the

house of twigs the "workaday counterpart" to the House of Fame (165). In this place, Geffrey finds absolutely no goal—not even an unworthy one—all is whirring, noisy chaos. Geffrey, for instance, hears noise there like "the rowtynge of the ston / That from th' engyn ys leten gon" (1933b–34); and he sees inside only people who roam aimlessly and, in the end, begin to run "as faste as that they hadden myght" (2146) until they are "alle on a help" (2149) and thus must climb over each other. The place, he finds, is a house of rumor, the cheap version of fame. As Bennett puts it, "there is no order, no hierarchy, not even a porter. All is constant jostling, plebeian fashion. The throng is noisy, miscellaneous, hurried" (171). Also, individual identities are lost, as this passage indicates:

> And, Lord, this hous in alle tymes,
> Was ful of shipmen and pilgrimes,
> With scrippes bret-ful of lesinges,
> Entremedled with tydynges,
> And eek allone be hemselve.
> O, many a thousand tymes twelve
> Saugh I eke of these pardoners,
> Currours, and eke messagers,
> With boystes crammed ful of lyes
> As ever vessel was with lyes. (2121–30)

Whereas the House of Fame contains at least some petitioners whom Geffrey can call by name, here, the people become mere types, mere representatives of their professions. Notably, too, the range of social classes in this place is located on a somewhat different area of the scale than in the House of Fame, where the upper range is represented. Here, Geffrey finds the lower end of the social spectrum: the plebeians.

Just as Geffrey visits the house of twigs, Nick goes to Tom and Myrtle's New York apartment. This tackier, cheaper version of Gatsby's house bears much resemblance to the ramshackle version of the House of Fame, although there are some key differences: Nick's visit to the apartment occurs early in the novel, before he attends Gatsby's party, while Geffrey's visit to the house of twigs occurs last. Also, Nick gets to know people's names in the apartment and at Gatsby's mansion while Geffrey knows names at the House of Fame, not at the house of twigs. Despite these differences, however, the similarities remain striking. As Nick describes it, the New York apartment contains all the most essential qualities of Gatsby's house, except to a greater and more blatant degree—just as the house of twigs is a blatant and grotesque version of the House of Fame. As Nick says,

> The living room was crowded to the doors with a set of tapestried furniture entirely too large for it so that to move about was to stumble continually over scenes of ladies swinging in the gardens of Versailles. The only picture was an over-enlarged photograph, apparently a hen sitting on a blurred rock. Looked at from a distance however the hen resolved itself into a bonnet and the countenance of a stout old lady beamed down into the room. Several old copies of "Town Tattle" lay on the table together with a copy of "Simon Called Peter," and some of the small scandal magazines of Broadway. (33)

The scenes on the tapestried furniture suggest much activity. With their pictures of ladies swinging in the garden of Versailles, these inanimate objects apparently seem almost alive to Nick; he feels in danger of stumbling over the women. The action involved in these tapestries is actually twofold: that of the artists who wove them; and that of the ladies themselves, who seem to be swinging both inside the scene depicted on the tapestries and in the living room. The photograph on the wall further suggests the action of an artist; its blurred quality has resulted from too many enlargements, as if art has been pushed beyond its bounds. Various copies of *Town Tattle* and some scandal magazines adorn the place, indicating creativity used only to spread rumor in tawdry, "popular" publications, similar to what occurs in the rumor-filled house of twigs. Notably, too, Gatsby's house is full of rumors: his guests spread them about Gatsby's mysterious background. But here, in the apartment, rumors are simply part of a tackier, cheaper atmosphere than at Gatsby's place—again, just as the house of twigs contains tackier, cheaper noise than that found in the cacophonous House of Fame.

When Nick speaks next of the people who arrive for a party, the impressions of exaggeration and chaos and jostling first established in his description of the furniture increase. Myrtle's sister, Catherine, wears many jangling bracelets, suggesting movement and production of a tuneless, chaotic sort of "music"; Catherine also has a blurred-looking face, the result of her eyebrows having been drawn on at odd angles. Mr. McKee, who took the aforementioned blurred photograph, reveals that he has taken 127 pictures of his wife since their marriage. The blurred photo and the many pictures of Mrs. McKee together imply art that is exaggerated and distorted. Further, the party that ensues is full of the chaos of arguments, chief of which is that of Myrtle and Tom:

> "Daisy! Daisy! Daisy!" shouted Mrs. Wilson. "I'll say it whenever I want to! Daisy! Dai—"
>
> Making a short deft movement, Tom Buchanan broke her nose with his open hand. Then there were bloody towels upon the bathroom floor and women's voices scolding, and high over the confusion a long broken wail of pain. Mr. McKee awoke from his dose and started in a daze toward the door. When he had gone half way he turned around and stared at the scene—his wife and Catherine scolding and consoling as they stumbled here and there among the crowded furniture with articles of aid, and the despairing figure on the couch bleeding fluently and trying to spread a copy of "Town Tattle" over the tapestry scenes of Versailles. (41–42)

Nick focuses on a multitude of signs of confusion and chaos here. The ladies on the swings now would appear to drip with Myrtle's blood—surely an incongruous and grotesque sight. Mr. McKee's fuzzy photograph of his mother is an artistic failure. The copies of *Town Tattle* serve not only to spread rumor but also to sop up blood, and they lie next to *Simon Called Peter*—certainly a stunning set of incongruities. Catherine runs about, her bracelets no doubt still jangling cacophonously, her blurred face indicating that she is as much a failed artist as Mr. McKee, and that, in her case, the failure is not just of a photo but of her own person as object of art. She cannot, in short, "paint" herself successfully.

Other of Nick's descriptions of events at this party indicate the confusion and chaos—the utter lack of goal—inherent in the atmosphere while also using a stylistic device common in Chaucer's dream visions: the list. At the end of the party, Mr. McKee shows Nick a catalogue of the photographs in his portfolio. The titles include, Nick says, "'Beauty and the Beast...

Loneliness...Old Grocery Horse...Brook'n Bridge...'" (42; Fitzgerald's ellipses). Additionally, Nick relates that Myrtle makes a list of future plans. He records her list as follows:

> "I'm going to make a list of all the things I've got to get. A massage and a wave and a collar for the dog and one of those cute little ashtrays where you touch a spring, and a wreath with a black silk bow for mother's grave that'll last all summer." (41)

Making his own catalogue of the party's events, Nick says that overall, "people disappeared, reappeared, made plans to go somewhere, and then lost each other, searched for each other, found each other a few feet away" (41). In short, in this place, Nick feels he has found "the inexhaustible variety of life" (40). But he also indicates how confused and incoherent this "variety" is.

Myrtle's list is, on one level, simply miscellaneous; she moves hastily from her physical appearance (the massage and wave), to her dog (the collar), to ashtrays, to death. On another level, Myrtle seems to have "organized" by association, moving from the idea of a living human being, to a living beast, to an inanimate object associated with death, to death itself. And this last item in the list is truly without signs of life, for in speaking of her dead mother, she mentions decorating her grave with a plant that will last an entire season (and a hot season at that); it must be an artificial plant she has in mind. Her planned actions thus represent a downward spiral into nothingness. In addition, McKee's catalogue, however suggestive of his activity as artist, also symbolizes the obsolete, the stationary, and the misdirected. The fairy tale *Beauty and the Beast* concerns an incongruous combination. The next title, *Loneliness*, implies stillness and stagnation. An old grocery horse is an obsolete means of conveyance, an active creature whose activity is no longer needed. Brooklyn Bridge is a means of traveling which is itself stationary. On a positive note, it is a structure much admired by artists and engineers for its beauty and usefulness. But negatively, this bridge takes travelers to (or from) New York City, which in this novel is associated with violence and confusion such as that found at this very party. It is also in the city that the confused confrontation scene at the Plaza Hotel takes place, and it is on the way back from the city that Myrtle is killed with such carelessness (though the bridge is not the setting for the wreck). The bridge is a bridge to nothing of worth.

One passage in Nick's description of the New York party seems at first especially similar to another part of Geffrey's dream account: that of the goddess Fame's behavior in the House of Fame. But it makes sense that this description is part of the New York party scene instead of the scene at Gatsby's party. The passage in question concerns Nick's perception of Myrtle's changing in size and revolving. Nick says that Myrtle

> changed her costume some time before and was now attired in an elaborate afternoon dress of creamcolored chiffon which gave out a continual rustle as she swept about the room. With the influence of the dress her personality had also undergone a change. The intense vitality that had been so remarkable in the garage was converted into impressive hauteur. Her laughter, her gestures, her assertions became more violently affected moment by moment and as she expanded the room grew smaller around her until she seemed to be revolving on a noisy, creaking pivot through the smoky air. (35)

Just after Nick views these changes, he starts seeing evidence of her seeming influence on her other guests. Mrs. McKee begins to speak to Myrtle about how well she looks in the dress and about how Mr. McKee could "'make something of it'" if he could "'only get you in that pose'" (35). Mrs. McKee is trying to gain recognition for her artist-husband and believes Myrtle can help. However, when Mr. McKee himself begins to press Tom for help, Tom's response reveals fully to Nick Myrtle's very different position: Mr. McKee, Tom sarcastically replies, should ask Myrtle, not him; "'she'll give you a letter of introduction, won't you, Myrtle?'"—a letter, Tom continues, that would give permission only for Mr. McKee to do some pictures of "'George B. Wilson at the Gasoline Pumps, or something like that'" (37). Tom's sarcasm and derisive laughter indicate Tom's opinion that Myrtle is the last person who could help the McKees; Nick thus sees Myrtle's actual powerlessness, her utter insufficiency as a goal for artistic efforts. She is merely a pretend Daisy, a pretend goddess Wealth.

This scene at first seems to parallel only the scene set in Fame's palace in which the goddess Fame undergoes similar changes. But it must be remembered that in Chaucer's poem, the goddess Fame is presented as the actual goddess, not a pretend goddess, not a substitute for some other real goddess Fame. She may not be a worthy goal for creative endeavors, but she is an actual one. In *Gatsby*, the situation with Daisy is more complex, since within the plot of Nick's dreamlike experience, she is a mere human being (albeit one with a prominent dark side), not a goddess. It is Gatsby's—and, at times, Nick's—perception of Daisy that makes of her an Alceste or a Good Fair White or, in this instance, a goddess Fame. Also, within the society pictured in Nick's dream, relative to Myrtle, Daisy is something of a "goddess," a wealthy woman who wields power as such. Myrtle, of a much lower social class than Daisy, is the pretender to the "throne"; her circling about in the middle of the room as though she were to serve as goal for an artist's attempts is merely laughable. Her actions of expanding and revolving are simply an attempt to imitate Daisy. They illustrate how much like the goddess Fame *Daisy* is, not Myrtle. Since the New York apartment is a "ghetto" version of Gatsby's place (with the utterly unrefined lower-class guests instead of the at least minimally refined West and East Eggers who attend Gatsby's parties), Myrtle is the "ghetto" version of Daisy. Sadly, Myrtle here denies her actual connection to natural fertility and growth (to Nature and to the goddess of Love, not of Wealth) and ultimately lets herself be destroyed by her contact with the one she would emulate, Daisy herself. When Daisy kills Myrtle, no sign of Venus is left in the valley of ashes; it becomes a much worse place than the desert in *The House of Fame*. The desert to the end contains a temple featuring at least a remnant of Venus; but here, the remnant is gone, leaving to "rule" the valley only a lifeless billboard with no such relationship to the eternal. And as for the New York apartment, it is always utterly bereft of Nature: the tapestries of the gardens are just that, tapestries, not real gardens; and Myrtle is not Myrtle when she is at the apartment. She is a pretend Daisy denying any connection to her "real" identity.

Like Geffrey, Nick finds no place that contains the right goal for creativity. The valley of ashes, like the temple of Venus and its surrounding desert, offers merely the remnant of an eternal goal (and ultimately not even that) and no accompanying creative activity. Gatsby's mansion, similar to the House

of Fame, has all the action the valley lacks but only an inap-
propriate—if potent—goal: Daisy Buchanan, perceived by
Gatsby and Nick in a way that makes of her the unnatural, undependable goddess Wealth.   The New York apartment, like
the house of twigs, contains no goal at all (Myrtle only pre-
tends to be one) and only the most chaotic of action.   And the
other places Nick visits have similar shortcomings: the Buchanan mansion is filled with drifting people—drifting not because they lack a goal for ongoing efforts to create something
but rather because they have "arrived."   The Buchanans have
wealth and thus are empty of a desire to seek it or anything
else; they are satisfied with their emptiness of any values other
than the material.   Even Nick's humble bungalow, which in
some ways seems at first like a microcosm of the Middle West,
ultimately is taken over by Eastern riches when Gatsby adorns
it so that it be an attraction with which to petition Daisy for attention.   In both of these places, then, the goddess Wealth
serves as the only goal for creativity.

   Yet another place figures prominently in Nick's dream ac-
count: it is Gatsby's place above the stars; and it parallels
Scipio's starry place as depicted in Chaucer's *The Parliament of
Fowls*, but with a key difference. In *The Parliament of Fowls*, the
poet-persona tells about his having read the part of Cicero's
Somnium Scipionis that concerns the appearance of the elder
Africanus to Scipio the younger in a dream. In Scipio's dream,
Africanus takes Scipio to a "sterry place" (43b), from which he
shows Scipio several sights: Carthage (Scipio's home); the
galaxy; the "lytel erthe that here is, / At regard of the hevenes
quantite" (57–58); and the nine spheres, which emit melodious
music (the music of the spheres).   Then Africanus tells Scipio
that, since the earth is so small and so full of torment, "he ne
shulde hym in the world delyte" (66).   When Scipio asks Africanus to tell him "al / The wey to come into that heven blisse"
(71b–72), Africanus replies that Scipio must

   "Know thyself first immortal
   And loke ay besyly thow werche and wysse
   To commune profit, and thow shalt not mysse
   To comen swiftly to that place deere
   That ful of blysse is and of soules cleere."   (73b–77)

In other words, Scipio must recognize both his immortal side
and his mortal one. He must see that he is a child of God who

owes his allegiance to the spiritual and eternal instead of the worldly—that is, his immortal soul must be in tune with a goal greater than the things of this little earth. But he must also realize that he is a mortal being among other mortal beings and therefore work busily for the "commune profit"—that is, for the good of all people. He must have love for other people as opposed to mere self-love.   In short, looked at as an artist, Scipio must balance an eternal goal (God or heaven) with action here on the temporal earth directed toward the good of all on earth. Only in that way can he eventually reach the perfect place of full unity, heaven.

Nick sees that Gatsby has in the past believed he could reach a starry place that Gatsby thinks would have given him heaven. However, beyond the traits shared by Scipio's place and Gatsby's lies a glaring difference. Nick talks about Gatsby's "place above the trees" as he recounts Gatsby's story of Daisy's assuming the identity of Gatsby's "paradise":

> The quiet lights in the houses were humming out into the darkness and there was a stir and bustle among the stars. Out of the corner of his eye Gatsby saw that the blocks of the sidewalk really formed a ladder and mounted to a secret place above the trees—he could climb to it, if he climbed alone, and once there he could suck on the pap of life, gulp down the incomparable milk of wonder. (117)

But Gatsby only thinks about reaching his starry place while Scipio really does so, at least within a dream.   There, Scipio gains the key to having a creative life: with the perspective borne of being far above the concerns of the mundane earth with a guide who can help him see the significance of his experience, he knows that his goal must be a universal, spiritual one—heaven—and that with it in mind, he must also be actively involved with the common profit of the people of this earth.   Similarly, Gatsby, as Nick relates, believes he needs communion with an entity above the mundane earth, that this contact would provide him with a valuable eternal connection. But Gatsby's place would, he thinks, bring him "the pap of life" and the "milk of wonder."   Though Gatsby may believe these items are the best anyone could hope for, they instead seem symbols of mindless, passive return to the womb, little like the insightful atmosphere in Scipio's starry place. Gatsby has had no "guide" truly comparable to Africanus to help him have insight into his dream. Nick tries to help him, but to no avail. What is worse, Gatsby ends up not even seeking this vague spiritual goal; he instead commits himself to an utterly earthly, temporal one, Daisy. When he kisses her, he himself realizes that he has "forever wed his unutterable visions to her perishable breath," that "his mind would never romp again like the mind of God" (117); but otherwise, he appears not to recognize fully his mistake. So, instead of accomplishing an effective combining of the universal and the particular as Scipio does, Gatsby never reaches a starry place of the eternal, above Daisy and all the riotous, imaginative parties and the "inessential houses" (189). Nick has the insight about Gatsby's starry place that Gatsby himself lacks. Nick comments that after Gatsby tells him about the place, "through all he said, even through his appalling sentimentality, I was reminded of something—an elusive rhythm, a fragment of lost words, that I had heard somewhere a long time ago" (118). Though Nick is aware of how gaudy Gatsby's imagination is, of the "appalling sentimentality" it produces, he also shows that Gatsby's story benefits him (Nick). It has made Nick almost remember a meaningful phrase. Although Nick cannot remember this phrase, surely the novel as a whole indicates that Gatsby has influenced Nick to produce many meaningful words.

In Geffrey's dream in *The House of Fame*, a man of great authority appears amidst all the failed efforts at meaningful creativity, perhaps to supply an eternal goal for them (perhaps Venus herself). In *Gatsby*, twice characters appear where one might expect such a figure to be, but neither of them fulfills the role. The New York apartment parallels the house of twigs, in which Geffrey's man of great authority appears; yet in the apartment, only Tom or Myrtle could possibly serve such a purpose, and clearly they do not. Tom has much authority, but only of the brutish variety; and he surely lacks knowledge of what a worthy goal for creativity could be. Myrtle rejects her connection to Love and Nature and can only pretend to have any other authority, the authority not of Love but of Wealth. Then, near the end of Nick's dream, Nick meets another man who conceivably could serve the function: Gatsby's father. However, instead of proclaiming a goal other than wealth, Mr. Gatz reveals to Nick that he, too, is encumbered with this insufficient goal. Nick tells about Mr. Gatz's comments and records his own thoughts about the man's attitude:

"Jimmy sent me this picture." He took out his wallet with trembling fingers. "Look there."

It was a photograph of the house, cracked in the corners and dirty with many hands. He pointed out every detail to me eagerly. "Look there!" and then sought admiration from my eyes. He had shown it so often that I think it was more real to him than the house itself. (180)

This man shows off a picture of his son's lavish house, not of his son; he obviously has very material values and offers no better goal for creative efforts. He is merely in a "slot"—near the end of the dream—where a man of great authority appears in Geffrey's dream.

With the unfinished *House of Fame*, it is as if two separate texts might exist for the artist (i.e., Fitzgerald) influenced by the work: the poem as it stands, with a man of great authority appearing but, because the work stands incomplete, never offering a solution to Geffrey's problem; or the poem as the reader might presume it was intended to end: with the man of great authority offering a solution that appears reasonable in light of the poem to that point. The bogus authority figures in *The Great Gatsby* are something like the man of great authority in the poem as it stands: none supplies an answer. However, there is another character in *Gatsby* who serves this purpose admirably: Nick Carraway himself. He becomes his own man of great authority, as though Fitzgerald were also influenced by one possible ending for Chaucer's poem, with the man of great authority succeeding in helping Geffrey attain full creativity. And perhaps it is not so glaring a contrast as it might first seem that Nick Carraway helps himself while Geffrey might have been helped by someone else. In a dream, after all, all characters are parts of the dreamer; the man of great authority is part of Geffrey.

Nick, in short, like Geffrey with the man of great authority, must look within himself, to the lessons he has learned as a whole during his dream: the quiet conversations with his shadow, Gatsby; his editing and rearrangements of these talks; his excursions to various edifices symbolic of various fragmented components of creativity. Only within himself, it seems, can Nick—the modern everyman and "everyartist"— find full creativity. Nick shares this inability to depend upon outward authority and consequent turning inward for solutions with the protagonist of Fitzgerald's *This Side of Paradise*, Amory Blaine. In the closing paragraphs of that novel, it is said that Amory's generation has "grown up to find all Gods dead, all wars fought, all faiths in man shaken." Instead of finding authority in any of these, Amory—like Nick Carraway—finds it within: "'I know myself,' he cried, 'but that is all'" (255).

The House of Fame has no closing frame; but, as has been explored earlier, *The Book of the Duchess*, *The Parliament of Fowls*, and the G text of The Prologue to *The Legend of Good Women* do. In them, the poets-personae report on their reentries into the waking world and reveal whether the dreams have solved their problems. Of these, the ending of *The Book of the Duchess* is most like that of *Gatsby*. In that poem, the poet-persona ends simply by stating that he has written the poem—which is, as the reader can see, evidence of the dreamer's newfound creativity. In *Gatsby*, Nick ends the novel with a stylistic and thematic tour de force that in its artistry reveals—as indeed the entire novel does—how successful an artist Nick has become. Capable only of composing solemn, obvious works before having the dream, Nick can now compose an imaginative *and* ordered account.

In three final subsections of this closing frame, Nick shows his newfound ability to keep in balance a sense of perspective and detachment and a vividly engaged imagination. The first of these is Nick's reverie about his past life in the Middle West. In it, Nick tells of his memory of coming back home at Christmas time from his school in the East:

> That's my middle west—not the wheat or the prairies or the lost Swede towns but the thrilling returning trains of my youth and the street lamps and sleigh-bells in the frosty dark and the shadows of holly wreaths thrown by lighted windows on the snow. I am part of that, a little solemn with the feel of those long winters, a little complacent from growing up in the Carraway house in a city where dwellings are still called through decades by a family's name. (184)

Here, Nick expresses both his vivid imaginative ability and his sense of order and perspective, and he exhibits an overriding concern with Nature. He imaginatively uses the evocative word "thrilling" to describe the trains, and he describes sensory details such as the street lamps and sleigh bells and holly wreaths to communicate the joy he feels in this largely natural atmosphere. Yet he shows perspective, too—and in several ways. He produces an effective, ordered description of his home; and he shows he is aware of his own solemnity. He also focuses on the stable and the orderly when he speaks of the Carraway house. Peter Lisca has in fact called this passage one of two "affirmations of order and continuity" with which the narrative is framed, the other being Nick's introductory remarks about his father's advice and his own Middle Western upbringing. (26).

Just after this reverie, Nick includes two passages concerning his dream of the East. The first of these is his account of his El Greco-like nightmare; the second constitutes the so-called "coda" of the novel. The nightmare account encapsulates many of the dreamlike features of the entire dream account, stressing exclusively the negative elements. It balances the earlier positive account of his trips to the Middle West at Christmas. Then, the coda within itself balances the negative with the positive. In these final six paragraphs of the novel, Nick concentrates on the one positive thing he has found in his dream of the East: Gatsby's dedication to his highly imaginative dream, a dream with implications for the American Dream itself. When he draws an analogy between Gatsby and the Dutch sailors, Nick evidences most clearly his hard-won understanding of these implications. Those sailors, he says, for a "transitory enchanted moment" held their breaths when faced with this continent, "something commensurate to his capacity for wonder." Likewise, there is "Gatsby's wonder when he first picked out the green light at the end of Daisy's dock" (189). But Nick also recognizes the dangers of dreaming too much, that Gatsby did not realize that his dream "was already behind him" (189). Gatsby's dream, Nick is saying, had its wonders, but it should have been but a part of his life, seen as a part of his past. He should not have lived in it.

Nick's inner search, then, has succeeded; he has met and embraced his shadow, and the result has been a successful piece of art. What R. A. Shoaf has said of the poet-persona of *The Book of the Duchess* holds true for Nick Carraway as well:

> The *poeta perfectus*, having as Dreamer confessed himself as Knight [as the Man in Black, his shadow], stands before the audience as the life-affirming response to death: that is, as the inventor of forms

which translate the past into a meaningful present.
(184)

There are dreams and there are dreams. Those of the Man in
Black and Gatsby—and those of the dreamers in some of Chaucer's and Fitzgerald's other dream visions—fail to produce
such forms; those of the dreamer in *The Book of the Duchess* and
of Nick Carraway do indeed produce them. Nick's return to
the Middle West does not mean failure; he is hardly retreating
to a life just like the one he had there before his dream. J.
Stephen Russell has commented that in a dream vision the
ideas of the narrator are not so much changed as transformed
("Meaningless Dreams" 24). Such appears to be the case with
Nick. His original view of his home has been transformed into
an insightful and imaginative one that bodes well for his future
as an artist.

As for Fitzgerald himself, the growth of his ideas about
creativity can be readily seen in his depiction of his artistic
counterparts Nick Carraway and Jay Gatsby. Still dealing with
the literary conflict between romantic/sentimental outpourings
and the perspective and objectivity hailed by the modernists,
Fitzgerald finally finds a way through the horns of that dilemma: he creates a first-person narrator to combine and comment upon two types of literature and two types of approaches
to life, showing how they can belong together. He truly is in
this respect as in others not so different from Chaucer, who
lets his poets-personae face and deal with an essentially similar conflict. In short, Fitzgerald, following Chaucer's lead,
puts the artist (both himself and Nick) in charge of the artist's
story and allows the artist to succeed.

CONCLUSIONS AND IMPLICATIONS

Did the dream visions of Geoffrey Chaucer influence F. Scott Fitzgerald? This study has presented strong external and internal evidence that they did. So, then, what is the significance of that influence? The comparison of their works has shown that Fitzgerald's use of Chaucerian structure and themes, along with his reflection upon similar artistic conflicts, helped Fitzgerald convey ideas about the artist and creativity. These ideas show Fitzgerald to be an artist who theorized about his craft to an extent that has previously gone unrecognized, perhaps because the theory is expressed almost completely in the dramatic terms of his fiction. The comparison reveals, too, important insights into Fitzgerald's knowledge of the medieval period and ability to relate aspects of that period to his own era. And it provides fresh insight into Fitzgerald's dilemma as a modernist with romantic inclinations, his attempt to portray women as artists, and his struggle with point of view.

Since these early works of Fitzgerald's manifest such strong connections to Chaucer's dream visions, later works by Fitzgerald might be profitably explored for evidence of similarly significant influence. The later works do not appear to have the overall dream-vision structure, but certainly other less comprehensive parallels may be worth scrutiny. For instance, *Tender Is the Night* (1933) has an artist-figure protagonist and some dreamlike passages, as well as a catalogue of trees and plants (the description of Nicole's garden) that might well prove similar to the catalogue of trees in *The Parliament of Fowls*. The fragmentary *The Last Tycoon* (1941) apparently would have had framing airplane flights, and its protagonist is also an artist-figure. Both of these later novels also indicate that Fitzgerald's continued struggle with point of view might be reapproached by critics in light of the insights afforded in the present study.

It would be particularly interesting to see how Fitzgerald's view of the artist developed during the later part of his career, often considered a period of decline—in his personal life, at least. Did he continue to perceive a conflict between romanticism/sentimentality and modernism? And did his view of the artist's ability to succeed in creating a work that "balances" the qualities advocated by these two movements continue the upward swing it takes with *The Vegetable* and *The Great Gatsby*? Or, as might be expected from the reports of personal decline, did his view peak with *Gatsby*, only to become again more pessimistic? As another alternative, did Fitzgerald's concerns simply shift away from dreams—as apparently happens with Chaucer—with Fitzgerald becoming more interested in what occurs when the dreamer awakens and must confront the waking world? Along with an examination of the later novels, another look at Fitzgerald's Pat Hobby stories, works of the 1930s that concern a down-and-out Hollywood screenwriter, might be most revealing in this regard.

Also, in view of the insights gained through a comparison of Fitzgerald's early female characters with Chaucer's, how did Fitzgerald's portrayal of female characters change, if at all, in later works? It is particularly interesting that Fitzgerald uses in each of his last two novels a woman as central consciousness (Rosemary Hoyt in *Tender Is the Night*), and as first-person narrator (Cecelia Brady in *The Last Tycoon*). How do these portrayals compare to those of Ardita and Sally Carrol, and to that of Nick Carraway, Fitzgerald's other first-person narrator?

Beyond these questions about Fitzgerald, this study brings up broader issues. This comparison of Fitzgerald and Chaucer has crossed conventional lines of periodization and genre and thus raises the question of what, after all, is the meaning of the influence of one author on another. Clearly, influence is *not* all about similarities between or closeness of historical periods, and it is *not* all about poet influencing poet or prose writer influencing prose writer. Critics clearly cannot afford to be too quick to categorize; they might miss the most intriguing insights!

And so this study returns to the question with which it began: was F. Scott Fitzgerald influenced by Geoffrey Chaucer's dream visions? It is said that the influence of one author upon another can never be proven absolutely, but if ever there were a case in which that rule of criticism cried to be broken, this one is surely it, for the evidence is quite compelling. The influence is there, and it is influence of much importance for the gaining of a fuller understanding of F. Scott Fitzgerald. As Fitzgerald himself might have put it, his works "ring...to the melody of Chaucer's lesser known poems."

NOTES

[1] Edward Gillin maintains that Fitzgerald may have consciously modeled his public persona on Mark Twain.

[2] See Mandel and Morgan for other treatments of Fitzgerald's use of courtly love.

[3] See "To F. Scott Fitzgerald from Harold Ober," 3 Sept. 1935, *As Ever* 223.

[4] Janet Miller, Department of English, Princeton University, personal communication with Hoffman, 1970, qtd. in Hoffman 157n.

[5] Gerould was to edit a collection called *Old English and Medieval Literature* (1929), and to write a book entitled *Chaucerian Essays* (1952).

[6] Qtd. by Janet Miller, who is qtd. in Hoffman 157n.

[7] Bishop 400; for Flahiff's comment on Bishop's statement, see Flahiff 98.

[8] I consulted the reproduction of the preface in Bruccoli and Clark's *Fitzgerald/Hemingway Annual: 1972* 1–2; it is also reproduced in This Side of Paradise: *The Manuscripts and Typescripts* 7–8.

[9] Facsimile from Princeton Library, qtd. in Janet Lewis 24.

[10] C. S. Lewis, *The Discarded Image* 63–64; Sharma 1-2; Higgs 6–7.

[11] In this study, the approach to the dream visions of Chaucer is chiefly that of Fulwiler.

[12] See [Schlacks]. In this thesis, I use Jungian theory in interpreting the novel, including Nicole and her garden. While I do not deal directly in that study with the possibility that Fitzgerald consciously used Jungian ideas in writing the novel, my interpretation suggests, I believe, that he may well have been sufficiently acquainted with them to have made such use of them in the novel.

[13] For informative discussions of modernism, see the studies by Clark, Quinones, and Gamache.

[14] Eagleton 41. Clark, 205–06n, also quotes this passage.

[15] Among the numerous studies of the influence of romantic authors on Fitzgerald, see the studies by Doherty, Grube, McCall, Trilling, and Wagner.

Chapter Two

[1] Jennifer McCabe Atkinson's article "The Discarded Ending of 'The Offshore Pirate'" includes a facsimile of the typescript of the original ending.

[2] See Kittredge 68–71; S. P. Damon, cited in Robinson 775.

[3] These works are mentioned not to suggest that Fitzgerald was influenced by them but rather simply to examine in what ways they might be enlightening in regard to Fitzgerald's use of women as dreamers. There is, I believe, simply not sufficient external evidence that Fitzgerald was familiar with the fifteenth-century imitations of Chaucer's dream visions.

Chapter Three

[1] The function of the town of Hades is complex. On one level, it is simply John's hometown on the Mississippi River. There people worship money yet do not have a lot of it. On an allegorical level, it is hell—not the hell spoken of in the Bible,

but rather the place of the absence of the god Wealth.   There, just as the demons in the Judeo-Christian concept of hell recognize God as God, the "demons" recognize wealth as god. Late in the story, when John states that hell no longer exists, he is talking about the Biblical hell.   He shows that for him, there would be no real difference between the literal and the allegorical designations for Hades: there is for him no supernatural, spiritual plane of existence; instead, the only god is earthly wealth; and the only heaven and hell, the state of having wealth and the condition of being separated from wealth, respectively.

2 Fitzgerald, *The Vegetable* 3. All stage directions in the published play are printed in italics; in such passages quoted in this chapter, the italics have been eliminated.

Chapter Four

1 Babb 338–40, Podis 64–70, and Tannenbaum all analyze these dreamlike qualities in *Gatsby*.

2 James E. Miller's scheme (112–14) provided the model for this one.   Miller's study concerns the idea that Joseph Conrad's influence resulted in the particular use of narrator and the sort of nonchronological structure found in *Gatsby*.   I contend that although Conrad may well have been an influence, so was Chaucer.   A third "influence" that has frequently been recognized is Fitzgerald's editor, Maxwell Perkins of Scribner's. As reported by Matthew Bruccoli in *Apparatus for F. Scott Fitzgerald's* The Great Gatsby, 15–19, after reading the typescript of the novel, Perkins suggested that Fitzgerald reorganize a part of it by breaking up a long block about Gatsby's history, which appears in typescript chapter eight.   In response, when the book was in galleys, Fitzgerald moved parts of Gatsby's biography to book chapter six from typescript chapters seven and eight.   Obviously, Fitzgerald made changes in structure more sweeping than Perkins' one suggested alteration.   Also, it is fairly evident from the nature of these changes that the structural affinity with the dream account Chaucer's *The Book of the Duchess* came partly into being at the galleys stage, though it is just as evident from an examination of manuscript, typescript, and galleys (as well as from Bruccoli's remarks about these

documents) that the structural changes made in reaction to Perkins' comments simply "intensified" the sort of structure Fitzgerald had already erected. Perhaps Perkins' suggestion led Fitzgerald to put to further use his models, including the dream visions of Chaucer. (See also The Great Gatsby: *A Facsimile of the Manuscript* and The Great Gatsby: *The Revised and Rewritten Galleys*.)

[3] Again, see Miller 112–14. In formulating this list, I have examined each chapter of the novel, counting not only Gatsby's conversations with Nick but also such things as depictions of Gatsby's parties; for I would contend that these events are as much a part of Gatsby's tale as are his comments to Nick. They are Gatsby's enactment of the "script" he has written for himself to play out in the novel's "present."

Chapter Five

[1] 22 Sept. 1919, *Letters* 456.

[2] See Dahl and Llamon regarding Fitzgerald's use of American architectural styles and use of symbolic edifices in *Gatsby*.

[3] I am indebted to Patricia Steed, then of Texas Woman's University, for the suggestion, made to me in a casual conversation in 1984, that Gatsby's mansion seemed to her quite similar to the House of Fame. Her brief comment provided the seed from which this study has grown.

[4] 120; emphasis added; last ellipses are Fitzgerald's.

[5] Interestingly, Fitzgerald was influenced by the dust jacket of *Gatsby*, which was created by the Spanish artist Francis Cugat months before Fitzgerald completed the novel. This Art Deco work features a pair of eyes, meant to be Daisy's, hovering over a carnival scene. A preliminary sketch for the jacket shows female faces hovering over the valley of ashes. Upon seeing one of Cugat's preparatory studies or sketches for the final jacket, or the final jacket itself (it is not clear which), Fitzgerald told Maxwell Perkins that he had written the jacket into the novel. Fitzgerald's statement has been widely taken to

mean that the jacket was the source for the billboard of Dr. T. J. Eckleburg's eyes; but, since it is not known which version of the work he had seen at that point, it actually remains unclear just what Fitzgerald meant. (See Scribner viii–xi.) In any case, it is intriguing that Daisy should emerge in this study as the goddess of Gatsby's party, symbolically hovering over it, influencing Gatsby and judging the people and events—just as Dr. T. J. Eckleburg's sign is god (or anti-god) hovering over the valley, influencing George Wilson and seeming to judge the valley.

BIBLIOGRAPHY

Adams, Henry. *The Education of Henry Adams.* 1905. NY: New American Library, 1961.

___. *Mont-Saint-Michel and Chartres.* Introd. Ralph Adams Cram. 1905. Boston: Houghton, 1933.

Arnold, Edwin T. "The Motion Picture as Metaphor in the Works of F. Scott Fitzgerald." *Fitzgerald/Hemingway Annual: 1977.* Ed. Margaret M. Duggan and Richard Layman. Detroit: Gale-Bruccoli Clark, 1977. 43–60.

The Assembly of Ladies. The Floure and the Leafe *and* The Assembly of Ladies. Ed. D. A. Pearsall. Manchester, England: Manchester UP, 1962.

Atkinson, Jennifer McCabe. "The Discarded Ending of 'The Offshore Pirate.'" *Fitzgerald/Hemingway Annual: 1974.* Ed. Matthew J. Bruccoli and C. E. Frazer Clark, Jr. Englewood, CO: Microcard Editions, 1975. 47–49.

Audhuy, Letha. "The *Waste Land* Myth and Symbols in *The Great Gatsby.*" *Etudes Anglais* 33 (1980): 41–54.

Babb, Howard S. "'The Great Gatsby' and the Grotesque." *Criticism* 5 (1963): 336–48.

Baldwin, Charles C. "F. Scott Fitzgerald." *The Men Who Make Our Novels.* Rev. ed. NY: Dodd, 1924. 166–73.

Barney, Stephen A. "Chaucer's Lists." *The Wisdom of Poetry: Essays in Early English Literature in Honor of Morton W. Bloomfield.* Ed. Larry Benson and Siegfried Wenzel. Kalamazoo: Medieval Institute-Western MI U, 1982. 189–223.

Becker, Raymond de. *The Understanding of Dreams and Their Influence on the History of Man.* Trans. Michael Heron. NY: Hawthorn, 1968.

Bennett, J. A. W. *Chaucer's Book of Fame: An Exposition of* The House of Fame. Oxford: Clarendon Press, 1968.

Bevington, David M. "The Obtuse Narrator in Chaucer's *House of Fame.*" *Speculum* 36 (1961): 288–98.

Bewley, Marius. "Scott Fitzgerald and the Collapse of the American Dream." *The Eccentric Design: Form in the Classic American Novel.* NY: Columbia UP, 1963. 259–87.

Bishop, John Peale. "Fitzgerald at Princeton." *Virginia Quarterly Review* (Winter 1937). Rpt. in *F. Scott Fitzgerald: The Man and His Work.* Ed. Alfred Kazin. NY: Collier, 1967. 46–48.

____. "Princeton." *Smart Set* Nov. 1921. Rpt. in *The Collected Essays of John Peale Bishop.* Ed. Edmund Wilson. NY: Scribner's, 1948. 391–400.

Box, Patricia Ann Slater. "The Image of the Artist in the Works of F. Scott Fitzgerald." Diss. Texas Tech U, 1978.

Brewer, Derek. *Chaucer and His World.* 2nd ed. Cambridge: Brewer-Boydell & Brewer, 1992.

Brody, Saul N. "The Comic Rejection of Courtly Love." Ferrante and Economou 221–61.

Bronson, Bertrand. "*The Book of the Duchess* Reopened." *PMLA* 67 (1952): 863–81.

Bruccoli, Matthew J. *Apparatus for F. Scott Fitzgerald's* The Great Gatsby. South Carolina Apparatus for Definitive Editions. Ed. Matthew J. Bruccoli. Columbia: U of SC P, 1974.

____, ed. *Fitzgerald Newsletter (1958–1968).* Wash. D.C.: NCR Microcard Editions, 1969.

____. Introduction. Bruccoli, *Price* xi–xx.

____. Introduction. Fitzgerald, F. Scott, *Facsimile* xiii–xxxv.

____, ed. *The Price Was High: The Last Uncollected Stories of F. Scott Fitzgerald*. NY: Harcourt-Bruccoli Clark, 1979.

____. *Some Sort of Epic Grandeur: The Life of F. Scott Fitzgerald*. NY: Harcourt, 1981.

Bruccoli, Matthew J., and C. E. Frazer Clark, Jr., eds. *Fitzgerald/Hemingway Annual: 1975*. Englewood, CO: Information Handling Services, 1975.

____, eds. *Fitzgerald/Hemingway Annual: 1971*. Wash., D.C.: Microcard Editions, 1971.

Bryer, Jackson R., ed. *F. Scott Fitzgerald: The Critical Reception*. The American Critical Tradition 5. Ed. M. Thomas Inge. NY: Burt Franklin, 1978.

Buell, Lawrence. "The Significance of Fantasy in Fitzgerald's Short Fiction." *The Short Stories of F. Scott Fitzgerald: New Approaches in Criticism*. Ed. Jackson R. Bryer. Madison: U of WI P, 1982. 23–38.

Burnam, Tom. "The Eyes of Dr. Eckleburg: A Re-examination of *The Great Gatsby*." *College English* 14 (1952): 7–12. Rpt. in Mizener, *F. Scott Fitzgerald* 104–11.

Callahan, John F. *The Illusions of a Nation: Myth and Mystery in the Novels of F. Scott Fitzgerald*. Urbana: U of IL P, 1972.

Carlisle, E. Fred. "The Triple Vision of F. Scott Fitzgerald." *Modern Fiction Studies* 11 (1965–66): 351–60.

Chaucer, Geoffrey. *The Book of the Duchess*. Robinson 267–69.

____. *The Canterbury Tales*. Robinson 1–265.

____. "The Complaint of Chaucer to His Purse." Robinson 539–40.

____. *The House of Fame.* Robinson 282–302.

____. "The Miller's Tale." *The Canterbury Tales.* Robinson 48–55.

____. "The Nun's Priest's Tale." *The Canterbury Tales.* Robinson 199–205.

____. *The Parliament of Fowls.* Robinson 310–18.

____. Prologue to *The Legend of Good Women.* Robinson 482–96.

____. *Troilus and Criseyde.* Robinson 389–479.

Chubb, Thomas Caldecot. "Bagdad-on-Subway." Rev. of *The Great Gatsby,* by F. Scott Fitzgerald. *Forum* 74 (1925): 310–11. Rpt. in Bryer 237–39.

Clark, Suzanne. *Sentimental Modernism: Women Writers and the Revolution of the Word.* Bloomington: Indiana UP, 1991.

Cleary, Barbara A. "The Narrator and the Comic Framework in Chaucer's *Parlement of Foules.*" *Delta Epsilon Sigma Bulletin* 24 (1979): 108–12.

Cowley, Malcolm. "Third Act and Epilogue." *New Yorker* 30 June 1945. Rpt. in Mizener, *F. Scott Fitzgerald* 64–69.

Crim, Lottie R., and Neal B. Houston. "The Catalogue of Names in *The Great Gatsby.*" *Research Studies* [WA State U] 36 (1968): 113–30.

Dahl, Curtis. "Fitzgerald's Use of American Architectural Styles in *The Great Gatsby.*" *American Studies* 25 (1984): 91–102.

Daniels, Cora Linn, and C. M. Stevans, eds. *Encyclopaedia of Superstitions, Folklore, and the Occult Sciences of the World.* Vol. 2. 1903. Detroit: Gale, 1971. 3 vols.

Davidoff, Judith M. *Beginning Well: Framing Fictions in Late Middle English Poetry.* Rutherford, NJ: Fairleigh Dickinson

UP: 1988.

Doherty, William. "*Tender Is the Night* and the 'Ode to a Nightingale.'" *Explorations of Literature.* Ed. Rima Drell Reck. Explorations of Literature No. 18. Baton Rouge: LSUP, 1966. 100–14.

Dodd, William George. *Courtly Love in Chaucer and Gower.* 1913. Harvard Studies in English. Vol. I. Gloucester, MA: Peter Smith, 1959.

Donaldson, Scott. "The Crisis of Fitzgerald's 'Crack-Up.'" *Twentieth-Century Literature* 26 (1980): 171–88.

———. "F. Scott Fitzgerald, Princeton '17." *Princeton University Library Chronicle* 40 (1979): 119–54.

Eagleton, Terry. *Literary Theory: An Introduction.* Minneapolis: U of Minnesota P, 1983.

Elmore, A. E. "Nick Carraway's Self-Introduction." Bruccoli and Clark, *Fitzgerald/Hemingway Annual: 1971* 130–47.

Ewald, Robert J. "The Jungian Archetype of the Fairy Mistress in Medieval Romance." Diss. Bowling Green State U, 1977.

Fahey, William A. *F. Scott Fitzgerald and the American Dream.* NY: Crown, 1974.

Farnham, William Edward. "The Sources of Chaucer's *Parlement of Foules.*" *PMLA* 32 (1917): 492–518.

Ferrante, Joan M., and George D. Economou, eds. *In Pursuit of Perfection: Courtly Love in Medieval Literature.* Series in Literary Criticism. Ed. Eugene Goodheart. Port Wash., NY: National U Pub.-Kennikat, 1975.

———. Introduction. Ferrante and Economou 3–15.

Fitzgerald, F. Scott. *The Beautiful and Damned.* 1922. NY: Scribner's, 1950.

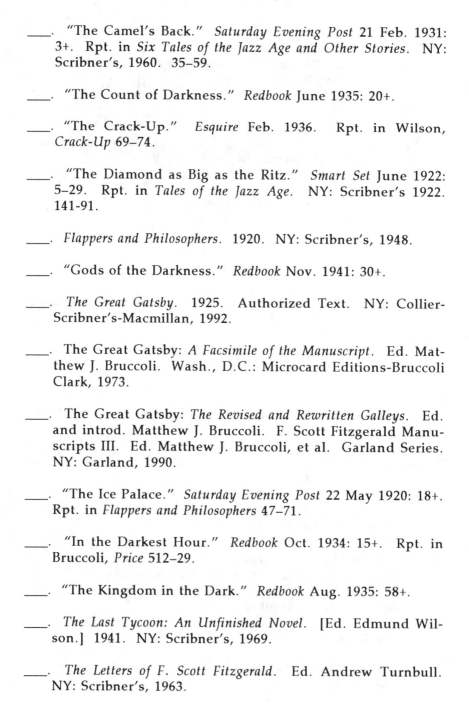

____. "The Camel's Back." *Saturday Evening Post* 21 Feb. 1931: 3+. Rpt. in *Six Tales of the Jazz Age and Other Stories.* NY: Scribner's, 1960. 35–59.

____. "The Count of Darkness." *Redbook* June 1935: 20+.

____. "The Crack-Up." *Esquire* Feb. 1936. Rpt. in Wilson, *Crack-Up* 69–74.

____. "The Diamond as Big as the Ritz." *Smart Set* June 1922: 5–29. Rpt. in *Tales of the Jazz Age.* NY: Scribner's 1922. 141-91.

____. *Flappers and Philosophers.* 1920. NY: Scribner's, 1948.

____. "Gods of the Darkness." *Redbook* Nov. 1941: 30+.

____. *The Great Gatsby.* 1925. Authorized Text. NY: Collier-Scribner's-Macmillan, 1992.

____. *The Great Gatsby: A Facsimile of the Manuscript.* Ed. Matthew J. Bruccoli. Wash., D.C.: Microcard Editions-Bruccoli Clark, 1973.

____. *The Great Gatsby: The Revised and Rewritten Galleys.* Ed. and introd. Matthew J. Bruccoli. F. Scott Fitzgerald Manuscripts III. Ed. Matthew J. Bruccoli, et al. Garland Series. NY: Garland, 1990.

____. "The Ice Palace." *Saturday Evening Post* 22 May 1920: 18+. Rpt. in *Flappers and Philosophers* 47–71.

____. "In the Darkest Hour." *Redbook* Oct. 1934: 15+. Rpt. in Bruccoli, *Price* 512–29.

____. "The Kingdom in the Dark." *Redbook* Aug. 1935: 58+.

____. *The Last Tycoon: An Unfinished Novel.* [Ed. Edmund Wilson.] 1941. NY: Scribner's, 1969.

____. *The Letters of F. Scott Fitzgerald.* Ed. Andrew Turnbull. NY: Scribner's, 1963.

____. *The Notebooks of F. Scott Fitzgerald.* Ed. Matthew J. Bruc-coli. NY: Harcourt-Bruccoli Clark, 1978.

____. "The Offshore Pirate." *Saturday Evening Post* 29 May 1920: 10+. Rpt. in *Flappers and Philosophers* 17–46.

____. "One of My Oldest Friends." *Woman's Home Companion* Sept. 1925: 7+. Rpt. in Bruccoli, *Price* 112–25.

____. "Pasting It Together." *Esquire* Mar. 1936. Rpt. as "Handle With Care" in Wilson, *Crack-Up* 75–80.

____. *The Pat Hobby Stories.* Ed. Arnold Gingrich. NY: Scribner's, 1962.

____. "A Penny Spent." *Saturday Evening Post* 10 Oct. 1925: 8+. Rpt. in *Bits of Paradise: 21 Uncollected Stories by F. Scott and Zelda Fitzgerald.* Ed. Matthew J. Bruccoli and Scottie Fitzgerald Smith. NY: Scribner's, 1973. 111–39.

____. "Preface to 'This Side of Paradise.'" Typescript, 1919. Harold Ober Associates. Reproduced in Bruccoli and Clark, *Fitzgerald/Hemingway Annual: 1971* 1–2. (Also reproduced in This Side of Paradise: *The Manuscripts and Typescripts.* Part I. Ed. and introd. Matthew J. Bruccoli. F. Scott Fitzgerald Manuscripts I. Ed. Matthew J. Bruccoli, et al. Garland Series. NY: Garland, 1990. 7–8.)

____. "Sleeping and Waking." *Esquire* Dec. 1934. Rpt. in Wilson, *Crack-Up* 63–68.

____. *Tender Is the Night.* 1933. NY: Scribner's, 1962.

____. *This Side of Paradise.* 1920. NY: Scribner's, 1948.

____. *The Vegetable or From President to Postman.* Ed. Charles Scribner III. 1923. NY: Scribner's, 1976.

____. "Winter Dreams." *Metropolitan* Dec. 1922: 11+. Rpt. in *All the Sad Young Men.* NY: Scribner's, 1926. 57–90.

Fitzgerald, F. Scott, et al. *Correspondence of F. Scott Fitzgerald.*

Ed. Matthew J. Bruccoli and Margaret M. Duggan. NY: Random, 1980.

Fitzgerald, F. Scott, and Harold Ober. *As Ever, Scott Fitz—: Letters between F. Scott Fitzgerald and His Literary Agent Harold Ober: 1919–1940.* Ed. Matthew J. Bruccoli and Jennifer McCabe Atkinson. Philadelphia: Lippincott, 1972.

Fitzgerald, F. Scott, and Maxwell Perkins. *Dear Scott/Dear Max: The Fitzgerald-Perkins Correspondence.* Ed. John Kuehl and Jackson R. Bryer. NY: Scribner's, 1971.

Fitzgerald, Zelda. *Save Me the Waltz.* 1932. Rpt. in *Zelda Fitzgerald* 1–196.

____. *Scandalabra: A Farce Fantasy in a Prologue and Three Acts.* 1933. Rpt. in *Zelda Fitzgerald* 201–67.

____. *Zelda Fitzgerald: The Collected Writings.* Ed. Matthew J. Bruccoli. Introd. Mary Gordon. NY: Collier-Macmillan, 1991.

Flahiff, F. T. "*The Great Gatsby*: Scott Fitzgerald's Chaucerian Rag." *Figures in a Ground: Canadian Essays on Modern Literature Collected in Honor of Sheila Watson.* Saskatoon: Western Producer Prairie, 1978. 87–98.

The Floure and the Leaf. The Floure and the Leaf *and* The Assembly of Ladies. Ed. D. A. Pearsall. Manchester, England: Manchester UP, 1962.

France, Anatole. *The Revolt of the Angels.* 1914. Trans. Mrs. Wilfrid Jackson. NY: Heritage, 1953.

Freud, Sigmund. *The Interpretation of Dreams.* Trans. and ed. James Strachey. NY: Avon-Discus, 1965.

Fulwiler, Lavon B. Lectures. Chaucer: The Dream Visions and *Troilus.* Texas Woman's U. Denton, Texas, 1984.

Funk, Ruth Christy. "Order and Chaos: A Study of Cultural Dialectic in Adams, James, Cather, Glasgow, Warren, and Fitzgerald." Diss. Syracuse U, 1979.

Gamache, Lawrence. "Toward a Definition of 'Modernism.'" *The Modernists: Studies in a Literary Phenomenon.* Ed. Lawrence B. Gamache and Ian S. MacNiven. Rutherford, NJ: Fairleigh Dickinson UP, 1987. 32–45.

Garbaty, Thomas J. "The Degradation of Chaucer's 'Geffrey.'" *PMLA* 89 (1974): 97–104.

Gerould, Gordon Hall. *Chaucerian Essays.* 1952. NY: Russell & Russell, 1968.

____, ed. *Old English and Medieval Literature.* 1929. Library of Old English and Medieval Literature. Freeport, NY: Books for Libraries, 1970.

Gillen, Edward. "Fitzgerald's Twain." First International F. Scott Fitzgerald Conference. F. Scott Fitzgerald Society. New York, 24 September 1992.

Graham, Sheilah. *College of One.* NY: Viking, 1967.

Grant, Mary Kathryn, R.S.M. "The Search for Celebration in *The Sun Also Rises* and *The Great Gatsby.*" *Arizona Quarterly* 33 (1977): 181–92.

Gross, Barry Edward. "A Note on F[itzgerald]'s Use of the House." *Fitzgerald Newsletter* 23 (Fall 1963). Rpt. in Bruccoli, *Fitzgerald Newsletter* 130–31.

Grube, John. "*Tender Is the Night*: Keats and Scott Fitzgerald." *Dalhousie Review* 44 (1964–65). Rpt. in Tender Is the Night: *Essays in Criticism.* Ed. Marvin J. LaHood. Bloomington: Indiana UP, 1969. 179–89.

Hanzo, Thomas A. "The Theme and the Narrator of 'The Great Gatsby.'" *Modern Fiction Studies* 2 (1956): 183–90.

Hieatt, Constance B. *The Realism of Dream Visions: The Poetic Exploitation of the Dream-Experience in Chaucer and His Contemporaries.* The Hague: Mouton, 1967.

Higgins, John A. *F. Scott Fitzgerald: A Study of the Stories.* Jamaica, NY: St. John's UP, 1971.

Higgs, Elton Dale. "The Dream as a Literary Framework in the Works of Chaucer, Langland and the Pearl Poet." Diss. U of Pittsburgh, 1965.

Hoffman, Nancy Y. "The Great Gatsby: *Troilus and Criseyde* Revisited?" Bruccoli and Clark, *Fitzgerald/Hemingway Annual: 1971* 148–58.

Joyner, William. "The Journey Motif in Chaucer's *House of Fame.*" *English Review* 50.2 (1973): 28–41.

Julius, Patricia Ward. "Appearance and Reality in Chaucer's Early Dream Visions." Diss. MI State U, 1976.

Jung, C[arl] G. *The Archetypes and the Collective Unconscious.* Trans. R. C. F. Hull. Vol. 9, Part 1 of *The Collected Works of C. G. Jung.* Ed. Herbert Read, Michael Fordham, and Gerhard Adler. Bollingen Series 20. NY: Pantheon, 1959.

____. "Archetypes of the Collective Unconscious." *Archetypes* 3–41.

____. *Dreams.* Trans. R. C. F. Hull. Bollingen Series 20. Princeton, NJ: Princeton UP, 1974.

____. "General Aspects of Dream Psychology." *Dreams* 23–66.

____. "On the Nature of Dreams." *Dreams* 67–83.

____. "The Psychological Aspects of the Kore." *Archetypes* 182–203.

____. "The Psychological Foundations of Belief in Spirits." *The Structure and Dynamics of the Psyche.* Trans. R. C. F. Hull. Vol. 8 of *The Collected Works of C. G. Jung.* Ed. Herbert Read, Michael Fordham, and Gerhard Adler. Bollingen Series 20. NY: Pantheon, 1960. 301–18.

Kerr, Frances. "Gender, Modernism, and the Failure of Art in *The Great Gatsby.*" F. Scott Fitzgerald session, American Lit-erature Association Convention. Baltimore, 29 May 1993.

Kittredge, George L. *Chaucer and His Poetry.* 1915. Cambridge: Harvard UP, 1967.

Kuehl, John. "Scott Fitzgerald's Reading." *Princeton University Library Chronicle* 22 (1961): 58–89.

Lehan, Richard D. *F. Scott Fitzgerald and the Craft of Fiction.* Carbondale: Southern IL UP: 1966.

Lewis, C. S. *The Allegory of Love: A Study in Medieval Tradition.* Oxford: Clarendon, 1936.

____. *The Discarded Image: An Introduction to Medieval and Renaissance Literature.* London: Cambridge UP, 1964.

Lewis, Janet. "Fitzgerald's 'Philippe: Count of Darkness.'" Bruccoli and Clark, *Fitzgerald/Hemingway Annual: 1975* 7–32.

Lhamon, W. T. "The Essential Houses of *The Great Gatsby.*" *Markham Review* 6 (1977): 56–60.

Lisca, Peter. "Nick Carraway and the Imagery of Disorder." *Twentieth-Century Literature* 13 (1967): 18–28.

Long, Robert Emmet. *The Achieving of* The Great Gatsby: *F. Scott Fitzgerald, 1920–1925.* Lewisburg, PA: Bucknell UP, 1979.

Lowes, John L. "The Prologue to the *Legend of Good Women* as Related to the French *Marguerite* Poems, and the *Filostrato.*" *PMLA* 19 (1904): 593–683.

Lumiansky, R. M. "The Bereaved Narrator in Chaucer's *The Book of the Duchess.*" *Tulane Studies in English* 9 (1959): 5–17.

Magoun, Francis P., Jr., and Tauno F. Mustanoja. "Chaucer's Chimera: His Proto-Surrealist Portrait of Fame." *Speculum* 50 (1975): 48–54.

Mandel, Jerome. "The Grotesque Rose: Medieval Romance and *The Great Gatsby.*" *Modern Fiction Studies* 34 (1988): 541–58.

Manning, Stephen. "Chaucer's Good Fair White: Woman and Symbol." *Comparative Literature* 10 (1958): 97–105.

McCall, Dan. "'The Self-Same Song that Found a Path': Keats and *The Great Gatsby*." *American Literature* 42 (1971): 521–30.

McMillan, Ann. "'Fayre Sisters Al': *The Flower and the Leaf* and *The Assembly of Ladies*." *Tulsa Studies in Women's Literature* 1 (1982): 27–42.

McNally, John J. "Prefiguration of Events in *The Great Gatsby*." *University of Dayton Review* 7.2 (1971): 39–49.

Michelson, Bruce. "The Myth of Gatsby." *Modern Fiction Studies* 26 (1980–81): 563–77.

Miller, James E., Jr. *F. Scott Fitzgerald: His Art and His Technique*. NY: NY UP, 1964.

Mizener, Arthur, ed. *F. Scott Fitzgerald: A Collection of Critical Essays*. Twentieth Century Views. Ed. Maynard Mack. Englewood Cliffs, NJ: Prentice, 1963.

____. *The Far Side of Paradise*. 2nd ed. Boston: Houghton, 1965.

____. Introduction. Fitzgerald, F. Scott, *Flappers and Philosophers* 11–16.

Moreland, Kim Ileen. "The Medievalist Impulse in America: Nostalgic Evocations of Courtly Love and Chivalry in Twain, Adams, Fitzgerald, and Hemingway." Diss. Brown U, 1984.

Morgan, Elizabeth. "Gatsby in the Garden: Courtly Love and Irony." *College Literature* (Spring 1984): 163–77.

Moses, Edwin. "F. Scott Fitzgerald and the Quest to the Ice Palace." *CEA Critic* 36.2 (1974): 11–14.

Moyer, Kermit W. "Fitzgerald's Two Unfinished Novels: The Count and the Tycoon in Spenglerian Perspective." *Contemporary Literature* 15 (1974): 238–56.

Patch, Howard R. "Precious Stones in *The House of Fame*." *Modern Language Notes* 50 (1935): 312–17.

Perosa, Sergio. *The Art of F. Scott Fitzgerald*. Trans. Charles Matz and Sergio Perosa. Ann Arbor: U of MI P, 1965.

Person, Leland S., Jr. "'Herstory' and Daisy Buchanan." *American Literature* 50 (1978): 250–57.

Piper, Henry Dan. *F. Scott Fitzgerald: A Critical Portrait*. NY: Holt, 1965.

Podis, Leonard A. "'The Unreality of Reality': Metaphor in *The Great Gatsby*." *Style* 11 (1977): 56–72.

Prigozy, Ruth. "Gatsby's Guest List and Fitzgerald's Technique of Naming." *Fitzgerald/Hemingway Annual: 1972*. Ed. Matthew J. Bruccoli and C. E. Frazer Clark, Jr. Wash., D.C.: Microcard Editions, 1973. 99–112.

Probert, K. G. "Nick Carraway and the Romance of Art." *English Studies in Canada* 10 (June 1984): 188–208.

Quinones, Ricardo J. *Mapping Literary Modernism: Time and Development*. Princeton: Princeton UP, 1985.

Rev. of *The Vegetable or From President to Postman*, by F. Scott Fitzgerald. *Shadowland* Aug. 1923: 67. Rpt. in Bryer 188.

Robinson, F. N. ed. *The Works of Geoffrey Chaucer*. 2nd ed. Boston: Houghton, 1961.

Rowland, Beryl. "Chaucer's Daisy (Prol. *LGW*, F 120–3; G (109–11)." *Notes and Queries* 208 (1963): 210.

Russell, J. Stephen. *The English Dream Vision*. Columbus: Ohio State UP, 1988.

____. "Meaningless Dreams and Meaningful Poems: The Form of the Medieval Dream Vision." *Massachusetts Studies in English* 7 (1978): 20–32.

Sanders, Barry. "Love's Crack-Up: *The House of Fame* ." *Papers on Language and Literature* 3.Supp. (Summer 1967): 3–13.

[Schlacks], Deborah Ann Davis. "Paradise Revisited: Garden Symbolism in the Novels of F. Scott Fitzgerald." Thesis. Texas Woman's U 1982.

Scribner, Charles III. Introduction. Fitzgerald, F. Scott, *Vegetable* v–xx.

Seymour, E. L. D., et al, eds. *Favorite Flowers in Color*. NY: William H. Wise, 1949.

Sharma, Govind Narayan. "Dreams in Chaucer." *Indian Journal of English Studies* 6 (1965): 1–18.

Shelton, Donna. "Malory's Use of Dream Vision: Medieval and Contemporary Strategies for Interpretation." *Arthurian Myth of Quest and Magic*. Ed. William E. Tanner. Dallas: Caxton's, 1993. 19-26.

Shoaf, R. A. "'Mutatio Amoris': 'Penitentia' and the Form of *The Book of the Duchess*." *Genre* 14 (1981): 163–84.

Sklar, Robert. *F. Scott Fitzgerald: The Last Laocoon*. NY: Oxford UP, 1967.

Smith, Scottie Fitzgerald. Introduction. Exhibition Catalogue of Zelda Fitzgerald's Paintings. Montgomery Museum of Fine Arts. 1974. Rpt. in *Zelda Fitzgerald* v–vii.

Spengler, Oswald. *Today and Destiny: Vital Excerpts from* The Decline of the West *of Oswald Spengler*. Ed. Edwin Franden Dakin. NY: Knopf, 1940.

Stallman, R[obert] W. "Gatsby and the Hole in Time." *Modern Fiction Studies* 1.4 (1955): 2–16.

Stearns, Marshall W. "Chaucer Mentions a Book." *Modern Language Notes* 57 (1942): 28–31.

Steed, Patricia Lou. "The World Turned Upside-Down: A Study of Chaucer's *House of Fame* and *Parliament of Fowls*." Thesis. Texas Woman's U, 1983.

Stein, William B. "Gatsby's Morgan Le Fay." *Fitzgerald Newsletter* 15 (1961). Rpt. in Bruccoli, *Fitzgerald Newsletter* 67.

Stevens, G. A. *Garden Flowers in Color: A Picture Cyclopedia of Flowers*. NY: Macmillan, 1934.

Stillwell, Richard. *The Chapel of Princeton University*. Princeton: Princeton UP, 1971.

Stoneback, H. R. "Hemingway and Fitzgerald's *Philippe*." First International F. Scott Fitzgerald Conference. F. Scott Fitzgerald Society. New York, 26 September 1992.

Tamke, Alexander R. "Michaelis in GG: St. Michael in the Valley of Ashes." *Fitzgerald Newsletter* 40 (Winter 1968). Rpt. in Bruccoli, *Fitzgerald Newsletter* 304–05.

Tenenbaum, Ruth Betsy. "'The Gray-Turning, Gold-Turning Consciousness' of Nick Carraway." Bruccoli and Clark, *Fitzgerald/Hemingway Annual: 1975* 37–55.

Tisdale, Charles P. "Boethian 'Hert-Huntyng': The Elegiac Pattern of *The Book of the Duchess*." *American Benedictine Review* 24 (1973): 365–80.

Trilling, Lionel. "Fitzgerald Plain." *New Yorker* 3 February 1951: 90–92.

Wagner, Joseph B. "*Gatsby* and John Keats: Another Version." *Fitzgerald/Hemingway Annual: 1979*. Ed. Matthew J. Bruccoli and Richard Layman. Detroit: Gale, 1980. 91–98.

Wasserstrom, William. "The Goad of Guilt: Henry Adams, Scott and Zelda." *Journal of Modern Literature* 6 (1977): 289–310.

Wilson, Edmund, ed. *The Crack-Up*. NY: New Directions, 1945.

____. "F. Scott Fitzgerald." *Bookman* Mar. 1922: 20–25. Rpt. in *The Shores of Light: A Literary Chronicle of the Twenties and Thirties*. NY: Farrar, 1952. 27–35.

INDEX